10K and Beyond:

One Runner's Story

By John Fischer

ISBN Number 978-0-578-17994-0

Table of Contents

Foreword

It's 5'oclock Sunday morning and in my dreams I hear an alarm going off. Slowly my body wakens and I realize it's time to get up. It's time to run. But before meeting my committed running partner there's much to be done – important stuff! Checking the weather one more time, carefully pulling on those restricting compression socks, munching a power bar, drinking just the right amount of water, getting dressed in a carefully preselected outfit, filling water bottles and GU flasks, applying gels, creams and goop to all kinds of places, acquiring a watch satellite, going to the bathroom – again, and finally tying my shoes JUST right. As I step outside I know that someone else is doing the exact same thing. After a quick head nod and "hello" we find our side of the road and begin our run.

Along the shops it feels like a ghost town. The streets are empty and quiet except for the pounding of our own two feet. During the course of 3 hours we see the sun rise, hear the birds wake up, feel the temperature rise, taste a mixture of GUs, and smell the sweat oozing from our bodies. As we turn for home the rest of the world is just starting to wake up. People are getting the paper, making coffee, and walking the dog. Bent over at the end of the driveway we congratulate each other and say good bye. I tip toe inside in the event the rest of the house is still asleep, peel off my clothes, and hobble into the shower. The rest of the house is now awake and ready to start the day. What will the day bring? We each have families ready for adventure and we put on a refreshed face and join in, despite having got up 3 hours before everyone else and having just run 20 miles. Why? Because we're distance runners and that's what we do.

I first started running with John during the summer of 2014. I knew from conversation that we were the same pace and could be good running partners. Running with someone for 3 hours when you're tired, physically and mentally, vulnerable, and irritable is another challenge though. Luckily, I discovered quickly that John was also good company and the conversations made the runs even more enjoyable. Over the past 2 years we've trained for anything from 5ks to marathons and it's been quite a journey. When you've run as many miles together as we have both training and racing, you really get to know someone. Of course with that many miles and races they're not all happy ones, they don't always go the way you want them to go, and they don't all end with PR's. But with John, they DO all end with a high five. John is the most positive person you will ever meet, or read about! As I've reread his blogs in the book that follows one word stands out time and time again, PRIDE. It doesn't matter if the run ends with a medal around his neck or ends with him limping to the finish, he finds something to be proud of. Other than fellow runners, few people know the toll that distance running takes, so to be proud of oneself is essential. Most people give you a skeptical look when you say you were up at 5am to run 20 miles, not a pat on the back. In addition to proud, John is meticulous when it comes to goals and training plans. He knows exactly what he wants to run and makes sure that EVERY day benefits that goal. For those that run you know that running is not typically a team sport, but the constant "we" John uses proves otherwise. He is determined to conquer obstacles together and work together to make each other better. If I've had a great run, I know I can count on John to send a thoughtful congratulatory email. If I've had a horrible run, I know I can count on John to send a thoughtful motivating email. It has been a privilege to get to know him and to share miles and miles of road with him. I hope you enjoy sharing the miles with him too.

Erika – neighbor, running partner, friend

Acknowledgements

I know it is customary to insert acknowledgements at the end of a book. But I gave this a lot of thought. And, in the end, for me and my running journey, I believe the acknowledgements belong at the beginning, front and center. In fact, I almost want to include them at the beginning and at the end. But I've restrained myself, and just included them once!

One of the themes of my running has been gratitude. So, when it comes time to write my acknowledgements, I've got a lot to say! Where to begin? Well, I think the best place is the beginning, with my Mom and Dad. I was raised with unconditional love and support and given every opportunity to succeed in this world. I've always valued that opportunity and vowed to myself to take advantage of it. And their love and support has continued throughout every step of my adult life. My Mom in particular has thrown herself into my running with great enthusiasm, traveling to watch my first three marathons and following my blogs and email updates with great interest and support throughout my running adventure. Mom and Dad, thank you for your love and support!

Speaking of enthusiasm and support, that brings me to my Mom's brother, my Uncle Jack. Jack has also traveled to see my first three marathons and reads my blogs religiously. Jack encouraged me to follow through with my writing and to eventually pull together this book. His enthusiasm has inspired me and energized me greatly. Jack, it has been a pleasure and a joy to share this journey with you!

Being married to a marathoner is not easy. Marathon training is a huge time commitment and requires a great investment of time and energy. Throughout this all, my wife Anne has stood by me, accepting each new marathon journey, but also sharing her love and support all along the way. I have tried very hard to balance my running with the rest of my life and to make time for my family along the way, but it has been a huge commitment nonetheless and has taken away from other things. Anne has been with me every step of the way. So many times I have returned from an exhausting run to be greeted by a delicious home –cooked meal. Anne, I love you and am thankful for you every day! You make my life whole!

Our home is filled with love and support and that brings me to my kids Eliza and Kevin. Eliza and Kevin have also put up with my extensive training schedule, sometimes at the expense of other parts of our lives. And they have added their support along the way. And, as far as Kevin in particular, Kevin was my inspiration to really get into running to begin with. His running inspired me to start and some of my favorite runs and races have been those I've done together with Kevin. Eliza and Kevin, I love you both and I am proud of you!

Kevin's running brings me to Heike Tuplin. Heike was both Eliza's and Kevin's third grade teacher. But, even more important than that, she coaches the South Shore Fireboltz, the youth running club which Kevin ran with from first grade all the way until high school. Heike is an incredible woman, a wonderful teacher, and a dedicated, caring and knowledgeable coach. She has been one of the most important people in Kevin's life, giving him a solid foundation in running and getting him immersed in a sport he loves. Along the way, she also got me hooked on running. And, while she is Kevin's coach, she has become a kind of coach and advisor to me as well. After I run a race that I'm really excited about, Heike is one of the first people I think to tell about it. Heike, thank you so much for all of your work and support through the years, you have made a huge difference!

Throughout my running journey, I have received great support from family, friends, and co-workers. If I tried to list them all, I would fail and I don't want to do that. But, for all of you who have posted Facebook comments, sent me supportive emails, or asked me how my running is going, I have appreciated all of it!

When I traveled to Chicago for the Chicago Marathon, my Mom's friend Junia Hedberg was incredibly gracious in driving us through the ENTIRE marathon course on the day before the race. Junia was so generous with her time and her efforts helped make Chicago a much better experience for me, as well as for my Mom and my Uncle Jack. And, since then, Junia has also been a source of support and advice in self-publishing a book. Junia, thank you for all of your support!

When Erika and I traveled to Philadelphia, we had the pleasure of staying with the world's most gracious hosts, Harriet and John Beckerman. I go way back with Harriet and John, as I went to high school with their son Pete, so I already knew all about how wonderful they are. They were the perfect hosts to both me and Erika, making us feel at home and helping to make Philadelphia such a fantastic experience for both of us. Harriet and John, thank you so much!

Several friends in particular do jump out for their running companionship. I'll start with my co-worker Mike. I ran a number of speed workouts with Mike last year, several in brutal snowy and icy conditions. Mike introduced me to my first track meet, which was a blast. And, along the way, he has been a supportive friend and colleague, always ready with advice and supportive feedback. Mike, thanks so much, and I'm looking forward to more runs together!

More recently, I started running with my co-worker Jordan, working specifically on speed and tempo workouts. Jordan is younger and faster than me, but has been a great running companion, helping to pace me on my weekly tempo workouts. In addition, to being a really strong runner, he brings a fun, positive and supportive attitude. Jordan, I'm looking forward to many more runs together!

Bear with me now while I grab a box of tissues. There's one more person to recognize and thank, my running partner and friend Erika. Erika and I did not begin running together until the summer of 2014, but I feel like we've always been running together. You will read much more about Erika throughout this book as we have run a lot of both training runs and races together this past year. And she wrote a foreword for me to introduce this story, sharing her perspective on running together. Our runs together have been marked by a combination of support, camaraderie, humor, toughness, gratitude, and joy. Many have been very tough and painful for one or the other of us, or sometimes both of us. And we've not just run together, but shared medical advice, consulted on training, provided pep talks, commiserated over setbacks, and celebrated accomplishments through email along the way. Through all of this we forged not just a running partnership, but also a wonderful friendship. We have had an incredible journey together. Erika, thank you for every step along the way. Thank you for being a fantastic running partner, and for being a thoughtful and supportive friend! It has been a joy and I look forward to many more running adventures together!

Introduction

There is nothing remarkable about me as a runner. There are many better runners out there in the world. Much better runners. There also are many people who are far more knowledgeable about running than I am. So I have neither special ability nor any particular expertise to contribute to a discourse on running. I also do not have a particularly dramatic story, as some runners do. What I do have is my own. My own thoughts and reflections about my time as a Runner.

I use Runner here in capital letters as a kind of title. It was in the fall of 2009, at the age of 40, that I first began to become a Runner. This happened gradually. But the more I ran, the more engaged I became and the more progress I made. 2012 was the first year when, in my mind, I really was a Runner. In January 2012, I wrote my first blog entry about my running, and I'm so glad I did. I wrote only sporadically during 2012. But then, as my running picked up, I wrote a little more in 2013. And then, in the most incredible running year of my life - in 2014, I wrote quite regularly. And, like my running, my writing has continued to pick up speed ever since. These blog entries are treasures to me now.

In this book, I've woven together many of my blog entries, adding an introduction to each one, reflecting back about each blog entry after the fact. In some cases I've used these introductions to fill important gaps that I did not get to write about. With the exception of minor editing, I have left these blog entries as I wrote them at the time. I want them to be an accurate reflection of my journey as a runner. I've not included every blog entry that I've written, but rather pulled the ones that I find most interesting to read now. Together they tell my story – so far.

I will continue blogging about my running, as it means more than ever to me now. So as my running journey continues, I will continue to tell my story. But my story to date is still quite rich for me. The title of this book, *10K and Beyond*, only seems fitting, as that is the title of my blog.

This book is divided into three sections based on my marathon experiences. The first section tells the story of my early days as a runner through my first marathon in Newport, RI in fall of 2013. The second section covers my 2014 running, culminating in the Chicago Marathon in October of 2014. The third section covers my most epic year of running to date when I trained for and ran three marathons in 2015. Each marathon experience is very meaningful to me in different ways. This book tells the story of all of them, along with many other races I've run along the way. My first two marathon journeys were largely solo voyages, whereas my 2015 odyssey was shared with my neighbor, running partner, and friend Erika.

As you read through this book, I hope my passion, joy, and gratitude leap off the pages for you. My running journey has greatly enriched my life, inspired me, and I believe, improved me as a person. I hope my story inspires you in some way too, whether it's to run yourself or to venture out on some other adventure in your life. Enjoy the journey!

Section 1

January 2012 – January 2014

From 5Ks to the Newport Marathon

This was the very first blog entry I wrote. And, in some ways, it means more than any other, as this was the start of all that came after it. This was when I decided to title my blog "10K and Beyond". I obviously had some idea then about where I may be headed, as it is a bit of a leading title. But I honestly had no idea that I'd have done so much just four years later. Looking back at my times back then, I realize that, while these are now slow times for me, at that time they really did represent meaningful accomplishment. While I know I can't improve forever, this gives me continued optimism as I strive to continue to improve four years later.

My Start in Running, January 28, 2012

This blog is about my path to running a 10K – and perhaps beyond. I'm now 42 and have been active and playing ultimate [Frisbee] for a decade. But I only began running in 2009. My son Kevin, who was 9 at the time, had been running track and cross country for South Shore Fireboltz, a local kids running club. He ran his first 5K at the Jeff Coombs Road Race in Abington, MA that year. It looked like so much fun, I was motivated to give it a try myself.

That Thanksgiving, I ran my first Turkey Trot and 5K in Hingham, MA. I ran with Kevin for most of the way, until he pulled away from me in the last 1/2 mile. But I had a blast and finished in a time I was very happy with – 25:15. Running with Kevin was a great part of the fun. It was also very energizing to have onlookers cheering us on – something that's totally missing when you just go out for a run.

I now have seven road races behind me – all 5Ks except for one 4.5 mile road race. And I've kept all the bibs! Along the way my 5K PR has dropped to 22:50. Of course Kevin has made great strides and improvement even faster. Although I've always been a little cautious about wear and tear on my knees, I've decided it's time to move forward and run a 10K. I've registered for Evan's Run in Norwell on May 20 as my first 10K – of course running with Kevin.

We did get out for our first 10K on our own on January 7 – with a baseline time of 54:00 for me and 53:30 for Kevin. We've been lucky this winter

– lots of mild weather for running. Today is in the mid 40's and partly cloudy – a nice day to run as January goes. So Kevin and I will be off shortly. Today's run will be 3.2 miles. I'll track my runs along the way to our first 10K here. At that point, if all goes well, my question will be what's next. But, that's a question for another day.

I was on a roll – two entries on one day! This one is interesting to me both for the times, and for what I considered to be "short" and "long" runs. At this stage, a short run was 1.6 miles, whereas 3.2 miles was a "long" run. Hah! Now I hardly ever run less than 4 miles, it's almost not worth bothering for that distance. And a long run today has an entirely different meaning to me.

Three New PRs, January 28, 2012

Today Kevin and I ran a relatively tough 3.2 mile route that we run. Thanks to Kevin's GPS watch, we know now that it's actually 3.26 miles. Today, I ran my PR for this particular run – 25:57. As usual, Kevin finished a little bit ahead of me at 25:45. We always run together until the last 1/4 mile or so and then he pulls away, despite my resolve to stick with him!

This continues a positive trend as 3 of my last 4 runs, at three different distances, have been PRs. Looks like our 6 mile run earlier this month is starting to pay dividends. Tomorrow's supposed to be another sunny day in the low to mid 40s, so I think I'm going to try to get out again tomorrow. Running two days in a row is always tough for me, so I think I'll keep the distance short – maybe 1.6 miles.

Kevin has indoor meets coming up on 2/5 and 2/12 so this will help keep him in good shape for those and hopefully he'll get good times in those. I believe he'll be running the 800m and mile in both events. Those have become his specialty.

Hard to believe, but I had just run my second 6 mile run at this point in my life, getting ready for my first 10K. I still remember the feeling of pride – not just in the time, but even that I was able to run 6+ miles period. Also an interesting look back at one of Kevin's indoor track meets, when he was 12 years old.

A Marathon Day, February 13, 2012

No, not that kind of marathon. Kevin and I spent 7.5 hours at the Needham Indoor Classic at the Reggie Lewis Center in Boston today. Was it worth it? In the end, absolutely yes. Kevin ran the 1500m and 800m. Although neither time was a PR, they were both just a few seconds off his best times, which is good considering this is basically out of season for track and he hasn't run sprinting races like that. We basically don't have an indoor track season, it's just running on our own. He also did the standing long jump today, but still it was a lot of sitting around in between the three events!

On Friday I went for the second 6.2 mile run in my life and did very well. I ran it in about 51 minutes, about 3 minutes faster than my first time. So I was thrilled about that. The only downside is that my knee bugged me a little bit in the end, but it doesn't seem to be bad. It was yet another mild day Friday. Tonight it's getting cold for one of the few times this winter – down to 12 degrees or so. But I believe it's scheduled to warm up yet again after that. I can't wait until we have enough extra daylight so that I can run after work – we're almost there!

Well, this was the beginning of the end and the moment when I think I first truly became a Runner in spirit. It didn't take me long to shift from my first 10K to thinking about my first half! As it turns out, it wasn't the BAA half, but rather a small half marathon in Wilmington, MA on September 23, 2012. I'll write more about that later. As far as this 10 mile run, this was one of the key moments in my running career, a moment when the seemingly crazy "What if...?" became real. I don't think I fully realized it then but, looking back at this moment with hindsight today, it seems inevitable that I would run the half and then run a Marathon. But I needed to take my time and go through a careful, logical progression to get to that point.

My 10K and My 10 Mile Run, June 10, 2012

My first 10K has come and gone and it was a success. It was May 20 in Norwell and the weather was beautiful. It was a little warm, but not terribly hot. I finished in 50:20, while Kevin finished in 49:20. He was the only boy under 18 who even ran the 10K so he got first place in his age group. He won a glass and a mug. We both felt pretty good and maintained a steady pace throughout. I even passed two people right before the finish, so I finished strong.

Now that I've completed the 10K, I've asked myself, what now? So, after a few weeks of some regular running, I had a personal day Friday and some free time. I decided to go for a LONG run and went for 10 miles, by far my longest run ever. (that had been the 10K). Although I ended up walking for three short stretches between 7 miles and 10 miles, I felt pretty good both during and after. I finished in about 92 minutes, so just over a nine minute mile pace, which exceeded my expectations. Now that I had run 10 miles and lived to tell about it, I started thinking a little bigger.

While we were out buying Kevin his new running spikes, I found a running calendar with races listed and started skimming through the half-marathons. I looked a little more closely at the Boston Athletic Association half-marathon in October, which looks very well supported and is at a nice time of year to run. And now I'm thinking about entering it. They have some training guidance on their site and I printed out a beginner's training plan for a half-marathon. Today I ran my first run off of that training plan and am on my way! I can't even register until mid-July so I'm not committed yet, but mentally I'm feeling pretty good and pretty certain about it. Stay tuned for updates.

In the meantime, Kevin, Eliza and I are entered in the "Finish at the 50" on July 3rd in Foxborough. It sounds like a blast – you get to finish at the 50 yard line in Gillette Stadium! Then, Kevin and I will run the Hingham 4th of July race (4.5 miles) the next morning. Those two together will test our endurance. But we've already run the Hingham race once and loved it and the Foxborough race looked too fun to resist.

I skipped over a lot here. My first half marathon in Wilmington, MA on September 23, 2012 was a fantastic race for me and worthy of a lot more attention. Running that half at just over an 8:00 pace at that stage in my running career was another of these milestone races for me. For starters it was my first half marathon, which is huge to begin with. But, to run it at that pace, and a very steady consistent pace at that, was really remarkable. This was when I first thought about the "magic of distance running". And, as you will see that success led directly to signing up for my first marathon. Again, it didn't take long! (One note, I think my math was off on the "nearly 1,000 miles" below, probably more like 800.)

It's A Marathon, Not A Sprint!, April 3, 2013

What holds true for 26.2 miles is exponentially true for marathon training! Today is the first day of my marathon training schedule. Ultimately, I will have run nearly 1,000 miles before I complete my first marathon in Newport, RI on October 13, 2013. Today, I ran 5.

I learned a little bit about the road ahead training for my first half-marathon last year. I never thought I could run that distance at the pace I did, just over an 8 minute mile pace, finishing in 1:46. I learned the power of distance running; how little, gradual improvements over months of training can ultimately make a huge difference. So, conceptually at least, the same should hold true for a marathon.

Between now and the race, I'll go out for over a hundred runs. Some will be great, some will be crummy. One down.

I believe this was the only time I wrote specifically about the 2013 Boston Marathon. I didn't write about it again later, but that 2013 Boston Run to Remember was a very special race. We ran with Sean Collier's badge number pinned to our backs. (He was the MIT police officer who was shot following the bombings.)

Marathon Training After the Boston Marathon, April 18, 2013

I'm now in the third week of my marathon training schedule. However, since the tragic events at the Boston Marathon earlier this week, running feels a little bit different. Our most direct connection to the Boston Marathon is that Kevin ran a 1-mile run up and down Heartbreak Hill the day before the race. (He did very well, by the way, running it in 6:24.) We considered going into Boston to watch near the finish, but decided we did not want to brave the crowds and decided to just watch the top runners on TV instead. We went bowling that afternoon and didn't find out about the bombings until that evening.

My first run after the Marathon – on Tuesday – was the toughest. The television images and videos were fresh in my mind and that was all I could think of throughout my run. Despite that, running felt right, and mildly therapeutic. Since then, I've run three days in a row and am feeling more comfortable with it. (Although I almost got hit twice by two drivers running red lights this evening!) As I continue my training, I will run in the Boston Run to Remember, a half-marathon scheduled for May 26 in Boston. I expect that to be a very emotional race setting, especially since it is sponsored by the Boston Police Dept. and Boston Police Runner's Club. As I train for that and as I continue to train for my first marathon in Newport, RI in October, I know that the Boston Marathon will be on my mind. I also know that my resolve to run is now even stronger.

This is not a particularly meaningful entry, but I always liked the title. It's also a good glimpse of how much heat and humidity affect my runs, especially on longer runs.

Northern Comfort, July 10, 2013

We recently returned from a family vacation to Florida, by way of Charleston, SC. After six runs in the hot and humid South, it was a joy to be home this AM and run in 70 degree weather. My pace, which had dropped off dramatically while in SC and FL, returned to its normal range this AM. It was nice to have that affirmation that the problem was not me, but rather the weather. I suppose if I ran in that type of weather regularly, I would adapt to it and get better – I had already started to – but it's certainly nicer and easier up here.

My marathon training is continuing to go well. My longest run so far is 17 miles and I'm scheduled to run 18 miles this Sunday. In June, I ran a total of 127 miles! Between my running and two track meets for Kevin this week, it will be a busy running week .

I never felt that I got a runner's high, but there are those days when running feels really good – just like the title of this blog. When those days happen, they are a real pleasure.

Smooth and Strong, July 25, 2013

I had an amazing 6 mile run tonight. In baseball, they talk about nights when a pitcher has "their best stuff." Tonight I felt like I had my best stuff running. It's a little hard to describe, but it was as if I had an internal engine powering me and I was just going along for the ride. Everything felt smooth and strong, even as I had a little soreness here and there. But the soreness was irrelevant because I just ran through it. Even when my pace flagged a little bit, my running still felt smooth and strong.

I ended up not running a PR, though it was close. My last mile, which had the greatest amount of climbs, was by far my fastest. It was like I had another gear to kick in. And it did. It's not that it was easy, I know I worked hard, but there was this inner power behind my running that made me feel like I was almost gliding across the pavement. I've gone on enough runs to know this is unusual for me. Just a time to sit back and enjoy the ride.

I always liked this blog entry for the insight it offers into my training for my first marathon. In my mind, while a marathon is a special event, the training is the really cool part and where the magic happens. And, regardless of how the race itself goes, the feeling of accomplishment over the progress achieved through six months of training is hugely rewarding. And that first marathon , when it's all new, is especially meaningful.

A Funny Thing Happened on My Way to the Marathon, September 8, 2013

Not funny in the sense of comical, but interesting. In fact, marathon training is full of interesting developments, not all of them pleasant. However one of the coolest is how one's perception of "a long run" changes over the course of the training. When I started my training in April, anything over 13.1 miles was unknown territory. And, for a number of my runs, I was running what at that time was the longest run of my life.

As I went, I became more comfortable with longer distances, as I should, and previously unknown territory became familiar and comfortable. Going for a 15, 16, 17, or 18 mile run became a more comfortable experience, albeit still challenging. Just a week ago, I ran a milestone run, my first 20 mile run. It went great, and I finished in 2:57, where I had hoped to be. But, most importantly, I did not "hit the wall" and felt strong throughout. So, I decided I would extend my training to run a 21 mile run, before tapering my mileage prior to the Marathon. I will do that run next week.

This week was a recovery week for me, so I lowered my long run distance to 16 miles so that I could be more fresh for my 21 mile run next week. Since I was doing a shorter run (returning to my original point above), I decided to push my pace and see how many miles I could run under an 8:30 mile pace. Turns out it was 13. I pushed my pace so hard, it was closer to 8:00 for many miles, that I ran out of steam at the end and ran/walked a very slow last mile in about 10:30. But, I still finished in 2:14, well under the 8:30 pace goal that I had set overall. Once again a successful run, in that I set a goal and met it!

One of the other equally important, though less exciting aspects of my training has been learning how I should drink and eat over the course of my long runs. This can be complicated because there is no one right answer, but I've found what works for me. About 20 ounces of water every 5 miles, with an energy gel about every 40 minutes, plus a Cliff bar about 20 minutes prior to the run seems to be the right formula for me. Similarly I think I've found the right clothes to wear as well to be (reasonably) comfortable on long runs.

Now all I have to do is make it through my 21 mile run next week, followed by 3 weeks of reduced mileage and I will be at RACE DAY! While I know the marathon itself will be the single most challenging and exciting event of this whole process, I believe that the real magic has taken place during this amazing 6 month training process. The transformation in me as a distance runner, while still an early work in progress, is really stunning looking back at where I was six months ago, or even more so compared to a year ago.

I did it! Wow, it still gives me goose bumps. Right behind me, my medal is hanging on the wall. I continue to be really proud of how well I trained for this race as a complete novice, staying injury free, but preparing myself well. I don't know if you can sense the feeling of momentum in my writing, but I certainly can. It's most obvious at the end, but it runs throughout the writing.

Reflections on My First Marathon, October 29, 2013

So my first marathon is now history. While I remain a relative distance running novice, I feel I've learned a lot over the past year. Here are my reflections about what I've learned training for a marathon – at least for me. Others may have different experiences, but this is what I found.

1. Your training Plan is the Key – I made a training plan beginning April 1 and running through October 13 (no pun intended) and followed it as closely as possible. I did make a few adjustments along the way about which days I ran and tweaked mileage up and down a bit along the way. But the only two runs I missed were when I had minor skin surgery with stitches on my leg along the way. I really believe that if you follow your training plan and stay healthy, you will succeed in your marathon. But I believe you have to make it a priority in your life and commit to it. I think I would have really struggled on Race Day without my regular, solid training foundation. Your plan should build mileage gradually from week to week, but I also like the idea of a low-mileage week every 4 weeks to allow your body a little rest and recovery.

2. *Your Plan Must be Right for You* – My plan had me running 4 days per week and peaking at a weekly mileage of about 40 miles. I know many people run more days per week (5 or even 6) and run more miles (some significantly more.) But, for me, I could not afford the time to train more and I think I may have caused some injuries if I did. As it was, I stayed healthy throughout, but also increased my stamina to the point where I could run 26.2 miles at a fairly steady pace. I do think it's difficult to train successfully for a marathon running less than 4 days per week or much fewer miles than I did. You might be able to get by with 3 days per week but, if you did, I think those would have to be long runs.

3. Get a good pair of running shoes – This is very basic advice, and repeated everywhere, but this is important. Spend a little more money to get a good pair, and go to a running store to buy them. They should examine your gait and fit you with a pair of shoes that's right for you.

4. Vary your Runs – I ran a lot of my runs off of the same core loop, but also tried to work in different runs along different routes. To the extent you can, finding good scenic areas to run in helps too. You will run a lot of miles on a lot of days so a little variety will be important. Build in speed interval training for your shorter runs, for the variety but also to work on speed at least a little bit.

5. Train for your Marathon Course – Most of all, if you are running a hilly course, you absolutely have to run hills during your training. Similarly, because you may get unlucky and it may rain on RACE DAY, don't shy away from running in the rain. Also do your long runs at about the same time that you will be running your marathon. Think carefully about what marathon you choose – especially for your first. I'd suggest not picking an especially challenging course. You'll also want to think about whether you want one locally, or want to travel. And, also what time of year. Living in the Northeast, I can't imagine doing anything other than a Fall marathon because I can't imagine training during the winter for a spring marathon, but that's me.

6. Training is about more than Running – Your training provides a great opportunity to figure out what you want to wear beyond your shoes. What shorts, shirts, socks, etc. are comfortable on long runs. This may be a personal preference thing, but I loved having a GPS watch. In addition, you need to learn what to eat and drink during your long runs. It's too far not to both drink and eat, so you need to figure out what works for you during your training. I'll tell you what worked for me, but you may have a totally different experience. For my long runs (> 10 miles) I would:

- eat a Cliff bar about 20 minutes before my run with a little water

- drink a 20 ounce bottle of water and take one GU gel about every 40 minutes

- drink a protein recovery drink after I finished (I used GU Recovery Brew)

7. You don't Need to run 26.2 Miles During Training

Unless you're an advanced runner, I've bought into the idea that you do not need to run 26.2 miles during training. My long run was 21 miles and I think that was about right. I think you definitely need to run 20 and I could see going 22 or 23, but I wouldn't have wanted to do more than that. I agree with the logic that the cost:benefit ratio is poor. You don't need to run that 26.2 mile distance to succeed and you put yourself at greater risk of injury. My only regret is that I didn't get in a couple more 20 mile runs. But there's always next time...

8. Run a Half First – If you are thinking about running your first marathon, you should absolutely, positively, definitely run a half marathon first. That will give you a pretty good idea of whether you can and want to handle running a marathon. I feel that if you can run a half strongly, then that's a good foundation to start training for a marathon.

9. Nothing New on Race Day! – As much as possible, RACE DAY should be an exact replica of your training experience. Your shoes and all your clothing should be things you've been comfortable with on your long runs. Your food and drink before and during the run should be the same as what you did on your long training runs. As much as possible, change nothing from your long training runs. And, especially on your first marathon, enjoy it! You've already accomplished so much just to be on the start line. While you can't control the weather or a freak injury, all your training up to that point will put you in a great position to be successful. Relax, and be positive every step of the way.

10. Just Do It! – If you're thinking about running a marathon, my advice is to do it, but to work your way up to it. If you're running 5ks, you should start by running at least one 10K, and then running a half. If that all goes well, as it did for me, my advice is to go for it. The whole experience is incredible and, now that I've done it, I can't imagine not having done it.

25

11. Tell Everyone – I told so many people about my marathon training all along the way – family, facebook friends, neighbors, co-workers, the guy at Tedeschi's whom I bought water from every Sunday, and so on. The support that you get from this kind of network is critical.

I'm planning run my second Marathon next fall. I don't know where or when yet. But, just two weeks after my first marathon, I'm already looking forward to the next one!

Well, if my enthusiasm didn't come through clearly before, it's virtually bubbling over now. 2013 was really a great and very meaningful running year for me. While I was primed for it, what I didn't realize then is how 2014 would be even better!

Last Race of 2013, December 9, 2013

Kevin and I finished our 2013 road races on a high note at the Mansfield Frosty Five 5K this AM. It was about 20 degrees when we got up and probably close to 30 by race time, but that did not deter us one bit. This race was an amazing deal, as we each received a $20 gift certificate to Marathon Sports, a winter running hat, and running socks for our $25 registration fees. In fact, we got paid to run this race. The course was through a business park in Mansfield, MA, which was completely flat – a very fast course.

It's amazing how 30 degrees doesn't really feel that cold once you get going fast. Kevin and I positioned ourselves right up front and got a good start in the race – which was a complete contrast with our ill-fated Thanksgiving Day race. We ended up running it in just over 21 minutes (21:07 for Kevin and 21:11 for me), and finished 26th and 28th overall out of 238 runners. I'm quite proud of the way that we are running these days, as we are routinely finishing in the top 10-20 percent of the local road races that we're running in. I had really hoped to break the 21 minute mark for the first time in this race, but that milestone will have to wait until 2014. My first mile was about 6:14, but I just couldn't hold that pace. But

I'm confident I'll reach that milestone then and be able to hold that fast pace longer.

Now I don't have any races planned until March. I had been looking forward to the break to give my body a chance to recover from all of the nagging ailments that have been wearing on me this fall. But, it's amazing how addicting running races can be. As soon as I crossed the finish line, my next thought was that I want to run again to hit that 21 minute milestone. I am really hooked on this.

2013 has been quite the running year for me. My marathon and the marathon training will always remain the primary highlight of the year. But along the way, I also set PRs at every distance I ran – 5K (twice), 10K (twice), and the half-marathon. What are the odds that I can wait until March to race again? Maybe nasty winter weather will change my mind but I'm already looking forward to our next race in March 2014. I'm not sure I can wait.

This isn't my absolute favorite blog entry, but I think it's an important one in trying to explain why I run and what I like about it. One thing that's become quite clear to me is that my enjoyment from running has continued to grow steadily, over the last couple of years in particular. I'm not sure how long it will continue, but I'm going to be sure to enjoy it as long as I can!

Why I Run, January 19, 2014

Why do you run? Everyone who runs is asked this question at some point by people who don't run. The more often and the farther you run, the more people wonder. Or maybe the question goes something like, "Why do you put yourself through it?" It may be prefaced by "I couldn't run a mile." Or, "I tried running, but it's too boring." That second one used to be me, But, since my first 5K in 2009, I've gotten increasingly hooked. The funny thing is, I can't give a simple, clear answer for why I do it. And, sometimes the answer varies a little bit depending on where I'm running and with whom. But I know some of the things I like about running that I think, collectively, form my rationale. So, not necessarily in order, they are:

1. I love the numbers! I love keeping track of miles run, cumulative miles, time, pace, and so on. It's very satisfying for me to know how far I've run and when I've eclipsed a personal best for a particular distance. And, so far, I continue to improve. I know I will reach a day and age, sooner or later, when I will no longer keep on getting faster. And then my goals will shift. But the great thing about running is that you can always set new and different goals that fit you. And, that's why they set up age groups for races. That brings me to my second point.

2. I love races! Don't get me wrong, I am not running races to win them. I'm not that kind of runner. But I enjoy the whole experience of getting your bib, warming up, stretching, running sprint outs and getting up to the line. I get a rush out of the thrill of lining up and preparing for the gun and the fast start of a whole pack of runners. Then, settling in to a pace after a few minutes. And, finally the final sprint (in relative terms) to the finish. As with all of my runs, races for me are mostly about competing against myself and trying to beat my previous PRs. Sure, I'm running with a bunch of other runners, and trying to keep up with or pass other runners can provide added motivation and focus. I also pay attention to how I finish overall and within my age group. Not every race will be a PR, but every race holds that promise at the start.

3. Kevin: My son Kevin's running is the reason I started running. I ran my first 5K with him and continue to run a few races with him every year. And, when he doesn't have his own training schedule, we run together. That will probably change next year when Kevin starts running high school cross country but I'm sure we'll still find time to run races together once in a while. My greatest experience running with Kevin was the 2013 Plymouth River 5K when we ran together at the front for nearly the entire race. We ended up finishing 1st and 2nd overall – Kevin 1st and me 2nd. Kevin almost always beats me (I can think of one exception), but so far we are closely enough matched that we can run together for most of the race, until he blows me away at the end. But the shared experience is fantastic!

4. Getting in shape: This is a secondary reason for me. And, it's balanced by the fact that running poses some injury risk. But, I've certainly gotten into much better shape through running. And, as long as I'm smart about training and pay attention to my body, I can reduce my risk of injury and lessen the length and severity of any injuries that I do get.

5. Because it's there! This is kind of tough to explain, but it kind of sums it up. It's the same kind of rationale for why someone may climb a high mountain. It may sound a little dumb but, for those who've experienced it, you probably know what I mean. I think this reason holds true especially for longer, more challenging races like a half marathon or marathon. Later this year, I'm planning to run a triple threat challenge: a 1-mile run, followed by a 5K, followed by a half-marathon. Why go through that? You guessed it.

Section 2

January – October 2014

The Chicago Marathon

At this point, I was just about to begin a planned month off to let my body heal – for all of February. But I was certainly looking ahead to a very active spring. I didn't know yet about Chicago, but I already had five races planned in April and May alone!

Spring Race Schedule, January 26, 2014

While we're still in the throes of icy January weather, I've already started to line up a full schedule of spring races, and am looking for more.

As of now, things kick off with the Cohasset Road Race by the Sea, a beautiful and very hilly 10K along the coast. Kevin and I ran this one together last year, and he beat me pretty soundly. This could very well be my toughest race of the spring, so I'd love to find something else to run before this – maybe a late March race.

After that, my next planned race is the 26.2 Relay Challenge, in Plymouth, on April 26. This race is a six-person marathon relay, with every leg starting and ending at the same spot. I'm working on finalizing a team for this one, but know that it will include Kevin. It sounds like a great time, and would be a very different race from anything else I've ever run.

Race #3 is my first half-marathon of the year, the Providence Rhode Race, on May 4. The course looks to be pretty flat, so this should be a relatively easy half and I'm hoping for perfect running weather, given the time of year. I spent a year in Providence right after college, so this will be a bit of a homecoming for me.

After taking Mother's Day weekend off, Kevin and I will run another 10K together, Evan's Run in Norwell on May 18. This will be our third straight year running this race and we've both done well there in the past. There are some hilly stretches, but it's nothing like Cohasset, so the course feels a lot more manageable.

Finally, May will wrap up with the Boston Run to Remember, on May 25. I ran this half-marathon for the first time last year and loved it. It's run in remembrance of police officers who have lost their lives in the line of duty. Needless to say, after the Boston Marathon last year it was a very special event. And the course itself is great. At least based on last year, it starts and ends at the Boston Seaport Convention Center and begins running through Downtown Boston, where the streets are closed to traffic. It then crossed the Longfellow Bridge (not sure about that part this year) and went down Memorial Drive to Harvard. Then we turned around, traveled back into Boston, looped past the Boston Public Garden and back to the Seaport. There were a lot of supporters along the way, including more than 100 police officers from towns across the state lining Memorial Drive and giving high-fives to runners. I ran a PR here last year and hope to build on that in 2014.

It's shaping up to be a busy spring, all of which will lay the groundwork for training for a fall marathon. I'm hoping that will be the Chicago Marathon in October – just depends on whether I get selected in the race lottery. I should know that by mid-April. Between now and these races, I'll be in a bit of a rest & rehab mode, trying to strengthen my foot and ankle, which has been bugging me off and on for about six months. Then I can hit the ground running :)

This seems like a distant memory now, but earlier this spring I had been worried about recurring pain in the top of my left foot. It still comes back from time to time but not enough to really affect my running. It seems to get aggravated in particular when my shoes get to the point where I have a lot of miles on them or when I lace them too tightly. So I'm working to continue to try to learn how my body reacts to running and manage it better. When I got a positive diagnosis after a couple of doctor visits, it came as a big relief to me!

A Green Light to Run, March 15, 2014

Ever since last September (starting just before my first marathon), I've had on and off pain in the top of my left foot. It's been something I can run through and was decent through my marathon. But, after it persisted for months, I decided to look into it more to ensure it wasn't anything that would be a further injury risk. So, after a visit to my primary care doctor, I had x-rays come back negative. Then, after the pain persisted, I had my first ever podiatrist visit. Long story short, he said it is not a big deal, and something I can manage through my choice of shoes, certain stretching, and maybe occasional icing.

For me, this comes as essentially a green light to dive headlong into my 900+ mile 2014 training schedule. This had been nagging in the back of my mind for months and now I feel free of it and feel like I can enjoy running without worry. Later today or tomorrow, I'll go to Marathon Sports to shop for my next pair of running shoes. I'll be off to the track with Kevin later this afternoon to run in fantastic running weather on a sunny 50 degree day. For the first time this year, we're going to run a timed mile – aka a fast mile.

There's a famous quote by Ernie Banks, the great Chicago Cubs shortstop, It's a great day for a ball game; let's play two!" Today, I'm feeling it's such a great day for a run, that I want to run twice! I'm looking forward to the joy of simply running on a beautiful day!

This 10K was the race that set me on my way in 2014, the beginning of 9 race PRs this year! This one was special because I trained specifically for it and I ran so strongly. What a great confidence builder to set me on my way!

Those Hills Aren't So Bad After All, April 11, 2014

I've been thinking about writing for a few days, but have had a bit of writer's block. I wanted to write about the recent Cohasset 10K that Kevin and I ran together, but just couldn't get inspired to get started. Then this title came to me and it clicked for me.

Kevin and I ran the Cohasset 10K together for the first time last year and I, in particular, found the hills really tough. I ended up doing OK, finishing just under 48 minutes but it really d

Wow, what an amazing spring I had – setting one PR after another!
Every race I entered was a PR! The best of these was the last one, the
Boston Run to Remember, when I set a Half marathon PR by more than 4
minutes and beat my time on the same course from the year before by
nearly 6 minutes!

A Spring of PRs, June 8, 2014

I've been meaning to write about my spring races for a while now, but
haven't had the chance and the energy to write until now. All told, I had
6 PRs (personal records) this spring. And Kevin, who's been running very
well, has had 6 as well. My four PRs that stand out the most for me are
my two 10K PRs and my two half-marathon PRs.

This sequence of races began on April 6, when Kevin and I both set PRs
in Cohasset. I finished in 45:46, beating my previous PR of 46:07 and
beating my time in the same race in 2013 by more than two
minutes. Cohasset is a hilly course so, to set a PR there is
noteworthy. Given that I set a PR on such a challenging course, I knew I
could set an even better time on an easier 10K course.

But first, I had the Providence Half Marathon to run in early May. This
was a fun race to run with decent crowd support and a pretty flat, easy
course. Here, on a great day weather-wise, I finished in 1:42 even, beating
my previous half-marathon PR of 1:43:20 from last year. But I had this
feeling that, despite getting a PR, I had not run my best race. My pace had
slipped at several points during the race and, while I rebounded and hung
in, it did not feel like I ran my best.

Up next was my second 10K of the spring, Evan's Run in Norwell. This
has become one of my favorite races and Kevin and I have run it together
for three years in a row. Now that Kevin will be running in high school
next year, this was our last race there together, at least for a few years. We
both ran well again and both set PRs. I finished in JUST under 45 minutes
(my goal for the year), finishing at 44:59. I was actually upset at the end
because I thought I had just missed 45 minutes due to fading down the
stretch. But, much to my relief, turns out I had just made it. Again, we

were fortunate to have really nice running weather, a consistent theme through this spring.

Finally, I ran the best race of all on May 25. I also think this was the best race I've ever run. This was the Boston Run to Remember, where I set a PR last year of 1:43:20. This year, once again, the weather was nice, partly sunny, mild, but not too hot. This race stands out for me in the way that I actually gradually improved my pace through the race. As I went, I grew a little concerned that my pace was too fast, but I told myself to just hold that pace as long as I could. I was shooting to get under 1:40, which means that I had to run about a 7:38 pace. I kept on running sub 7:30 miles and, once I got to around 10 miles, I was even running sub 7:00 miles. Unfortunately my GPS watch was a little funky in this race, so I don't know exactly what my paces were. But, I know I was definitely under 7:00 miles. Ultimately, I finished in 1:37:38, more than 4 minutes under my previous PR, which was only three weeks old.

This is one of these races that's kind of a revelation. I honestly had no idea I could run like this for this distance. While it is hard to imagine ever running any better than this, the fact that I broke my previous best by such a large margin suggests that I can still do better, even though my future improvements may be more incremental.

I really like this entry. I'm not sure what I like so much, I guess it just really gives a good sense of my typical thought process during a long run. This run was a pretty solid run, which of course makes it more fun to look back on.

A 16 Mile Run – Mile by Mile, June 24, 2014

Yesterday, I went for a 16 mile run on a beautiful morning. As I thought along the way (2 hours and 12 minutes is a long time!) I thought I'd try writing a mile by mile account. Not sure how it will turn out, but I'm going to give it a crack.

Mile 1 – 7:47: This was an absolutely beautiful morning for a run! I started just before 8:00 and it was right around 60 degrees with bright sunshine. This was an easy mile – mostly downhill to Jackson Square! The 7:47 mile was an auspicious start to a long run.

Mile 2 – 7:58: Another solid mile and feeling very comfortable. Crossed the commuter rail tracks on Commercial Street, turning into Fort Hill Street. A little knee soreness and back tightness, but not bad.

Mile 3 – 8:00: My pace is dipping a little bit, but only to 8:00, which is actually right where I would like to be. Hung a right past Bare Cove Park onto West Street/Beal Street. (These street names are always changing.) So, all things considered, things are going well. The mild knee pain continues a little bit, but it fades in and out, and isn't worsening. Saw my first wildlife of the run to speak of – a rabbit.

Mile 4 – 8:08: My pace continues to slide little by little, mile by mile, but I'm still feeling solid. For some reason I always slow on this Beal Street stretch. The terrain isn't hard, I think it's partially due to needing to cross the street three times to stay on the sidewalk. But again, the dip wasn't bad. I'm still feeling cool, due to a combination of the relatively cool morning, the slight breeze, and the fact that there's still a lot of shade.

Mile 5- 8:07: Nice and steady now. I hung a right onto 3A in bright sunshine, which actually felt invigorating! This is a nice, flat stretch and I'm running well.

Mile 6 – 8:10: Took my first GU gel (Chocolate Outrage) at the start of the 6th mile. Very good pace, considering that I usually slow to take my gel. I stopped for water at a Tedeschi's at 5.3 miles. Normally I've drained my first 20 oz of water by then. But, today, I had a little extra left at that point. Saw my regular Tedeschi's clerk whom I see almost every Sunday in the summer. I was a little stiff coming out of the store, so I did a little stretching prior to starting up again, especially for my back. My other wildlife highlight of the run was a chipmunk. Ok, not that exciting, but more interesting than the countless squirrels I see.

Mile 7 – 8:13: A lot of times on long runs, I count other runners I see. I don't see a ton, but typically see at least 1 or 2 per mile. Today, I didn't see my first fellow runner until the end of mile 7. Just ran by Hingham Harbor, which is such a nice, quaint New England scene – lots of small boats floating serenely on the calm water. The calm harbor view was followed by my first significant climb up Summer Street.

Mile 8 – 7:55: My pace really picked up again in this mile – which I find to be one of the more boring stretches of the run. Summer Street, bearing right onto Rockland Street. But it had a slight downhill and then was flat, so it made for good running.

Mile 9 – 8:12: So my pace dropped a little bit. Again, the weather was still cool with a nice breeze and some decent shade, so I was able to skip my customary 2nd water stop at about the 9 mile mark. A pack of about 10 cyclists rolled by me – looks like fun – amazing how easily they pass by…

Mile 10 – 8:20: Turned for home onto 228. Ok, I'm feeling some fatigue now and it shows in my pace. This is nice rolling stretch along 228. Saw only my 2nd runner of the run, very unusual.

Mile 11 – 8:34: Sigh, I'm tired. I took my second GU gel, Vanilla Bean, which is just about my favorite flavor. I need it. Part of the pace drop was probably due to taking the gel, but I was fading. Seeing a couple more runners now. For any fellow runner reading this, I always wave and say hi to other runners, and it always gives me a little boost when someone says hi or waves back. Kind of makes that connection, especially when I'm out running on my own.

Mile 12 – 8:30: My goal here was for a negative split (pace faster than the last mile) and I got it – barely. The nice stretch along 228 rolls on and on But it's nice. Hingham has great streets to run on with nice sidewalks set back from the road and lovely yards and houses to run by. This is where I tell myself these long runs will pay off in races and focus on my pace, stride, and posture.

Mile 13 – 8:25: A second slight negative split in a row. I'm working hard now and happy with this slight improvement in pace this late into the run. Stopped at the small general store for my 2nd water break. I had to stretch out again after getting the water I was starting to tighten up. Sometimes the rest provided by a water break helps. But, often times, the break does me more harm than good, as it breaks my momentum and I lose the pace that I'm working hard to maintain. This one went OK.

Mile 14 – 8:22: A third straight negative split. Not quite the pace I want to be at eventually, but this is pretty good for now. Turning onto High Street now. I'm in very familiar territory now, in a stretch that I run very often. There's a slight uphill, but I crested it quickly and am still running steadily.

Mile 15 – 8:28: Back to Jackson Square. For my long runs, I try to stay focused in the moment – focused on each mile at a time. But now I'm admittedly fading and thinking ahead to finishing. Not where I want to be mentally and I keep on bringing myself back to the moment, back to my stride, posture, and pace. What's kind of cool, and what I didn't notice until I thought about it, is that my knee soreness and back tightness faded some time ago – an encouraging result!

Mile 16 – 8:47: Up a couple of hills, including a steep climb up Putnam/Chard Street and almost home. My slowest mile of the run and I know it. But I'm happy with my overall time of just under 2:12, more than 11 minutes under where I was at this same time last year.

The Aftermath: I'm feeling pretty good. Had a bottle of GU Recovery Brew (kind of like chocolate milk) to help rebuild. I lost 4.5 pounds on this run, so I know I need to rehydrate and refill protein and carbs. Overall, a very successful long run.

I think the take home message from this entry and about this run is that I struggled badly at the end and still beat my 17 mile run from last year by

*17 **minutes**! It was great running with Erika in the second half though my first nine miles on my own clearly wore on me.*

Running With a Pacer, June 29, 2014

My long run today was a little bit different. I ran 17 miles total, but ran 9 miles on my own first and then ran the last 8 miles with my neighbor Erika, who paced me. My aspirational goal for this run was to run the 17 miles at an 8:00 pace, or as close to that as I could get. My first nine miles on my own were solid, just under an 8:00 pace. I was motivated in part by the fact that Erika and I had agreed to meet at about 8:15, which was based on me running an 8:00 pace. I should also note that she has no problem running 8 miles at an 8:00 pace. In fact our first mile together, and my 10th, was at a 7:35 pace! No worries though because I felt strong.

When I started at 7:00, it was reasonably cool (low 60s), but it got up into the upper 70s by the end of our run. And, I could feel the humidity from the very beginning. I think next time I'm going to try to start even earlier. I was very strong through 13 miles, under an 8:00 pace, but I could feel my fatigue building. In short, my pace slid for miles 14-17, all the way down to a 9:00 mile at one point. My right foot bothered me a little bit, though that was helped by loosening my shoe and stretching a little bit. But in the end, I was just flat out exhausted. I do think that 1) I stuck to my 8:00 pace longer because I was running with Erika and 2) my slide would have been even worse if I were not working to try to stay with her. For her part, she was very patient with my fading pace!

I finished the 17 miles in just over 2:18, at an 8:08 pace overall, pretty close to the goal I set for myself. And, looking back at last year, my 17 mile time at about the same time of year was, drum roll…2:35! This year to year improvement is amazing for me and very promising as I look ahead to the Chicago Marathon in October. My goal there is to run at an 8:00 pace. I've read often that you should not run your long runs at "race pace" and I've ignored that advice so far. Since I'm not running 26.2 miles in my training, I'll get up to 21 miles, my goal is to push my pace on these "shorter" long runs. I feel like, if I can run at close to 8:00 pace for 20 or

21 miles on a training run, I have a pretty good shot to do it for 26.2 miles in a race.

Next week, I will reduce my miles in advance of a half the following week. After that, I'm back to regular long runs. I'm hoping that I will be able to run an even 8:00 pace for my next true long run, which I've planned for 15 miles. And, hoping that Erika will run a piece of that run as well!

This was the point when I decided to up my Chicago Marathon goal from 3:40 to 3:30. This made sense given how I had run my half marathons earlier this year and I think was important in shifting my mindset to think and believe that I actually could run a marathon at 8:00 pace.

In Search of an 8:00 Mile – 26.2 of 'em Actually, July 17, 2014

I usually do not write about upcoming races. I much prefer to write about a race after I've completed it. I suppose that's driven by a bit of superstition, but there's also much more to say after a race is over. Everything up until then is just conjecture. But I feel a little differently about marathons. There is so much that goes into them for so long, that I feel a need to write as an outlet for my thoughts. Already, I've been working towards this since March and I still have nearly 3 months to go.

So I've run loads of 8:00 miles, in fact it's a pretty comfortable pace for me. I've now run four half-marathons at sub 8:00 pace, so I know I can handle it. Up through 13.1 miles anyway. But my quest now is to run a marathon at 8:00 pace, and 26.2 8:00 miles in a row is a little different. But that's my goal, to run the Chicago Marathon on October 12 in about 3:30, or an 8:00 average pace.

I ran my first marathon last year in 3:52, or just under a 9:00 pace, so this is a big step up. Initially, when I started training this year, I started working with an 8:30 pace goal, which would put me at about 3:43, a pretty solid improvement of 9 minutes. As I've gone through my spring races though, and I set one PR after another, I began to get more confident and more ambitious.

Pace calculators tell me I can do this – at least potentially. According to the McMillan running calculator, my half marathon PR would equate to a full marathon time of about 3:27, presuming the proper training, similar conditions, etc. So, with the blessings of good health and decent weather on October 12 in Chicago, I can't help but shoot for this goal.

Absent an injury, sickness, or poor weather that affects my time, here are the potential concerns and reasons why I might fall short:

1. This is an aggressive goal and I will have to be running my best. While I will do everything humanly possible to ensure this, I just may not be at my best on that day. I may not really even know why. Sometimes I'm just a little slower. And, marathons can be inherently unpredictable.

2. Will my training be enough? I am very disciplined about my training and hardly ever miss a scheduled run. I'd say, on a net basis, over the past year and a half, I have run 99%+ of the miles I planned. And I plan my runs with focus and intent. But, I have very clear limits to my training. I allow myself to run 4 days/week, peaking at about 40 miles a week, and that's about it. I know high school kids who run a lot more than that to train for 5-mile races. And certainly, marathon runners who run both more days and many more miles per week. But, at least at this stage of my life, this is non-negotiable.

3. So far, I've yet to meet this pace beyond a half marathon. I know that I can, but 26.2 miles is just a really long way and there's lots of time to break down. But, that's what training is for. This Sunday, I will be running 15 miles with a 2 hour time goal – i.e., 8:00 miles for 15 miles. The last time I ran 15 I was only 2 minutes off this, so I believe I can do this. And, the weather forecast for Sunday looks decent. This will be an important milestone for me. If I do that, I only have to keep it up another 11 miles. :)

So, there are my doubts. Now, it's time to turn to positive thoughts!

1. The pace calculators tell me I can do this. And, while my training days and miles are limited, I believe in my training plan. I have significantly improved my training, 10K race, and half race times this year and there's no reason to think I can't make a similar improvement in a marathon!

2. The Chicago Marathon will feature flat terrain and a decent number of spectators – like 1.7 million! I've never experienced anything like that before and the adrenaline rush will obviously be tremendous. For much of the race, my biggest challenge may be making sure I don't run at too fast a pace.

3. While the weather on any given day is a wildcard, odds are the weather in Chicago in October will be a lot better running weather than what I'm training in – likely in the neighborhood of 20 degrees cooler. Assuming that holds true, this will make a big difference in how I last beyond 2 hours of running.

4. This is now my 2nd marathon, and the doubt and jitters of a first-time marathon runner are behind me. Though I have to say I was not real nervous the first time. But I can approach this race with more confidence and focus and know better what to expect from myself.

5. I will of course taper going into the Marathon and be well-rested, though mildly insane.

In the meantime, I've got plenty of training runs to focus on and use to build both my endurance and speed. In the roughly 85 days between now and then, give or take a few, I will likely think about the Chicago Marathon at some point on roughly 85 of those days.

This entry tells the story of one of my best training runs of the year. The pacing on this run was about as good as it gets for me, 15 miles within a 28 second pace range. Really, really solid. This piece also could have been titled "Smoother, Not Harder", a mantra that became one of my mental keys in my running this year – as in run smoother, not harder.

15 Miles in 2 Hours!, July 20, 2014

I've been looking forward to today's run all week and it did not disappoint. First of all, this morning was made for running, mostly cloudy with temperatures in the low 60s. Just a great, great morning to run. I was out on the road by 6:25.

I am not always this aggressive in my long run pacing, but today I had a goal of averaging 8:00 miles for this 15 mile run and being as steady as possible in my pace. At the end, I'll list my mile my mile paces. I know that's a little tedious – but they were awesome and really tell the story of this run.

My first mile, as it turns out, was my slowest of the entire run – at 8:15. But, I felt steady so that didn't bother me. I knew I had plenty of miles in which to make up 15 seconds. In fact, I almost made up the whole difference in my 2nd mile! I was headed to Webb Park, out along the water, where there are beautiful views, almost 360 degrees around on this neck of land.

My pacing was pretty steady throughout the run and I felt really strong. On this run, the mantra I kept on repeating to myself was "quick and light". Every time that I felt my pace flag, rather than trying to run **harder**, I tried to run **smoother**. I've never had a lot of luck with that approach, especially when I get really tired, but it really clicked for me today. When something like that works, it comes as a revelation!

I stopped for water at a CVS at mile 6, which turned out to be my only water stop of the day, because I was feeling so good. That 6th mile was the last mile of the run when I would be above an 8:00 pace. My neighbor

Erika lent me a small clip on bottle for GU gels, which made taking GU on the run a lot easier and smoother as well.

After that, I headed into Bare Cove Park. There's a stretch on the road coming out of Bare Cove (it was in mile 9 on this run), when I sometimes slow down a little bit – for whatever reason. Today, as my pace started to flag there, I told myself that slowing down was not an option and just pushed through it – feeling fine. What's the Yogi Berra quote? — it's 90% mental, and the other half is physical – something along those lines.

From there, I took North Street to Main Street in Hingham. My pace stayed strong from here on it, again focusing on running smoother every time I would start to feel fatigued. My last mile of the run, which is also the hilliest, always presents a challenge on these long runs, but I ran that last mile in 7:58 and finished very strong!

So the mile splits were:

1. 8:15

2. 7:47

3. 7:57

4. 8:11

5. 7:58

6. 8:04

7. 7:50

8. 7:49

9. 8:00

10. 7:47

11. 7:50

12. 7:47

13. 7:56

14. 7:50

15. 7:58

Everything within a 28 second range! And I actually got steadier and more consistent as the run went. Great run for today and a big milestone for my training!

Although this entry seems like it's all about Kevin, and much of it is, it's also quite a bit about my involvement and engagement with Kevin's running and how that came to inspire me in my own running. Kevin's longtime coach, Heike Tuplin, will always be an important figure in Kevin's life and, by extension, mine as well.

Kevin & South Shore Fireboltz, July 27, 2014

Back in 1st grade, Kevin started running track with the South Shore Fireboltz, a running club coached by Eliza's third grade teacher (and Kevin's eventual third grade teacher) Heike Tuplin. Yesterday those 8 years of our lives wound to a close. For 8 years, Kevin ran track with the Fireboltz and for six years he ran x-country.

Fortunately, Kevin is moving on to an exciting new phase in his running, running high school x-country. But I know I, and I believe Kevin and Anne too, will miss the Fireboltz experience greatly. It wasn't always easy and there were lots of days standing out in the rain, the cold, or in the blistering heat at a day long track meet when it was brutal. But, when we look back at Kevin's childhood and where he goes from here, I believe this will be the defining foundation of his life. His times improved greatly through these years, but it's not about numbers. And, it's not just about running. It's about competing, and building character, discipline, and mental and emotional strength.

I get very emotional about sports, and I'm having to take breaks as I write this to wipe tears from my eyes. Yesterday's track meet was similarly emotional for me. We were at the Needham Youth Classic, on the 2nd day of a 1.5 day event. For the most part, it was a mediocre meet for Kevin personally. But, it was a great meet for us as a team, as we finished 2nd with fewer athletes than we've had at many times in the past. And then, Kevin ended the meet on the perfect note for him, running a PR in the 800 meter run – the last event of the day. I held myself together, but it was very hard.

Next week Kevin will compete in the AAU National meet in Des Moines, IA as a South Shore Fireboltz. But, other than another summer meet alumni appearance in the next year or two, that will be the end. From an emotional standpoint, yesterday was really the final team event for him. This is not just about Kevin. Anne and I have spent hundreds of hours helping to time races and run field events at practices and even a few meets, as well as standing out in the woods in Wompatuck, making sure the kids are safe. It has been a big investment in time and energy for all of us, but the returns have been awesome.

This is a happy and exciting time as Kevin moves on to high school x-country. But, as we look ahead, I also find myself looking back quite a bit. While the memories and experiences are very positive, transitions like this always have a bit of a bittersweet note. Through Kevin's Fireboltz years, he has grown from age 7 to 14 and has progressed through three schools. So, in many ways, this transition is more meaningful than graduating from middle school to high school.

I'm finding myself searching for the words to sum this up and bring it to a close and they aren't coming. Perhaps it's a little too soon for this level of reflection. Suffice it to say, this has been a very special and meaningful experience for all of us and despite the exciting times ahead, it is a little painful to say goodbye to such a wonderful phase of our lives.

Wow, four minutes faster in a month, that's pretty good! You can feel the momentum in my running through the momentum in my writing. As my progress, confidence and energy grew, I wrote more often and wrote longer pieces. Kind of like my running...

A Tale of Two Runs, July 29, 2014

At first I wasn't going to write about my most recent long run, which was 16 miles. But then I was reading about my last 16 mile run and struck by the difference in about a month, so I couldn't resist.

First of all, my overall time was significantly faster, 2:07:45 vs. 2:11:56, a > 4:00 difference. But, it's the pacing and how I felt during the run that made the difference and is driving me to write. My run this past Sunday was different to start in that I ran the first 10 miles with my neighbor Erika. And, we did a couple of 10 minute tempo intervals – aiming for 7:25 pace. While our pace was not precise there, this did make the start of the run (particularly miles 2-4) a lot faster than it normally would have been for me. But the real story for me is what happened after that.

Here's the mile by mile story with the splits from my prior run in parentheses:

Mile 1 – 8:11 (7:47) – Into Jackson Square. This was a "slow" mile by design, although the fact that I now consider an 8:11 mile on a long run as slow is saying something!

Mile 2 – 7:19 (7:58) – This is where the tempo part of this run kicked in and we got a little carried away with a 7:19 mile! That's getting close to 10K pace for me!

Mile 3 – 7:36 (8:00) – Still running the tempo part of the run, although the pace settled down a little bit.

Mile 4 – 7:31 (8:08) – Past the entrance to Wompatuck. The last mile of the tempo part of the run. No big deal to run that pace for a few miles, but doing it as part of a 16 mile run is a little different.

Mile 5 – 8:01 (8:07) – Here we settled back in and sought to re-establish a steady pace for the rest of the run. This was a good one, as we reached a turnaround point, just past Hingham High.

Mile 6 – 7:54 (8:10) – If anything this mile was a little fast, but I was just feeling strong. On the way home now for the 10 mile section of the run.

Mile 7 – 8:04 (8:13) Right where we want to be pace-wise.

Mile 8 – 8:10 (7:55) Again right on track with the target pace for this part of the run, a little bit over 8:00 miles.

Mile 9 – 8:05 (8:12) Still steady as we head back into Jackson Square.

Mile 10 – 8:22 (8:20) This is the one mile where our pace flagged though I think it's to be forgiven, given a couple of hills in this last mile home, including a short, steep one in the last half mile. This was my last mile with Erika and, without redoing the math, I believe we were about a minute under 8:00 pace overall – about 1:19 for the 10 miles.

Mile 11 – 7:54 (8:34) This was the moment of truth mile for me. One, I had to re-establish my momentum after stopping briefly at home. And, two, I was now running on my own after running with Erika for 10 miles. I passed with flying colors, finishing this mile under 8:00. This is also the mile when my paces really start to diverge from my last 16 mile run. Last time, I was hanging on for the last six miles, really struggling to keep my pace under 8:30. This time, I got my pace under 8:00 AND I was feeling good! What a difference a month of training can make!

Mile 12 – 7:52 (8:30) – Another great mile and I am feeling strong. Headed past the commuter rail station. Tired, yes, but strong.

Mile 13 – 8:16 (8:25) – My pace finally slowed on this mile, but not too badly and I'm still feeling good. At the end of this mile, I turned around to head back home for my out and back 6 mile 2nd leg of the run.

49

Mile 14 – 8:09 (8:22) – An 8:09 mile for me at this stage of the run is great! But, what's more the pace feels OK. I'm not dying to run this pace and it's feeling pretty steady for me.

Mile 15 – 8:04 (8:28) – Another very strong mile for me, when I was just barely hanging on at this stage a month ago. Back through Jackson Square yet again and one hilly mile left to go.

Mile 16 – 8:18 (8:47) – OK, I may finally starting to be fading a little bit, but my pace drop is not terrible, just down to 8:18, so still reasonably steady.

Overall, this was a very steady, strong run, and I'm feeling really great about my progress. Part of that is about the times, but it's also about how I felt along the way and at the end. Even as my energy faded, I was still able to stick pretty close to 8:00 pace. This was even more impressive to me given that these later miles were on the heels of the 20 minutes of faster tempo running earlier in the run. This is good stuff!

This is the story of my Triple Threat Challenge race, when I set 5K and half marathon PRs back to back – on the heels of a 1 mile race too, and after returning from Des Moines, IA and getting to bed at 1:30 AM. I didn't expect to set any PR in these races, I was just looking to test my endurance to get through them, so to set PRs in a 5K and half back to back is, well, shocking.

A Mild State of Shock, August 3, 2014

This morning, I ran the Triple Threat Challenge in Rockport. That's a 1 mile run, followed by a 5K, followed by a half marathon, in fairly rapid succession. This was on the heels of spending a 1/2 day at Kevin's track meet in Des Moines, IA, yesterday, spending most of the rest of the day in airports and on planes, getting back to Boston after midnight, and getting to bed after 1:30. So I was not exactly well-rested.

The results were shocking. I didn't quite know what to expect from this kind of race, but one thing I was certain about was that I would not set a PR. There was just no way. Well, turns out I set two! (The footnote to that is the general consensus among those with GPS watches was that the half was a little short and maybe the 5K too. But they called it a half and 5K, so I am too!) The courses were somewhat hilly too, especially late in the course, so the races were challenging.

So, first things first, I ran the mile in 6:45, which is about what I had in mind – came in 4th in my age group and 24th of about 240 runners overall. Could have been much faster, but I didn't want it to be with the two races coming up. So, this was about what I expected. It was a very good race and just about what I planned.

The 5K started at 9:20, 20 minutes after the start of the 1 mile race. That time passed very quickly. I ran the first mile of the 5K in 6:40, a little fast for a conservative pace. But it was just the first mile and I wasn't real concerned. But, when I ran the 2nd mile in 6:35, that really gave me pause. This was not what I had planned, and I had a decision to make. But the decision was an easy one. Anytime I have a chance to go for a PR, I'm doing it. So I kept on pushing my pace through a couple of tough hills in the last mile, and finished in 20:52, a 19 second PR! I finished 2nd in my age group and 18th overall of about 340 runners!! It was basically at mile 2, when I had 6:40 and 6:35 splits, when I said "Forget the half, I'm going for a PR." In some ways, I felt it was a dumb decision, but my thinking was to sacrifice my time in the half to get a 5K PR. After all, it is a race.

The half started at 10:15, so I had a little more time to regroup. After the 5K, I was sure I would have a slow half, but mile after mile I kept on ticking off good splits, sub 7:30 pace. I decided to just try to hold that pace as long as I could, thinking it would fade eventually. But, even though my pace started to drop off a little bit, I still kept churning out sub 8:00 miles even in the final miles. This was getting tough as the miles went by, but I was hanging in, one mile after another. I ended up finishing with a great sprint up the hill right before the homestretch and through the finish, finishing in 1:37:19, another PR, beating the prior PR of 1:37:38.

I was 8th in my age group in the half, and 68th overall of about 770 runners! In addition to my 2nd place age group finish in the 5K, I also got the prize for 2nd place in my age group for combined place across all three races. And, I think I was 13th overall of about 180 runners who ran all three, though those results look a little off.

I remain in a state of shock about how well I ran, both the PRs and my age group finishes. I really didn't expect anything like this and still don't quite know how it happened. Overall, I ran the combined 17.2 miles in 2:04:58! So I'm pretty much stunned by this, but completely thrilled! I did not know I had this in me and am still in a state of shock, turning it over in my mind, trying to figure out how it went so right. I'm not sure I'll ever really figure it out, but in the meantime, I'm enjoying it!

I like this post a lot. As I say at the end, the theme that runs through this is how much support from other people, in various forms, has helped me in my training and races. I especially like the last sentence, "While I will be physically running on my own in Chicago (aside from the other 44,999 or so people), I really won't be on my own."

How Did I Get Here?, August 17, 2014

2014 has been a great running year for me and I've been asking myself why that is. I'm quite sure that having one marathon and one year of marathon training under my belt helps both physically and psychologically. But, given how significant and consistent my improvement has been, I think there's more to it than that. So, I've given some thought to what have been the key factors that have led to this success. Because there are so many variables, it's a little tough to attribute specific effects to each. Here's what I think, in rough order of importance from top to bottom:

1. For Christmas, my Mom got me a book called Chi Marathon training, or something along those lines. Although a lot of that book is deeper than I want to go, there have been some important takeaways for me in terms

of running form. Most important is the concept of short, quick strides and rapid leg turnover. It's almost like my legs are a wheel spinning. This has led to my mantra of running smoother and quicker, rather than harder, which has helped me a great deal on long runs.

2. This year, I've run track intervals, typically repeat 800s, virtually every week. Although I did these here and there last year, I didn't do them consistently. I believe these have helped a lot in enabling me to sustain a fast pace late in runs when I'm tired.

3. In January, I started participating in a 100 mile challenge set up by Lisa Quine Brini. To my surprise, I stuck with it and ended up running 100 miles in January. Although I did take all of February off from running, I rode an exercise bike and did light core workouts to keep my endurance and strength up and hit the ground running in March. OK, sorry, I couldn't resist. Perhaps more important though is how it expanded my running support network. Several people from this group are now a very important part of my support system. And I believe vice versa!

4. Recently, I've started running with my next door neighbor Erika on a lot of our long runs. Since she is training for a half, my long runs are longer, but we have run her long run together, followed by some bonus running for me. Prior to this, I hadn't run a run longer than a 10K with anyone else. While I often like running on my own, having Erika's company on some long runs has been a breath of fresh air. This has also helped my long run pacing a lot, both to be faster and more consistent. One run in particular that comes to mind is a 10-mile run that we did together. I think I went a total of 16 that time. During this run we ran a couple of faster tempo intervals early in the run. That run was a revelation to me, as I was able to keep up my pace later in the run, despite the tempo intervals. This run did a great deal to improve my confidence in my long run paces.

5. Over the course of the 100 mile challenge, I got to know a friend of a friend, Margaret. Even though we've never met, we exchanged a bunch of emails about our running. Although I knew the importance of doing some lifting and core workouts, it has been Margaret's encouragement that

has gotten me over the hump to do this quasi-regularly. Although I still don't do these quite as regularly as I should, I've been doing them a lot more than last year. I think these have helped increase my speed and perhaps ward off some injuries.

6. This may seem like a little thing (it actually is!), but Erika also gave me a small bottle that slips onto shorts' waistbands and makes it a lot easier and quicker to take GU gels. Prior to this, I would take GU gels on the run – open up the packet while running, squeeze it in and take water with it. This always slowed me down while taking it and sometimes even had a longer term effect, as it broke up my rhythm and stride, sometimes slowing me down for a mile or more. No longer. Now I mix them with water and just squirt it in as I'm running, just like drinking water. A subtle improvement, but I bet this shaves a minute or two off my longer runs.

7. Last but not least is all of the writing I have done about my running – either through FB posts or this blog – AND all of the support and encouragement I have received in return. While it's fuzzy to say how this affects my times, I know it has greatly improved my morale and positive energy about my running, which has been wonderful. Keeping a positive outlook while running is critical, especially on days like these when I have a tough run.

If I had to pick a theme that runs through these, it's the support of other people that has made a world of difference to me. While I will be physically running on my own in Chicago (aside from the other 44,999 or so people), I really won't be on my own.

This was perhaps my worst training run of the year, but valuable in its own way. This was one of the few, maybe the only, long run that I did in the afternoon and it was quite a warm day. The heat and humidity really crushed me on this run. It was not a poor effort, but it was a poor result. But in the long run view of marathon training, any run that doesn't get you hurt can be a valuable run. And, looking back, I think this one was. Humbling, but valuable nonetheless.

A Grind, August 26, 2014

It's not like I like having my butt kicked by a run. Of course, I always want to have success and run well. But, it just doesn't always work that way. And, I believe that in the long run, the runs that are struggles are at least as useful as the ones when I fly along. Not necessarily fun, but useful.

Today was one of those days. I set out for a 16 mile run on a very warm afternoon, feeling pretty good and strong. I was scheduled to run 11 miles on my own and then 5 with my neighbor Erika. Despite being liberal with water and GU and trying to stay in the shade when I could, it felt even hotter than I thought it was going to be. I was already running on fumes when Erika joined me after 11. I managed to struggle through 14 miles, but just felt that I couldn't go on at that point. Well, not so much that I couldn't, but that I may hurt myself if I did. So I stopped and we walked for a bit. I managed to pick back up and jog after maybe a 1/4 mile or so. Or maybe a 1/2 mile, I don't know.

Anyway, we picked up jogging again until we got to the North Street/Commercial Street hill. If you know the hill, you know it is daunting. About a 1/3 mile up and it gets a little bit steep. Normally, I can handle it fine, but this was not a normal day. I had no interest in running up that hill, but Erika cajoled me to at least try. I managed to keep going through one of Erika's targets, then the next and, before I knew it, we were essentially at the top. The pace was unspeakable but, for this stage of this run, that wasn't really the point. To run up that hill at any speed was a big victory. I paused at the top as I was a little shaky on my feet and then we jogged the last bit home.

A triumphant run? Well no, not exactly. But I managed to run 14 miles at an 8:06 pace. And, while the last two miles were ridiculously slow – I didn't even time them, getting through as much as I did based on the way I felt was a moral victory. And, just for perspective, the 14 mile part was 4 minutes faster than I ran in June and 8 minutes faster than last year. Even so, I won't look back on this run as an impressive one, it was really pretty ugly late in the run. But I will look back at climbing that hill and know that, when I felt I had literally nothing left, I still climbed it. I don't think I could have possibly run any slower up that hill, but I did run up the hill. And that was the take-away from this run.

This is the story of a really strong 20 mile training run. Certainly not my best run, but it was right up there. And, taking into account the heat and humidity, perhaps this one was even better than I'm giving myself credit for. The mile splits tell the story of how much I was struggling but, at the same time, how hard I worked to hang in on this run. It's runs like these that lead to great marathon races.

I Wear My Sunglasses at Dawn, August 31, 2014

This is the story of my 20 mile run this AM. Although I didn't meet my goal, I feel it turned out to be one of my best runs ever.

When I set out at 5:45, it was just starting to get light and it was overcast. But with Rx sunglasses you have to choose one or the other. So, looking ahead, I picked sunglasses. It was fairly cool when I started, like mid 60s, but the humidity was oppressive and I knew that would be a factor later on.

Miles 1-5 – 8:01, 7:53, 8:07, 8:07, 7:53 – Right on 8:00 pace. I headed out to Webb Park, looped around, and headed back towards 3A. I was feeling nice and steady through the first 5, but I could really feel the humidity. Although it wasn't that hot, I was sweating a lot and losing a lot of fluids. Started taking GU at 4.5 miles. Vanilla Bean GU really hits the spot. Seriously, when you're running, it's like the nectar of the gods!

Miles 6-10 – 7:54, 7:55, 8:06, 7:59, 7:55 – Actually a little ahead of pace and I was reminding myself to stay within myself and my pace goal. I got my first water at CVS at mile 6. Then I headed into Bare Cove Park, through the park and out onto Beal Street. I'm starting to feel a little fatigue, but my pace is steady and I'm feeling strong. This was a strong stretch.

Miles 11-15 – 7:55, 7:51, 8:08, 8:09, 8:35 – During mile 11 the sun is blazing right into my eyes on 3A. Although it may have looked a little odd to have sunglasses when it was virtually dark out earlier, I am glad to have them now. I stopped for my 2nd water fill-up just past mile 11. I'm going through water in a hurry and losing even more. I had already finished 2 GUs and filled my GU flask with the 3rd and final GU. I'm thinking now why didn't I bring a 4th? This stretch took me along 3A, onto Lincoln Street, into Hingham Harbor and up several tough hills. First, in mile 13, I climbed two hills on 3A. Then, after turning onto Rockland Street, I turned right onto Kilby and faced two more uphill stretches. I worked hard up those hills and the effect showed in mile 15, headed back on 228.

Miles 16-20 – 8:36, 8:39, 8:40, 8:45, 9:00 – It was those hills. I just can't regain my pace, but at this point, I am OK with hanging in at this slower pace. I'm headed home on 228, with a right onto High Street, through Jackson Square and back on Commercial Street past Legion Field. My 3rd and final water fillup comes just after the 16 mile mark, when I also finish my last GU. My mile splits kind of tell the story here, but this is the part of the run that I'm most proud of. I was really hurting and fighting through exhaustion. But my pace, albeit declining, stayed relatively steady. Particularly in the last two miles, I really wanted to walk and was fighting the urge constantly. But I hung in and finished steady through the 20 mile mark.

The Aftermath – I am spent. The tightness started kicking in right away. I had burned an estimated 2,750 calories and lost 5+ pounds. Overall, I finished in 2:44:08, at an average pace of 8:13. Although I had hoped to do this run in 2:40, at an even 8:00 pace, I was still really happy with the result and with the effort. And I know the slower pace at the end was directly due to 1) the hills in miles 13 and 14 and 2) the really high humidity, neither of which I should face in Chicago. For now it's time to rest.

This is a very simple blog post, short and sweet, but I think it carries a really important message. When you're running, especially training for longer events like a marathon, you have got to want it, deep down in your soul. Your reasons can vary, but you have got to want to do it very strongly. And, in the big picture, it's got to be fun and enjoyable. After all, it takes up a lot of hours.

I Get to Run Today, September 6, 2014

Just like "15 minutes can save you 15% on your auto insurance", everyone knows that little words can make a big difference. You know, obvious things like: yes/no, off/on, and/or, etc. Ask any lawyer, One slightly less obvious pair of words that makes a critical difference to me in my running is get/have, as in "get to" and "have to".

When I look at my running schedule coming up, I usually think to myself, "I *get* to run today." When my thinking slips into, "I *have* to run today," I try to change that outlook. Of course, when you're running on a schedule, some days you're just not at your best and may not really feel up to it. But, more often than not, when I know I have a run planned later in the day, I'm thinking to myself that I *get* to run that day. And, that little word makes all the difference.

Every chance I get to run really is an opportunity and, like all of the other wonderful things life has to offer, opportunities like that shouldn't be taken for granted. While I'm not sure I'd go so far as to call every run "fun", almost every run is satisfying and rewarding. And, having been through enough training by now, I know that even the bad runs can help me get better. I've written in an earlier blog about why I run, and I won't repeat that here, but suffice it to say that I get a lot out of it.

Sometimes I wonder what might have happened if I had discovered running earlier in life. Who knows, but I'm certainly glad I have now. Most days that I get to run I am buoyed by this feeling of opportunity and the sense of gratitude that goes along with it. Every now and then, as a runner, you come upon a run that is a revelation, a pure joy, perhaps a runner's high. On those days, running can be euphoric. But, even on the ordinary runs or the crumby ones, deep down I end with that feeling, that I got to run today.

Looking back at this run, the mile splits were really solid, especially late in the run when I was struggling. But it gives you a good idea of the combined mental and physical toll that marathon training can take on your mind, body, and spirit. This is not easy.

Another Cool, But Humid, Run, September 7, 2014

Today's scheduled run was 20 miles, for the second week in a row. When I started out, it was nice and cool (low 60s), but felt pretty humid. I didn't want to run an easy pace today, but wasn't really looking to push my pace and didn't have a specific time goal. My primary goal for this run was to run at a relatively consistent pace. I ran this run in the reverse direction of my normal long runs, looking to change my perspective late in the run. Often, the last 4 miles of my long run are always the same and this tends to lead to a little mental fatigue – you almost feel like you should get tired at that point. So I decided to change course.

Miles 1-5: 8:24, 8:14, 8:22, 8:32, 8:28

This was a slow start for me. I didn't really mind, but was a little surprised to see the 8:24 for the first mile, because my adrenaline alone usually takes me out of the chute faster. Since I didn't have a specific time goal, this wasn't really an issue and starting out slow is not a bad concept, but it shook me a little bit. I continued to run at a relatively slow pace for me, as I headed through Jackson Square, onto Ward, Cushing, and then 228. I had planned to stop at the little general store on 228 for my first water stop at about 4.5 miles. This was a bit of an early stop, but I was pounding water. So my first setback of the run was that the store was closed. This was a drawback of reversing direction, as my normal water stops were off. But, despite the slower than normal splits, I'm feeling good.

Mile 6-10: 8:10, 8:06, 8:02, 8:06, 7:57

I don't know where this was in the first 5 miles of the run but, in mile 6, my running was transformed. My cadence picked up, my strides were quick and light – I was running like I dream I will run in mile 26 in Chicago. I didn't think about it – it just happened. The times reflect the change, and it felt so good. When I run like this, it's so much more smooth and efficient, I feel like I'm not working hard, and almost gliding. I ran along 228 to Rockland Street and turned back on a sharp left, towards 3A. I stopped for my first water stop at Tedeschi's at about mile 8.5. A little late for me, and my water bottle was long since empty, but I hung in OK. I'm taking GU now, but it's Espresso something and I'm not loving, it. The pitfalls of a variety pack. I twisted my ankle a bit just before the water stop, but it seems like there was no harm done. Although it's a shade warmer, I think the humidity has dropped and there's a nice breeze. Actually feels pretty good.

Miles 11-15: 8:03, 8:11, 8:13, 8:12, 8:29

I'm losing track of exactly where I was at which point, but I took 3A down into Hingham Harbor, and headed back on North Street and back onto 3A. Stopped for water again, just after mile 12. This was a little soon, but I didn't want to run dry again. I also filled my GU flask with Chocolate Outrage. For future reference, this seems like about the thickest GU ever and it didn't dissolve well. A little gross. I'll have to go with better flavors next week. Headed north onto 3A, and hung a left on Beal, heading towards the entrance of Bare Cove Park. I was tiring a bit now and taking a lot of chocolate GU – reluctantly. Lots of people out walking dogs in Bare Cove Park this AM!

Miles 16-20:   8:27, 8:24, 8:36, 8:17, 8:14

I am really getting tired now and my legs are really getting sore. Maybe the hill repeats the day before my long run weren't such a good idea after all. Back onto 3A yet again, uphill over a small bridge and stopping for water for the last time at CVS at about mile 17.5. Ouch, my legs are really tightening up. Ankles, calves, knees, quads, hips – all sore and tight. I stretched out a little bit and managed to start running again. But it's painful now and wearing. Just thinking to myself that I have just over 2 miles left and I DO NOT WANT TO FADE. Mile 19 is an awesome one, as I regrouped to run at an 8:17 pace. My strides and cadence are a little better and I'm fighting through the fatigue well. This is the long run finish that I want! I'm heading back on Green Street, onto East, Unicorn, and then Commercial Street, dodging the real steep hill I did repeats on yesterday. As I make my way through mile 20, especially late in the mile, I am really picking up steam and running fast. I looked at my watch just before I finished and I'm at a 7:25 pace. Absolutely fantastic finish, but I'm physically, emotionally, and mentally drained.

It's not just the run, it's that now I need to go home and mow the lawn, paint more trim on the front porch, get ready for the work week, etc. Sometimes I wish I could be a professional athlete who could focus solely on training and not have to get up and go to work the next week.. I think this is a matter of the grass being greener on the other side of the fence, and actually think this would quickly get old. But, right now, it sounds pretty good.

Forget about the marathon itself, marathon training is a real odyssey. It's incredible how much time, thought, and energy I put into this. And not just while I'm running. But, this is a case where the mantra of, you get out of it what you put into it, absolutely holds true.

One Month To Go!, September 12, 2014

My marathon is now just one month away – 30 days to be exact. Actually, at this time, one month from now, I'll be having a nice, big beer and a huge dinner, nursing my increasingly sore body. But I'm getting ahead of myself. This one month milestone is a good time to take stock, both looking back and looking ahead. Since I began my training schedule in March, I've run 110 times and run about 760 miles. Although a few of those 110 runs have been real struggles, overall my runs have been largely positive. I've set PRs at virtually every distance of training run and I've run PRs in 6 of the 9 races I've run so far this year. My intervals have been both faster and more consistent than they were last year. In short, I've become a better runner through this spring and summer. Absent an injury or illness, I know I will run the Chicago Marathon faster than I ran my "rookie" marathon in Newport last year. That's a great way to feel at this point!

So, the question becomes "How much faster?" I've already written about my race goal of a 3:30 marathon, which would equate to running at an 8:00 pace. No turning back from that now. While I'm not confident that I WILL do this, I'm confident that I CAN. And, I suppose that makes for a good goal. In evaluating my training runs, the one area where I think I've fallen short a bit is not achieving consistent pacing on long runs. Given that all of my long runs have been faster than last year, I'm not running poorly. But, I know that I will need to be both faster and more consistent come RACE DAY! Again, this is sort of a given – of course I should be faster on race day than on training runs. But I would like to be running steadier paces on my long training runs.

I've been looking ahead to the Chicago Marathon for months now, envisioning how I will run at different stages of the race as I fall asleep at night, or picturing strong finishes in my mind during my commute to and from work. I'm a big believer in positive thinking and imagery and working to block out negative thoughts and I've been practicing it early and often. But, right now, it's tough to look beyond the 22 mile run that I've got planned for Sunday. This will be my longest training run EVER, as I'm only up to 20 miles so far this year, and peaked at 21 miles in my training last year. Needless to say, a 22 mile run is a challenge that has my full running focus right now.

The run will at least seem a little more manageable, as I'll be breaking it into two parts. I will run the first 12 with my running buddy Erika, followed by 10 on my own. Of course those 10 will be the key. Honestly, at this stage, running 12 miles, especially with a running companion is, well, easy. The last 10, on the other hand, will be a challenge. My focus will be on running a slightly slower than target race pace – say 8:15 miles, and doing so relatively consistently. The biggest challenge with the first 12 will be to keep my pace in check and not go flying along with reckless abandon.

After this run, it's all downhill, so to speak. Both my long run and weekly mileage will drop from Sunday until race day in Chicago. I will also drop off the intensity of my interval and tempo runs, as I "taper" towards race day. I have bought into tapering, especially for a marathon, but it's a lot harder than it sounds. You would think this would be the easy part of training and, from a physical standpoint, I suppose it is. But, psychologically, it's tough! If you've ever been through it, you know what I mean. You've been running so hard for months and then you gradually drop to virtually no miles at all. The idea is to build all of this energy for race day, but it gets you very antsy. During tapering, you also tend to question and worry about just about anything – especially training and injuries. You worry about getting hurt doing yard work, walking to work, getting in and out of bed, eating breakfast – you get the idea. With training, there's also the tendency to think perhaps I trained too hard? Or maybe I didn't train enough? Should I have done a longer long run? Shorter? More miles per week? Less? Oh no, I didn't do enough core work. And so on. There's also the tendency to check weather forecasts relentlessly, even before long term forecasts for race day exist. After Sunday, my peak training will be over and I will be entering the beginning of this tapering phase.

So, 6 + months of training down, 1 month to go. With marathon training, I've come to feel that it is not just a means to an end. The training is an end in itself. While running the actual marathon race completes the experience, the training is really the heart of running a marathon. The past 6 + months of training have been an incredible experience for me and I'm looking forward to one more. Gotta run.

This was an absolutely amazing run – one of my best ever – and perhaps my best training run ever. 22 miles in 2:57:25, but that time doesn't tell the full story of this run. Fortunately, this blog post does!

WOW, September 14, 2014

I've had an amazing year running, including a few runs that have left me quite simply stunned by the result. Today was one of those runs and, I believe, the single most important and meaningful run in my life – so far. I feel like the first thing I should do here is grab a thesaurus to compile a list of superlatives, but I'm just going to give this a whirl. This is one of three runs this year that stand out for me above all the others. On these runs, I completely shattered my goals, almost to the point where they look silly. As I think back on this run, I'm just shaking my head, still not quite believing I'm capable of this. But running results, for better or worse, do not lie.

I started off with my neighbor Erika at about 6:30. It was shaping up to be a beautiful morning, although I think the first thought we each had was, "Brrrr". It was chilly, just over 50, and I was cold in my short-sleeve running shirt and shorts. But, on the running weather scale of 1-10 for me, this was a solid 10. It would warm slightly as we went, but the temperature was perfect for running and felt really comfortable over the course of the run. This certainly worked in my favor, as I had absolutely no heat fatigue.

Our first mile was 8:21, which turned out to be the slowest mile of the entire run. We're heading out to Webb Park, down Commercial Street to Green Street. We're running at a conversational pace to start, which helps make the time pass. Mile 2 is a little quicker at 8:05, as we cross 3A. Did I mention that the weather is gorgeous? Clear blue sky, bright sun, and perfect temperatures. As we passed by Lane Beach, there was a really strong crosswind – brisk! Mile 3 was 7:54 and I'm thinking this was a little fast. If I only knew what lay ahead.

Miles 4 and 5 featured Webb Park and excellent splits of 8:09 and 8:03. At this point, I'm not feeling particularly good or bad, but know that these splits are nice and steady, which is what I'm looking for from today. At the end of mile 6 (8:08), we stopped at CVS for water. We're heading into Bare Cove Park for miles 7-9, running one consistent mile after another – 8:04, 7:58, and 8:06. This is all great, but I know that I've faded on one long run after another, so I'm not getting excited about splits through 9 miles. It's early and I've basically got a full half marathon to go. The last part of my 12 miles with Erika continued to feature one steady mile after another – 8:07, 8:06, and 8:08 for miles 10-12. I think we we're at an 8:08 average mile pace which was great, though I was afraid it was maybe a shade fast. I'm feeling some fatigue now and know that a solitary 10 miles lies ahead. I made a quick pit stop and filled my water bottle at home, took a deep breath, and headed out for the key 10 miles of this run.

Leading up to this run and throughout the run, I knew this would be the hard part. I decided to try to shift my mental perspective a bit and think of this just as a 10 mile run, to block out the fact that I'm actually running 22 miles, which is a tiring thought. So, in my head, mile 13 became mile 1, and so on. I think this really helped a lot, so I reinforced this in my head constantly through the last 10. Mile 13 (aka mile 1) was a good start at 7:58. I headed down into Jackson Square, heading towards Hingham on High Street. Over and over I'm telling myself I'm now in mile 2 and I finish mile 14 in 8:09. I'm reminding myself to take my GU now. I will need it. I had Strawberry Banana for the first half and am on to Jet Blackberry for the 2nd half of the run. As I hit 228, I finish mile 15 in

8:02 – man is this a steady run. But I'm still telling myself not to get excited yet and just stay focused on my pace in the moment. I finished mile 16 in 8:10 as I passed by Wompatuck State Park, slowing a bit, but still hanging in. One more mile 'til I turn around to head home, a key mental milestone for me. I finish that mile (#17) in 8:16, my slowest mile since the start. I was affected a bit by a strong cross/head wind as I ran past the Hingham fields. But, I've finished the first half of my second 10 miles and am buoyed by the fact that I'm now heading for home

Virtually every mile on this run was awesome, but mile 18 was one that really stands out and was a pivotal mile in this run. After the 8:16 mile in mile 17, I ran my 18th mile in 7:58. This is where I know this is going to be a special run and my spirits and energy are through the roof right now. Four miles left and, right at this moment, I KNOW I've got this run nailed. Sure enough, I run miles 19-21 in 7:59, 8:00 and 7:53. Am I tired? Yeah I guess, but I'm not even thinking about that, because I'm smelling blood now and my energy and confidence are building with each mile. As I start my last mile, which includes a couple of steep hills, I am, in relative terms, flying. For late in a 22 mile run anyway...My energy and confidence are sky high and I feel like I could do this all day. Mile 22 turns out to be the fastest mile of the entire run, in 7:50! After running 21 miles, I just ran my fastest mile split. Unbelievable. This is an absolutely amazing accomplishment and, as I look ahead to running 26.2 in Chicago, this is a massive boost.

I finished the run in 2:57:25, at an average pace of 8:04. Last year, by comparison, I ran 21 miles in 2:59+. I had been hoping for an 8:15 pace overall, so this pretty much blew that away. Even more remarkable, is that my final 10 miles on my own were run at a faster pace than my first 12 with Erika. I really don't know how to put this into words, but this is special stuff. My recent pattern of fading on long runs is now ancient history, replaced by 100% positive thoughts. This is the run that I will have in mind when I run Chicago.

This blog post lays out a really well thought out race strategy. However, on race day, this strategy pretty much went out the window in mile 1 and I never saw it again. But the mental discipline and fortitude that I worked on leading up to the race were still really important to me on race day. That's what enabled me to hang in as well as I did, even though my pacing worked out much differently than I had planned.

A Look Ahead to Race Day, September 24, 2014

I haven't had the energy to write for a while or, when I have had the energy, I haven't had the time. Finally both are coming together for a few minutes tonight. I've now got less than 3 weeks to go 'til Race Day – actually just over 18 days – so I'm starting to think in more focused terms about The Race. So here's the strategy (shhh, don't tell anyone!) I'm thinking in terms of 4 phases of the race, as follows:

Phase 1 – Miles 1-12: This is the easy part. Perhaps that's a bit of an exaggeration but, in relative terms, these miles are easy ones. For this part of the race, I should pretty much be coasting, boosted by the adrenaline from the start and the crowd as I get carried along. I expect to maintain an 8:00 pace easily for this part, but do not want to go faster than that. Perhaps the most important aspect of phase 1 is ensuring that I'm doing a good job with hydration and taking my GUs. This has been part of my training over the past few months, so I've got this down; I just have to pay attention. I will need this later on – very badly!

Phase 2 – Miles 12-20: During this stage of the race, the fatigue will start to build and I may have to work a little harder to sustain my pace. Of course, this is also a critical stage to make sure I'm taking my water and GU right on schedule. Somewhere along this stretch, the fatigue will start to build to the point where my pace, energy, and motivation start to fade. Soreness will build, my breathing will become labored, I will start to get tired in every way. It may not happen until mile 20, or it could happen sooner – I won't really know this for sure until I'm there. But, whenever that happens, whether it's mile 16 or mile 20, I will shift to phase 3.

Phase 3 – Miles 21-26: I don't usually think about baseball analogies with regard to running because it's not usually a good fit but, in this case, I'm thinking about pitch counts – i.e., balls/strikes during an at bat. During the microcosm of an at-bat during a game, there are certain pitches that are pivotal pitches in the at bat. In baseball, the biggest is strike 1, but this also happens with 1 ball/1 strike and 2 ball/2 strike counts. Those pitches often determine the course of an at-bat, giving either the pitcher or batter a distinct advantage depending on how they turn out. Well, in my marathon, the start of phase 3 of the race, whether it begins in mile 21 or in mile 17, is like the 2-2 count. For me this transition is what will make me successful. When I get to this point, which I will know by feel and by gut, I will shift gears both physically and mentally. Assuming this begins after mile 20, at that point, I will completely forget about the first 20 miles of the race and will now be thinking of this as a 6 mile run. And I can run an 8:00 pace for 6 miles in my sleep. Well, I haven't actually tried that, but anyway 6 miles at 8:00 pace is a routine distance and pace for me. And that's how I'll think of it. (If this shift happens at mile 18 instead, no biggie, it just becomes an 8 mile run.)

But this is going to be the aggressive part of the race for me, so there's a little more to it than that. Running a marathon is, in the bottom line, an individual pursuit. This is no relay, I'm running this race start to finish. But I think every runner draws on all kinds of external sources of support, energy, and motivation. When I walk to the starting line in Chicago, in addition to being fueled by a light breakfast, Cliff Bar, and water, I will also carry an auxiliary fuel supply – the support of family and friends. It will weigh nothing, but be very powerful. Every Facebook like, comment, question about my training, expression of support, and more will be set aside in my mind for this moment. As I start to pick up my pace here, I will draw on this energy source and gradually increase my pace mile by mile. So I'm not just going to be running 8:00 miles here, I'm going to be looking for negative splits with each mile faster than the last. I've done this on a couple of training runs and, if I do it right, I will gain energy and confidence as I go, almost like a runaway locomotive. Or, thinking of it another way, a piece of music gradually building to a crescendo (though that would be an exceptionally long piece of music!) As I go through this phase, this is where I plan to draw on the support of family and friends, my auxiliary fuel source that I'll be saving for this critical stage of the race. Miles 21-26 should be faster than miles 1-6. The timing of this is very important because I know I'll be dealing with limited energy at this point. If I wait too long, I won't be able to keep up my momentum. If I go too soon, I'll waste it. Can I do this? Absolutely yes. Will I? I'll get to that in a minute.

Phase 4 – The Last 0.2 miles – aka a lap: Hardly worth breaking out from a distance standpoint, but very important to the overall experience. I should have good speed heading into this stage and plan, and fully expect, to kick here. Will I have the energy to kick after going so hard in the third phase? Well, truthfully probably not really. But this is the Chicago Marathon, where I'll be surrounded by thousands of other runners and hundreds of thousands of spectators along the way, so this is pretty much non-negotiable. I will sprint to the finish. It may not look much like a sprint, but it will be all I've got at that moment. There's a reason I've been running a 400 meter split at the end of each of my track workouts this summer – it's to prepare for this very moment, the moment when more than 7 months of training and planning bears its fruit. Doesn't matter how I feel, you bet I'm going to sprint.

My job over the next 18+ days is to strengthen my belief and my conviction for phases 3 and 4, to shift from thinking that I can accomplish this to knowing for an absolute fact that I WILL. This will be an exercise in willpower that will be as much about psychological strength as it is about physical strength and conditioning. Will I have doubts? Sure, hordes of them! I need to take those doubts, cast them aside, crush them, bury them, whatever it takes so that, by 7:30 on October 12, my confidence and resolution are absolute.

At last! What a great race and a great experience! I am so glad I chose to run Chicago. I think it was a great choice for me and it met all my expectations – which were quite lofty. Among other things, the Chicago Marathon is a great way to see the City and to learn about a lot of the different neighborhoods which were such a great part of the race experience.

Chicago Marathon, October 13, 2014

I've got so much to write about this marathon, but I am one tired and sore puppy here, so not sure how much I'll write tonight. It's about 6:00 here and I'm about ready for bed! But I don't think it's a good idea to go to sleep quite this early.

I think I've got to start with the 12,000+ volunteers, who were awesome! So, positive, enthusiastic and competent. They really made the race work. Also, the marathon was really well run and well organized. Then come all the spectators, including my Mom and Uncle Jack, who were so numerous and so supportive. There were 50 "entertainment stations" – DJs, a mariachi band, school bands, bagpipes, and even cross dressing cheerleaders! It was really an incredible spectacle – seemingly something new to look forward to around every corner.

As for me, I started out way faster than I had planned and just couldn't slow down – until after the 20 mile mark. So my whole race strategy was basically out the window from the beginning. Here's the breakdown:

Pre-race: It was cool (mid 40s) and I had my sunglasses on in the dark, walking the 1.3 miles in the dark. The sidewalks were filled with runners by 6:30. I brought a throw-away sweatshirt that I tossed out of the corral just a few minutes before the start. There were shirts and pants flying all over the place. When I first got in the corral, there was plenty of room, so I was able to warm up. Then I moved towards the front of corral C and waited. It took me just over 5 minutes to get up to the start. I was planning to run with 3:30 pacers, but lost them at the start and never saw them again until mile 22 – when they caught up with me.

Mile 1 – Whoa this was fast – 7:36. But it didn't feel like I was working hard, so I just kept on plugging along.

Mile 2 – Even faster in 7:15 . Saw my Mom and Uncle Jack for the first time here.

Mile 3 – 8:08 – Finally slowed down a little bit, but it took a focused effort to relax and take my foot off the gas.

Mile 4- 7:35 Well, that didn't last long – right back to 7:35. But the fact is I don't feel like I'm running fast here. My stride and cadence are smooth, my breathing is easy, and I'm relaxed and running easy. So, while this was not the plan, I'm feeling good and the pace feels right.

Mile 5 – 7:35 Ditto – just flying along easily. I'm up in Lincoln Park along the Lake now. This reminds me that wind was not an issue at all throughout the race.

Mile 6 – 7:49 This pace is a little more of what I had in mind, but still sub 8:00 and solid. I am feeling so strong at this stage.

Mile 7 – 7:42 Out of Lincoln Park and about at the far northern end of the course. Just solid pace, more of the same. I'm absorbing the crowd as I go, checking out all the signs, listening to the cheers and taking it all in.

Mile 8 – 7:50 More of the same. The crowd is great in this stretch, really for the next 8 miles or so, the crowd is almost entirely lining the street.

Mile 9 – 8:01 Dropped off a shade here, but still feeling solid and strong.

Mile 10 – 7:50 Right back to it and the miles are just flying by for me. Keeping up with my GU and water very nicely.

Mile 11 – 7:48 Another solid, steady mile – one after another now.

Mile 12 – 7:59 Ditto

Mile 13 – 6:49 This can't be right, maybe 7:49? I was basically steady here.

Mile 14 – 7:44 Another steady mile. My left foot started hurting a little bit here, which was a concern. I had been running on the edge of the street

71

to better absorb the crowd, but decided to shift to the center of the street, as it was a little more even there. There was a bit of a slope going down towards the gutter. That shift seemed to help as my foot soon felt better.

Mile 15 – 8:08 I'm having to work a bit harder now and my pace dropped off a little bit. After the half mark, we headed west and I'm now at the far western edge of the course. I'm heading back towards the skyscrapers of downtown, but I know that's just a tease, because I'll soon be heading south away from downtown.

Mile 16 – 7:59 Still strong and back at it with another solid mile.

Mile 17 – 7:59 Still hanging in with another steady mile and still feeling strong.

Mile 18 – 7:57 Ditto. The crowd has been a bit thinner and I miss that, but it's about to pick up.

Mile 19 – 8:01 Another solid mile.

Mile 20 – 8:14 Now we're into Pilsen, a Latino neighborhood, where there is a great mariachi band.

Mile 21 – 8:07 Then onto Chinatown, which is a really great cheering section! I'm starting to fade now and I know it. I'm feeding off the energy of the crowd and that's helping me to hang in.

Mile 22 – 8:13 The 3:30 pacers caught up to me here and I managed to stay with them for a bit, but then fell back. I'm fading now, but hoping the homestretch will spur me on.

Mile 23 – 8:18 The crowd is a little lighter and I am hurting, feeling sore.

Mile 24 – 8:24 Finally heading back north on Michigan. I'm working on reeling people in and am passing a bunch, but they're fading even worse than me. But the strategy of hooking and reeling people in is helping and keeping me from fading too badly.

Mile 25 – 8:27 Still focusing on looking ahead, catching people and passing them. It's the only way I can keep going now. I skipped the last couple of water stops as I don't want to do anything to slow down now and I have enough in my bottle. I did not walk a single step of this race and I'm not planning on it now.

Mile 26 – 8:48 Slow now and just focusing on one foot in front of the other and trying to stay steady.

Mile 27 (0.6 miles on my watch) – 4:48 The last 0.2 miles featured a small hill just before the finish, but I handled it fine and finished strong through the line.

The aftermath – I was hurting. Really sore and limping badly. I really worked hard today and was feeling a lot of pride over my race. There were several points during this race when I nearly burst into tears thinking of meeting this goal and thinking of my family and friends rooting for me. That was especially true at every 5K mark, when I knew my time would be posted. Had to walk about a mile through the finish chute to get to the post-race party and it took a long time. Picked up my heat sheet, medal, beer, food bag, Gatorade and more along the way. Eventually got to reunite with my Mom and Uncle Jack and relax at the post race party for a bit.

7:00 here and time to get ready for bed soon. I expect I'll be asleep by 8:00. Just exhausted now.

After so much success in 2014, it will be interesting to see how I do re: my goals in 2015. I know at some point I will face diminishing returns – I can't possibly keep improving at this rate. But, then again, I'll be training quite a bit with my neighbor Erika, and boy has she got a training plan! I do think that, with increased focus, I can still keep getting better. Time will tell...

Mission Accomplished! Now What?, October 15, 2014

Note: I wrote this on the plane, but am just getting to post it now.

I'm now on my way home from Chicago after a great trip and a highly successful race. When I first set out to run the Chicago Marathon, my goal was to finish under 3:40. As I went through my training and spring races though, that goal didn't seem ambitious enough, so I set my sights higher and aimed to finish under 3:30. While I fell just shy of that at 3:31:03, I think that was the right goal for me to strive for. And, in the end, while I fell just shy of meeting that time, I feel very positive about the entire experience, including:

- Setting PRs at virtually every long run training distance that I ran.

- Setting PRs in 6 of the 9 races that I ran leading up to Chicago.

- Setting a 21 minute PR in Chicago!

The bottom line of all this I that I am a different and much better runner that I was a year ago. I am faster, stronger, and have better endurance. Up to this point, I've been mostly focused on just recovering from the marathon, along with enjoying the rest of my time in Chicago with my Mom and Uncle Jack. But now as I head home, I'm drawn to the inevitable question – now what?

I've met every race goal that I set to start the year and fell just 1 minute shy of my revised Chicago Marathon goal, so the first part of this answer is that it's time for new goals. The one race I definitely have on my calendar (though I've not registered yet) is the Burlington Marathon on Memorial Day Weekend 2015. I'll be running that one with my neighbor Erika, and we're hoping that we'll be able to do many of our long runs together. The other race that I'm planning to do in the short term is the Julie Roddick Dreamcatcher in Weymouth on Thanksgiving AM. That is a 5 mile race. The nice thing about that distance is that I've never run it before, so it will be an automatic PR! :)

Aside from that, I don't have much planned. But I know I will soon grow restless and want to sign up for some more races. I will likely try to work in a 10K and a half into my spring marathon training. And, I expect I'll try to do a 5K or 10K in addition to the 5 mile Thanksgiving run later this fall/winter.

The other change I'm thinking about is joining a gym to train better after daylight savings ends and the weather grows colder. I've never joined a gym before – based on the logic that I wouldn't go regularly and it would just be a waste of money. I think that's always been true in the past. But, given my spring marathon plans, running more in winter has become a greater priority for me and I think I'm going to want to run more often and for longer distances than I want to do on our home treadmill. Plus, I'm more motivated to do some strength training 2-3 times per week to help support my running. Since Planet Fitness has a $10/month special, this seems like a pretty low risk investment. Not sure I would want to join year round, but it seems like a good idea for maybe November – March at least. So I think I'm going to give that a shot for the first time.

Next comes the question of what my new goals should be? For the marathon, I think continuing to strive for a sub 3:30 time remains the right goal. That's Erika's marathon goal as well, so that seems like a good fit. For the half, my new PR this year was 1:37:19. I expect to run several halves later next summer and fall, so I expect to have a few chances to beat this. I'm looking now at a goal of 1:35, if for no other reason than it is a good round number to shoot for and isn't crazy ambitious compared with my current PR. That's about a 10 second per mile pace difference which seems at least reasonable, especially given that I improved my half marathon PR by about 6 minutes, or almost 30 seconds per mile, this past year!

I also feel I can improve my 10K PR time, which is currently 44:59. That was big to get under 45:00, but pace calculators suggest that I could get in the 43 minute range, which seems reasonable to me. But, to keep this manageable for a one year period and because I'm not sure how many 10Ks I will run, I am going to set my 10K goal for 2015 at sub 44 minutes.

I'm not sure what to say about a 5K goal, because I'm not sure how many 5Ks I want to run. I got just under 21 minutes this summer, which was a big milestone for me. The clear milestone to set would be sub 20 minutes, which would be really cool to get to. But, to do that, I would likely need to run a bunch of 5Ks and train specifically for them, and that's not really where my strongest interest lies. Through May, I'll be fully focused on marathon training, and any races I run then will be part of my marathon training. (which likely will not include 5ks). Then, for the fall, I'd like to run mainly halves and 10ks, so again doesn't really fit with 5K training. So, for now I'm not going to set a specific 5K goal and will come back to that later when I'm more focused on 5Ks.

So here's what I've got for 2015 goals:

Burlington Marathon – May 2015 (my only planned 2015 marathon): < 3:30

Half Marathon (I expect to run 4-6 halves): < 1:35

10K (I expect to run maybe 2-3): < 44:00

The other goal I have that's a little bit different is to run races in all six New England states in 2015 – specifically (Mass, CT, RI, NH, Maine and VT). I've already got VT covered and I can easily get to races in all the other NE states within a 2 hour drive – really more like an hour in most cases.

Section 3

October 2014 – December 2015

Running With a Partner:

Burlington, Newmarket, and Philly

This was my first entry about running after the Chicago Marathon. At this point, I was running without a schedule, running as often and as long as I wanted to. But, I definitely wanted to run. While I was still recovering physically and mentally, this was the story of one of my stronger post-Chicago runs.

Getting My Legs Back, October 28, 2014

The nice thing about running without a schedule is that you can run as little or as much as you want, whenever you want. Most of the time that may mean taking it easy. But tonight I saw the weather and decided I had to get out for a run. I decided to go for 6 miles but, after I got out there, I realized that it's Tuesday night and Kevin's old running team, the South Shore Fireboltz, was having practice in Wompatuck State Park – 4.25 miles one way. Well, despite some soreness, which I'll get to, I was feeling so good and strong that I said, "Why Not!?"

For the first time since my Marathon, I was really running at a good clip, covering the first 4.25 miles at a 7:40 pace. And I wasn't pressing either – it was coming naturally. It's such a great feeling when that happens. Then I got to talk with Kevin's previous coach Heike, for about 20 minutes, and see some former teammates and their parents. After a really nice visit, I headed back home. By this time it was getting dark and my soreness was mounting a little bit, so my pace coming back wasn't nearly as aggressive. I started the return trip fast, but ended up at about an 8:08 pace for the return trip – still very solid.

I'm still more sore than I should be for the runs I'm doing, so I know I'm not quite fully back yet. Now I'm icing my left foot and knee, so a little caution is in order. But, for that few minutes, it felt great to really run again and open it up a bit. It's such a joy to just go out and run sometimes – with no purpose beyond just running.

Now I was building my momentum back up. This run was the beginning of another amazing stretch of running for me. At this point, I didn't realize how amazing November and December would be. I thought 2014 would always be about Chicago and all of my training and races to get to that point. And one thing I definitely did not expect, especially in the wake of Chicago, was running so well in November and December. But, I'm getting ahead of myself a bit.

An Unexpected PR, November 11, 2014

Well, it was just a training PR. But, a PR is a PR no matter how you slice it.

Today was a gorgeous mild day here in Weymouth and I was off for Veteran's Day. Kevin and I are running in the 5 mile Julie Rodick Dreamcatcher race on Thanksgiving AM. Since neither one of us has run it before, I decided to scout out the course today. Most of the roads are main roads that we know well, but it's always different to run it – you pick up things that you don't notice driving around town. And, knowing the little back streets on the course helps too so that you can anticipate the turns.

I think it was about noon when I started, partly cloudy and about 60 degrees, As long as I'm not going super long, that's just about my favorite running weather – T-shirt and shorts running weather – a treat for November. I drove to the start of the course at the Weymouth Elks with the course map in my pocket. As I got going, I felt good, but not great. I don't think I've had a totally pain free run since my Marathon – there's always something nagging me a bit. But, all in all, I felt good. I wasn't trying to run fast, just running at the pace I felt like. No plans for a PR. Turns out the first mile pace was 7:21 – yikes. I still wasn't thinking about a super-fast run at this point, I figured I'd slow as I went and I had no problem with that. After all, I was just scouting the course.

Mile 2 featured the biggest hill on the course, up Washington Street, towards Middle. Nothing huge, but noticeable for a runner. My pace for this mile was 7:36, still pretty quick, especially given that hill. So after that, I really felt I would fade, Not that I planned to, but I didn't really care one way or the other.

Well, mile 3 along Libbey Pkwy turned out to be a 7:23 mile. This was mostly flat with just a mild uphill and, at this point, I couldn't help but notice that I was having a fast run. Mile 4 was mostly along Pleasant Street, towards the High School, on to Elm, then Pine and back – for those that know the streets. This was pretty flat too, but I faded a little bit, to 7:48. But I thought I knew my 5 mile PR (I was right) and I knew I had a chance to beat it.

So, for mile 5, I decided to be aggressive and push my pace – just for kicks. I was really flying down Pleasant and finished that 5th mile in 7:19 – for a total time of 37:26 – beating my previous 5 mile PR by about 25 seconds! Generally speaking, a training run PR is no big deal. And, the way this year has been going, I've set many for myself. But this one really matters to me. I've been working, not entirely successfully, to recover from my Marathon. This isn't so much a confidence issue, not exactly. But I've been missing running really well and, looking ahead to a race in about two weeks, a little confidence boost doesn't hurt.

This was an interesting and tricky time for me in my training. With just over 7 months between Chicago and Burlington, I was stuck a bit in-between in terms of how to handle my training. I ended up keeping up my base mileage, but at least giving myself a bit of a mental break by running without a set schedule. Looking back with hindsight I think this was a good way to go.

Schedule or No Schedule?, November 16, 2014

I've now got six and 1/2 months to go until the Burlington Marathon. That time period is interesting because I had already started my training schedule for Chicago with 7 and 1/2 months to go. But, right now, I do not have a training schedule planned for Burlington until the beginning of February. The reason for that is that, over the past month, I have been focused on my mental and physical recovery from Chicago.

But, I have been gradually ramping up my miles over the past couple of weeks. And, despite having no schedule, I am now back up to 20+ mile weeks – at least for this past week anyway. With two races now scheduled over the next three weeks, I have a feeling of increased momentum and energy about my running. Recently, I joined Planet Fitness, the first time I have ever joined a gym/health club. I believe I will need that in order to keep up with the running I need to do this winter – with or without a training schedule. That would also enable me to do more supporting core workouts.

So the question I face now is – Schedule or No Schedule? I am leaning towards "No Schedule". Here's the thinking. All I really need to do is keep up my base miles of 20-25 miles per week and do some supporting core workouts 2-3 times per week. The general plan is to run 2 times during the week and then run on Saturday and Sunday. The mid-week runs will be at Planet Fitness, where I can easily do the other workouts I need to do. I think that, as long as I can keep up with 20-25 miles per week without a specific schedule, then I should just leave it at that. Running without a schedule is a little more relaxing and, given that I've been running with a schedule for so long, I think it would be helpful to take advantage of this chance to run without a schedule while I can. That will give me a mental break, even though I'll still be running. Once I get to February, I know that I will have to be on a specific training plan, so I won't have a choice at that point. If I feel like I'm slipping and not keeping up with my mileage and workouts like I should, then I'll write down a training plan to keep me on track.

The other good thing I have going for me now is that I'm routinely doing a long run of 7-8 miles each week, keeping up my distance stamina. And, with each passing week, I feel my stamina and speed returning to me a little bit more. Next up is the Julie Roddick Dreamcatcher on Thanksgiving Day (11/27) and then a 5K on December 7. For me, there is nothing like having a race to look forward to to keep me motivated and energized. While I enjoy training runs for their own sake, races are what really drive me. Assuming that I set a PR in the 5 miler, but not the 5K, that would bring me to 8 race PRs for the year! So I think that will be my short-term focus now – to wrap up the remarkable year of 2014 on an up note,

My 5K on December 7 will be the Frosty Five in Mansfield – the same race that was my last race of 2013 – perhaps a budding tradition? The difference is that I ran this one with Kevin last year. But now he has moved on to high school indoor track so he's not able to run these races any longer. Fortunately, I won't be running this one alone, as my neighbor Erika will run it with me. That's always welcome, especially when staring down who knows what December weather that may face us on that day.

To be fair, this was likely to be a PR by default, as I've never run a 5 mile race before. But, it was a legitimate PR, because it was my fastest 5 mile run ever. And the time was really good for me.

PR #8!, November 28, 2014

The weather here in Weymouth, MA was dicey before, during, and after Thanksgiving. But, things worked out for a pretty decent stretch on Thursday AM, when it was about 34 degrees, without precipitation, and partly cloudy. Given the rain before this and the snow later in the day, this was super. Kevin and I were running the Julie Rodick Dreamcatcher 5 Mile Road Race for the first time and we took advantage of the weather window to have a great race!

This was my 12th race of 2014 and my 8th personal record! As I've written along the way, this type of progress is incredibly gratifying. I've met virtually every goal I've set in virtually every race I've run this year. My goal yesterday was to finish the 5 mile race in 35 minutes or less. This was likely to be a PR by default because, while I've done lots of 5 mile runs, I had never run a 5 mile race. But, as it turned out, this was much better than a PR by default and there's really no asterisk associated with this one.

Leading up to the race, I was able to regroup enough from Chicago to do a decent amount of both speed and distance work and, just before the race, my legs felt GOOD. I felt strong and I felt fast. This feeling, combined with the decent weather, made me very optimistic as I warmed up pre-race. The race start was, well, kind of spontaneous. So, as a result, I didn't start my watch right on time and my mile splits were slightly off. And, from the paces they posted, it appears that the course was a shade long, more like 5.1 miles. But the splits I got on my watch give the general idea of how the race went.

Mile 1 was fast as it should be, but not stupid fast. My first mile split was about 6:27, pretty much where I wanted to be. There's something kind of special about running in your "hometown", seeing so many people you know in the race with you. It gives you a little extra boost of adrenaline and happiness. I was further buoyed late in mile 1 by seeing our neighbor Erika and her kids cheering us on. I felt good and strong, right on track with the pace I wanted.

Mile 2 featured the biggest hill of the race and my pace slowed to 7:01. Again, this was about where I wanted to be for this mile and, while I knew I was working hard, I continued to feel strong and on track. My steady pace continued in mile 3, where I hit 6:58. I was surrounded by several of Kevin's teammates at that point, kind of cool. At this point, I knew I was ahead of my pace goal and there was no need to do anything aggressive. I just needed to hang at this pace.

In mile 4, I passed by a house playing music – Eye of the Tiger! I'm steady as I go, at 7:02. Looking back at this race, I thought I ran a really good race, but definitely not my best race. It's miles 4 and 5 that I have in mind when I reflect back. At this stage, I knew I had my goal nailed, and I was running that way. I certainly wasn't coasting, as mile 5 was 6:50. But, I wasn't exactly flooring it either. I was content with the race I was running and probably left a bit in the tank. Anyway, there was an extra 10 seconds in there at the end, as my watch showed a shade over 5 miles and I finished strong. I finished in 34:26 and Kevin finished in 33:24.

Depending on what distance you use, I ran this race at either a 6:53 or 6:45 pace. Comparing that to my 5K PR pace of about 6:43 and my 10K PR pace of about 7:15, this was a legitimate PR and definitely an improvement over my prior races. I had a similar feeling after the Providence 1/2 earlier this year. I ran a PR time then, but knew it wasn't my best effort. Three weeks later, I beat that time by more than 4 minutes. So I can't wait to run the Dreamcatcher again next year – and to have a new, more aggressive goal to shoot for.

Burlington was different than Chicago from the very beginning. Burlington was all about Erika – both training together and, hopefully, running the full race together. While training with someone else, especially someone so well matched with you, is great, I think we are each burdened with additional expectations at times. We each want so badly to hold up our end of the bargain. The other thing that was totally different about this marathon for me is that it is a spring marathon, so I needed to train through the winter. I didn't know it at this point, but man did that turn out to be tough!

Building The Base, December 3, 2014

It doesn't really seem like it, but right now I'm training for the Burlington Marathon. I started my training for Chicago more than 7 months out and, I'm a little surprised to note, Burlington is now less than 6 months away! Starting in early November, I picked up my running again, running pretty much 4 days a week and 20-25 miles a week. That will pretty much be my pattern from now through late January. At that point, the weekly and long run miles will start to pick up.

Although this base mileage period doesn't seem like much, it's a critical component of my training. This solid base will enable me to pick up my mileage in February looking ahead to Memorial Day weekend. When I look back on this marathon, whatever success I have will be based on the foundation I'm building right now. This is admittedly not the most inspiring part of training for a marathon but, fortunately I continue to like it and look forward to and enjoy my runs. Yes, even the treadmill runs! But it also helps to remind myself that this base mileage is an integral component of training for Burlington.

I have already begun the process of envisioning the Marathon in my mind – thinking particularly of the last 6.2 miles. While you want to be able to prevent and deal with setbacks, and you have to consider potential problems to do that, I believe there's no place for negative thoughts and energy in a runner – especially a marathon runner. It's just too hard as it is, so positive energy is critical. So I strive to keep everything positive and turn every negative thought that pops up into a positive one as I go. Time and time again, in my mind, I plan, envision, and commit to a strong finish in the last few miles. My training will give me the physical strength and fitness I need – everything else is will.

Every boring treadmill run, every brutal run in snow and ice, and every core workout is a chance to strengthen my physical and psychological resolve for those late marathon miles. When you've run to and past the point of exhaustion and then have to run a few more miles. But not just run a few more miles, but run them at a 8:00 pace. With each race I run, with each training run, with each workout, I learn that I can do a little better and also gain a little better sense of what I can do differently and better. So tonight's 6 mile treadmill run at Planet Fitness wasn't just a 6 mile treadmill run. It was another step towards the finish line in Burlington. And that's something to get pumped about!

This was a great race for me, and a completely unexpected PR. I really thought that my 5K times had maxed out, so I was amazed to get a 30 second PR in this 5K, and my 9th PR of the year. This was also my first race ever with Erika. 9 PRs, at 4 different distances. Just an incredible, awesome year.

Last Race of 2014?, December 8, 2014

Well, if this was the last race of 2014, it was a great way to go out. Today, I ran the Mansfield Frosty Five 5K with my neighbor Erika. About a year ago, this was my last race of 2013, that time with Kevin. This time, it MAY be my last race of 2014. In a year that has been filled with almost surreal running superlatives for me, today was yet another one. I ran a 5K PR of 20:21 – 30 seconds faster than my previous 5K PR. In the world of 5K times, that is huge.

There have been times in Kevin's running career when it seemed like nearly every race he ran was a PR. I was always particularly proud of him at those times because I knew those PRs were the result of all of his practices and hard work along the way. But he's 15 and at an age when you would expect him to improve, at least over time.

I, on the other hand, am 45. Not old by most means, but certainly not moving into my running prime. Or, at least not what most people consider prime running age. But in this year when I turned 45, I set PRs in 9 of the 13 races I ran, which is purely awesome. Now, the cynical view is maybe that's because I had so much room to improve. And, to a degree, that is true. Having only started my running at age 40, I'm still a relative newbie and have gotten into better and better running shape with each passing year. But I've been around enough people doing enough running to know that this streak of PRs is exceptional for anyone at any time.

To sum up, my 2014 PRs were:

4/6, Cohasset 10 K, 45:46

5/4, Providence 1/2, 1:42:00

5/18. Evan's Run 10K, 44:59

5/25, Boston Run to Remember 1/2, 1:37:38

8/3, YuKan Triple Threat 5K, 20:51

8/3, Yukan Triple Threat 1/2, 1:37:19

10/12, Chicago Marathon, 3:31:03

11/27, Julie Rodick Dreamcatcher 5 Mile, 34:24

12/7, Mansfield Frosty Five 5K, 20:21

So, I'm a numbers guy. Having set 9 PRs in a year, I can't help but think how great it would be to get 10 in one year. There aren't many race options this time of year, but I've been looking around and thinking about it. Perhaps one more 5K or 10K!? Because, here's the thing – it's about more than numbers. In my recent PR races, I've had this post-race feeling that I still did not run my best race. This is about competing – competing against myself to continue to get better. And when I run races these days, soon after the finish, I am left with one recurring thought that I just can't shake. I go on with the rest of my day, I do other stuff, I think about other things. But, one thought just keeps coming back – driven by that competitive desire that is still burning strong.

I want to go again. I want the next race.

Although I fell short in my bid for my 10th PR of the year in this race, looking back this was a really strong race and a great effort. This race, along with the Mansfield 5K, came as revelations to me that I could still get faster in 5Ks – and definitely in 10Ks. I will also always remember this race for the email psyche-up message that Erika sent me prior to the race. I read over that again as I was writing this, and it is one of the most amazing messages/letters that I've ever received. While that was great for this race, it also filled me with excitement looking ahead to running Burlington together!

Hungry for More, December 14, 2014

I could start the story of today's race at a number of different points, but I'm going to pick my 5 mile scouting run for the Julie Roddick Dreamcatcher in November. That was my first really solid run after the Chicago Marathon when I felt I could run with some pace. And that led to a very good run in the Dreamcatcher on Thanksgiving Day. After the Dreamcatcher, I felt good enough and inspired enough to sign up for the Mansfield Frosty Five 5K last weekend. That was a great race for me, my 9th PR for the year, and it made me a little greedy. I turned this over in my head a lot but, eventually decided I wanted to try for one more PR – #10 for the year. Given all of my times, I think my best shot would have been in a 10K, but my options were limited. So, after hemming and hawing for 4 days, I signed up for the Amica Downtown Jingle 5K in Providence today.

It's worth noting that, in the Mansfield race, my watch registered the course as 3.07 miles, and I ran it in 20:21, a 6:39 pace. This was a solid 30 second PR for me, a very big step up. But, after the race, I felt really good – just a little too good. And, I couldn't help but think that I could have run just a little bit faster. And, perhaps, if clicking on all cylinders, finished under 20:00.

Leading up to Providence, I was working on getting my head off of getting the PR and focusing more on just how I was going to run the race. I got a huge boost from a "psyche-up" message from my running partner Erika. After that, I knew two things for certain:

1. I was going to run this race very hard – with an edge.

2. I have an awesome running partner!

I also felt very confident about getting that 10th PR.

On race day, Anne, Eliza, and Kevin all decided to come with me – kind of a last minute decision. it was great to have the company, the support, and a cheering section! The weather was beautiful running weather for December – about 40 degrees, sunny, and not too much wind. No excuses. Warming up, I felt good, strong, and confident. This was a big race, about 1,300 people total, and I maneuvered my way into a spot in the first three rows. They played the National Anthem and I was chomping at the bit.

I came out of the chute very fast – running the first mile in 6:06. I wasn't quite aiming for that, but I wanted to run this race with an edge and was thinking about 6:15 for the first mile. So this wasn't too far off. I slowed in mile 2, as we ran along the Providence River. I finished that 2nd mile in 6:31, so just 12:37 for the first two miles, average of 6:18 per. FLYING. I was in great shape time-wise at this point, but I could feel the fatigue building.

Early in mile 3, maybe around 2.2 or so, I felt a wave of fatigue that almost made me buckle. I was hurting and started to get a little concerned about my pace. I was able to push through that, but my legs just weren't there for me. I wanted to push so badly but I just didn't have that explosive kick left. I continued to work hard and used my Marathon tactic of passing a couple of people to try to give a jolt to my pace. I ended up finishing the 3rd mile, in 7:00, a disappointing result.

Through 3 miles, I was still actually 19 seconds ahead of my Mansfield pace. At this point, there was a subtle but key difference between the Providence race and Mansfield. Where the Mansfield race came out to be 3.07 miles, this one measured at 3.13 miles. At my pace, that .06 mile difference accounted for about 24 seconds. I finished in 20:24, just three seconds off my Mansfield time, on a course that measured .06 miles longer. So my pace was actually 6:31 today, vs. 6:39 in Mansfield. So, while it was technically not a PR today, I actually ran faster.

I ended up finishing 28th overall and 6th in my age group, numbers that I am very proud of. I am particularly proud of these 5K successes because these 5Ks were really an afterthought for me this year. In a year when I focused on the Chicago Marathon and running halves, it was really pretty cool that I set two 5K PRs and nearly a third. I really hadn't trained for 5ks at all. Perhaps you can guess what's coming next?

Between now and Memorial Day, my running focus will be on the Burlington Marathon. I am very much looking forward to that race, but also the marathon training. That is a really awesome experience and I am psyched for it. And, I am going to be 100% focused on this goal between now and then.

But, after I recover from Burlington, I already know what my next focus and goal will be. I plan to focus on both 5Ks and 10Ks after that. My 5k goal will be to finish sub 20:00 – getting that time in the 19s will be a great milestone. My 10K goal will be to run it at under a 7:00 pace, or 43:24. My current 10K PR is 44:59 and I should be able to best that easily at this point. I will adjust my training to focus on more shorter speed work so that next time I will not waver in that last 1.1 and will push through it fast and hard.

Looking back on 2014 it will always stand out for me for the 9 PRs. But, in addition to that, I think it's noteworthy that I set PRs at 5 different distances (marathon, half (3 times), 10K (2 times), 5 mile, and 5K(2 times). Through this awesome year, I have continually adjusted my expectations upward (or downward in terms of times) as I've improved. One of the points that Erika made to me is that, if I don't get this PR today, that will leave me hungry for more. OH YEAH!

I really like this blog entry, as it blends my disappointment over falling just short of a PR, with my resolve and commitment looking ahead to Burlington. And, again looking back at 2014, I continued to be struck by what an amazing year it was. I especially like the last paragraph looking ahead to Burlington, as this really summed up my mindset that remained strong through very difficult periods of training.

Licking My Wounds, December 15, 2014

I am definitely feeling my effort from my 5K yesterday in my legs. I think this is the most sore I've been since the aftermath of Chicago. In addition to this physical fatigue, I'm also feeling emotional fatigue and letdown, as I really laid it on the line Sunday in Providence. Although I ran a great race (my 2nd fastest 5K ever by just 3 seconds) and my effort was excellent, it's still disappointing to lay it on the line like that and fall short of your goal. It stings a bit.

I was struck by this emotion and realized how unfamiliar it is for my running this year. I have spoiled myself with success. Other than this race, when I fell just short of a PR, I failed to get PRs in only 4 more of my 14 races this year:

• two 5Ks this spring when I was just running to get into shape and wasn't even thinking about PRs (and still nearly did in one of them)

• a July 1/2 in Easton when I beat my time on the same course last year by nearly 4 minutes!

• the mile run in the Triple Threat Challenge when I was purposely trying not to get a PR!

In fact, the only other race that I can think of when I failed to meet my goal was the Chicago Marathon when I fell one minute short of my goal! But that race was the biggest success of all because I set a 21 MINUTE PR!

Out of about 180 training runs this year, I could count the truly poor runs on the fingers of one hand, maybe even with some fingers left over. So, out of nearly 200 runs this year spanning more than 1,200 miles, I've had barely a handful of disappointing ones. So this disappointment, even in a limited way, is an unfamiliar emotion to me in my running this year.

I will be spending the next six weeks rebuilding physically and emotionally as I work to build a strong foundation for training for Burlington. This is an important time to rest and nurture my running spirits and morale as well as my body. But rest is relative for a marathon runner. Even during this "rest period", I will be running a total of 20-25 miles/week, running 4 days per week and doing core workouts three days per week. Even tonight, I will drag my tired, sore body through a core workout.

I could rationalize my way out of this (I just ran a hard race, Burlington is still more than 5 months away, it wouldn't hurt to miss one...). But I am in marathon training mode now and there are no shortcuts. Training for a marathon is not an 80% commitment, a 95% commitment, or even a 99% commitment. It's a 100% all in mental, emotional and physical commitment. Every run and every core workout is a building block for Burlington. I don't plan to miss a single one. (Of course excepting a real injury or illness, but soreness and fatigue don't count.)

When you're a marathon runner, it's not just for one day. I will be a marathon runner for each of the next 160 or so days leading up to Burlington. The work habits and discipline that go into this training are critical not just for my physical conditioning, but also for my mental and emotional conditioning. As I've written before, being successful on RACE DAY is based on my core workout tonight, along with every other run and workout over the next 160 days. So, yeah, I'm tired and I'm sore. And it's about time to work out.

At this point, my focus was beginning to shift from my 2014 runs to looking ahead to Burlington.

Settling In, December 20, 2014

Not for a long winter nap, but for a long winter training schedule. I had a little flurry of races recently, which lent an exciting twist to the end of the year. I'm just now settling down from the adrenaline and excitement of those races and shifting gears mentally. I will probably write an end of year blog post later, as this time of the year always brings out my sentimental side. But my thoughts now are more forward-looking.

Big picture, I am now a totally different runner than when I started the year. I mean like an order of magnitude difference. I'll write about times later, but qualitatively, I've risen to a new level. That much I know. I read an article the other day that suggested that it takes about three full years of solid training before you can really realize your running potential. Although I'm in my 5th year of running now, this is really only the 2nd year that I've trained consistently and in volume. So, I'm hoping that I've got another year of significant improvement still to come!?

I'm already feeling stronger from my core workouts. I've been doing this regularly now, something I've never managed before. Looking ahead, I'm hoping these will be very valuable in supplementing my training runs and making me both faster and stronger. The potential of the year ahead is really exciting for me. But it's not exciting in a dreamy, wistful way. It's exciting in a more tangible, real sense. I know what I can do and I know what I will need to go to get there – and I'm committed to making it happen. This includes the Burlington Marathon as the top priority – and the first priority. That training plan is the appetizer if you will, with the marathon being the main course of the 2015 running year. But I'm confident I'll be hungry for a dessert of a few 5Ks and 10Ks. Maybe even an after dinner liqueur!

I'm not sure I've ever been able to fully peg why I enjoy and value my running so much. I've tried in past posts (see **Why I Run**?) and I think I've gotten a lot of it out. There's a sense of momentum for me now that's very powerful and compelling. Each new success furthers my drive to be even better. I don't know where and when this will end, but I'm riding this wave for as long as it lasts. And, who knows, that could be a very long time.

Although I focus on my own times when I run races, I can't help but notice that I'm starting to place pretty well in a lot of my races. And, of course, my place finishes have improved along with my times. And there's a little latent ripple of excitement below my emotional surface when I take a moment to think about this. It's not that I think I'm going to go win races, but the idea of placing well is kind of a tease for me. You know, in case I need a little motivation.

For now, I'm settling into the long stretch of marathon training. That will give me all I can handle over the next five months. And, as is always the case for me, it's really all about the journey.

This blog entry was all about 2014, and rightly so. I think this one pretty much speaks for itself. I especially like how I framed it in the introductory paragraph. 2014 was a special running year for me, especially noteworthy in how I progressed so well at so many different distances.

Top Ten Runs of the Year, December 27, 2014

Reflecting back on 2014, I've had a lot of great runs – both races and training runs. I began to think some more about what were my best runs of the year and decided to come up with a list of my top ten runs of 2014. It was a lot harder than I thought it was, as it wasn't immediately clear what made a run one of "the best". I decided it didn't necessarily mean the fastest time, though it could be. It didn't even have to be a PR, though many of these ones were PRs at the time. I also decided that a run could be on my top ten list even if wasn't a great run, but if it was a meaningful run for some other reason. This was an interesting exercise to think through, as it made me think about what I value about my runs. Below are the choices I selected, along with a little description and explanation of why each run is on this list.

#10. Mansfield Frosty Five 5K, December 7 This race was meaningful for several reasons. This was my first race with Erika. Even though we ended up not running the full race together, we ran much of it together, and it still made the whole experience a lot more fun. This was also my 9th race PR of the year. I finished in 20:21, a full 30 seconds faster than my previous

5K PR. This came at a time when I thought I had perhaps maxed out my 5K times, so this was a bit of a thrill to realize I could still get faster at this distance. This race, perhaps more than any other, helped inspire me to look ahead to 2015 and realize how much better I can still be at shorter races like 5Ks and 10Ks.

#9. 16 Mile Training Run, August 25 This was perhaps my worst run of the year, so it may seem like an odd choice for this list. On this run, I did 11 miles on my own, followed by 5 with Erika – at least that was the plan. I did this run on a very warm afternoon, which was unusual for me for a long run, as I did most of my long runs this year in the early AM. It was a bad choice! I got through the first 11 OK but, by the time Erika joined me, I was already spent. I hung in for three miles, up until mile 14, when I felt like I had to stop. From there, Erika helped me salvage what could have been a dismal run and give it a nice upside. We picked up jogging again until we reached a large hill in the homestretch. Erika cajoled me to start running up the hill and, little by little, to run up the full hill. The pace was terribly slow but given how I was feeling at this point, this was a great moral victory. A run like this is very humbling on one hand, but also potentially inspiring.

When you're running with a relatively new running partner, you want to run well. Not necessarily super-fast, but the last thing you want is someone waiting on you, especially when you've recently started running with them. So, yeah, this was a humbling run. But, it helped me realize that you can have a terrible run and still be a very good runner. And Erika, for her part, was incredibly patient when she was basically fresh and I had nothing left.

#8. Julie Roddick Dreamcatcher 5 Mile Race, November 27 This was my first race after the Chicago Marathon. It was a fun race, because it was right here in Weymouth, Kevin was running it too, and we knew a lot of people there. I had a solid run on the course a few days prior to the race and had set a goal of finishing in under 35 minutes, a 7:00 pace. I ended up finishing the race in 34:24, and still felt like I had a little left in the tank. This was gratifying for me to set a race goal like this and meet it so solidly.

This race also inspired me to run a couple more 5Ks late in the year (including #10 above) and continue to push my pace in shorter races.

#7 16 Mile Training Run, July 27 I completed this run in 2:07:45, under an 8:00 pace, and more than 4 minutes faster than a 16 mile run I had done about a month earlier. On this run, I was doing the first 10 miles with Erika and then the last 6 on my own. As part of the run with Erika, we did two 10 minute tempo stretches, aiming for a faster 7:25 pace. I've done lots of running at that pace, but never by design as part of a long run, so this was new to me. We wrapped up the tempo part of the run in the 4th mile. The real story of the run is how well I ran after that point. The rest of the 10 with Erika went very well and we wound up back home at that point. I took off for the last 6 miles all by my lonesome and managed to run the last 6 miles at a steady, strong pace. This was an exciting run for me, in that I could run fast tempo stretches early in the run and still be able to hang in with my pace at the end.

#6 15 Mile Training Run, July 20 This was my strongest long run early in my training this year. I was aiming to run 15 miles at a steady 8:00 pace (in 2 hours) and nailed it! My slowest mile of the run was the first in 8:15 and every single mile was between 8:15 and 7:47, remarkably consistent for me. Even more impressive was that every mile after mile 6 was under 8:00. Just a really, really strong run. And, perhaps the first time that I felt really confident that I could run the Chicago Marathon at an 8:00 pace. This may have been my most consistent run all year!

#5 Boston Run to Remember Half Marathon, May 25 I ran this half marathon in 1:37:38, more than 4 minutes faster than my previous PR, which I had set just three weeks before. This was a great race for me and noteworthy for how I increased my pace as I went. I typically go out fast in races, and rarely get negative splits, especially late in a race. In this race, I kept on running sub 7:30 miles and, once I got to 10 miles, started hitting sub 7:00 miles. This was one of several races in 2014 when I dramatically exceeded my expectations and ran at a level I just didn't know I was capable of. This was a revelation in helping me realize how much better I could be and how I could still improve my times not just incrementally, but by leaps and bounds.

#4 Cohasset 10K, April 6 This was the race that really set me on my way in 2014. I had been a little nervous about this race because of the hills. I had struggled on it the year before and, while I had set a PR then, had a tough time with it. So I trained specially for this race, doing hill workouts leading up to the race. It paid off in a big way, as I ran this race very strong, handling the hills with relative ease and at a nice, steady, fast pace. I finished in 45:46 which was a 22 second PR. But, more important than that, I finished the course more than 2 minutes faster than I had the year before. And, most important of all was how strong I felt through a very challenging course. Mentally and emotionally, I think this was a huge confidence builder and springboard for all of the great races I ran later in the year.

#3 22 Mile Training Run, September 14 It's a little hard to say, but this may have been my single best, i.e., highest quality, run all year. In any case, it certainly belongs in the top three. I ran this 22 mile run in 2:45:45, at an average 8:04 pace. My blog post on this one was titled "WOW". This was a cool morning, starting in the low 50s – no coincidence there. Also, no coincidence that I ran part of this great run with Erika. We started out running together and ran the first 12 together. The first mile turned out to be the slowest mile of the whole run at 8:21. It was a beautiful day for running, crisp and clear, and the miles went by smoothly.

But the real test of this run, and the part that makes it great, was the last 10 that I ran on my own. I did a mental trick, thinking of this as a 10 mile run, not the last 10 miles of a 22 mile run, and it really helped. I ran mile 13 (aka Mile 1) in 7:58 and I was on my way. That was a pivotal mile in my run. The other pivotal mile was mile 18. I had slowed to 8:16 in mile 17 and it appeared that I might slow down the rest of the way. But then I nailed mile 18 in 7:58 and I built a huge amount of energy and momentum off of that mile. The last 4 miles were all under 8:00, with the last mile, mile 22, finishing in 7:50. My fastest mile of the whole run was mile 22! Just an amazing, powerful run. And, looking back on it now, I do think this was my best single run of the year. But still not good enough to be #1 on this list.

#2 Triple Threat Challenge, August 3 As the name suggests, this race was three races in one, a 1 mile run, a 5K, and a half back to back to back. On a warm summer morning. No big deal :) I ran the mile in 6:45, a conservative mile as it should be. One thing I knew about today is that there would no PRs. I just wanted to manage my way through three back to back races and not get hurt. The 5K came next and I was feeling strong. A little too strong. I ran the first mile in 6:40 but thought, "It's just the first mile and I'm a little jazzed." But when I ran the 2nd mile in 6:35, I was a little taken aback. I knew a PR was in reach then and just decided to go for it, figuring I'd just coast in the half. I finished in 20:51, a 20 second PR! Ooops, I didn't mean to get a PR!?

Getting ready for the half, I planned to run a more subdued pace, knowing now that I definitely wouldn't get a PR in the half. I didn't come out flying, but I was routinely hitting sub 7:30 miles, mile after mile after mile after mile. And so on. It kind of snuck up on me, but I realized that, somehow, I was running a very, very strong half. Wow. I still wasn't thinking about a PR, just trying to hang with sub 7:30 miles as long as I could, for as many miles as I could. I figured this way I'd at least keep my time respectable. As I got closer to the end, I realized the stupendous possibility that I could get a back to back PR. I ended up with a very strong kick up a hill at the finish and a 19 second PR in 1:37:19. To this day, I still shake my head at this race, really having no idea how it happened, but being very proud of my accomplishment.

#1 Chicago Marathon, October 12 If you've been following my running this year, you knew this would be #1 before you started. It was a great race, a 21 minute PR, at 3:31, and just over my very aggressive goal of 3:30. But this was about more than just my race. The entire marathon was an incredible experience, and I had an awesome 5 days in Chicago with my Mom and my Uncle Jack. For any runner who's not run a big city marathon, I highly recommend it. And, though I know there are several premier ones in this category, I certainly recommend Chicago. Running in front of, and really through, those crowds is just an awesome experience. I ran this race faster than I should have, but felt so strong and ran with so much adrenaline, I almost made it through at that aggressive pace. And, even when I slowed at the end, I hung in for a decent finish. A great race following an incredible year of training.

This run was one of many that Erika would work through together in 2015. We were not always at our best but, on these runs, we always worked through them together. And the story of these runs was not about how I ran, or about how Erika ran, but rather how WE ran together.

Looking Ahead, January 3, 2015

As I reached the end of the calendar year, New Year's Eve, and New Year's Day, I thought I would want to write more about what a great year I had running in 2014. But I really didn't. My heart just wasn't in it. Don't get me wrong – my thoughts of my success running this past year continue to be overwhelmingly positive. And I still think back on those successes fondly. But I've already written about that to my heart's content and, at least for the time being, I have moved on.

Today I went for a 5 mile run with Erika. She had struggled on her last run, coming back from being sick and a few days off. Ironically the course we ran today was the same one that I struggled so mightily with this past summer. That was the one and only run this summer that I had to cut off and walk. Of course I had run 11 miles before that on that day and it was about 50 degrees hotter then. So this was not a daunting run for me today by comparison. But I found it ironic that, at a time when Erika was struggling a bit, that we were running the course that I had struggled on so badly. This was the first time since that day that I had run this particular route and I found the negative memories popping up in my head as if they were just yesterday. It's amazing how clear the images were, especially at the point when I had stopped. It mattered to me then and it still matters now. Sometimes the bad runs fill you with more motivation than the good ones.

I wasn't sure how I felt about this irony, and hoped that today would go well – especially for Erika. My hope for this run was just for a steady pace – nothing special or fast – just a solid run. When we started off at 8:13 for the first mile, and it didn't feel particularly fast, that was promising. When we did the second mile in 8:07, with both of us feeling good, this was really encouraging, We finished mile 3 at a 7:52 pace. This was where I had cut off that run this past summer, so it was nice to be hitting it with negative splits now. Miles 4 and 5 went well too, at 8:03 and 8:09. This was especially good given that mile 5 featured a big uphill climb. We ended up in 40:25 for the 5 miles, nothing splashy, but a nice solid pace and pretty decent splits.

So, the thing about this run, and the part where I was looking ahead, is that I cared more about how Erika ran today than how I did. I was feeling OK, but she was coming off a struggle of a run and I know how that feels. It was so gratifying to have such a solid run together. With the Burlington Marathon less than 5 months away all of a sudden, I was reminded yet again about how excited I am to train for this marathon with Erika.

Now, I am happy to run on my own, and perfectly comfortable doing so. I've had many long runs on my own, and I can handle it, both physically and mentally. But, every time we run together, I'm reminded of how much it can help to run with a training partner to help you through the rough patches. I know she helped me through several this past summer, and I know I was at least a little bit helpful to her today. The longer runs are right around the corner, and a run like today's really helps to build the emotional momentum as the intensity and duration of our training schedule builds.

Only 20 weeks to go and it's starting to get real.

Although we had a very long way to go at this point, and we really had not picked up our training yet, I was feeling very confident about the road ahead. My confidence was properly placed and turned out to be justified. But it turned out to be an awfully tough road for both of us, especially with the brutal winter weather that would arrive soon.

18 Weeks to Go, January 19, 2015

So we're now at the critical 18 week mark – 18 weeks to go until the Burlington Marathon. The swing point in our training. Actually, I'm just kidding, 18 weeks is really a completely random milestone as far as I'm concerned. But I still feel like checking in on how things are going.

Both Erika and I are working on treating minor injuries – Erika for her knee and me for my back and side. I think we've each improved over the past few days, so I'm feeling better about that. When you have injuries like that, they tend to nag at your mind in addition to your body. But, given our progress over the last few days, I'm feeling really confident right now. Our schedule calls for picking up our long runs soon, first with some tempo pace, then with longer long runs. We clearly want to go into that phase feeling as close to 100% as possible. So our days are filled with a lot of extra stretching, heating, icing, rolling, and ibuprofen. And I think all of that, together with common sense, has helped a lot. Erika has cut back on her runs a bit and I've skipped core workouts for the past week.

In addition to feeling better about our recoveries, my confidence stems from two primary sources that will carry us to the start line and through the finish line in Burlington:

– my confidence in myself

– my confidence in Erika as a training and racing partner

Training for a marathon brings you through an odyssey of expectations, concerns, worries, anxieties, dreams, and visualizations – in addition to a lot of miles! Training for a marathon together means you share a lot of that odyssey together. It is awesome but, make no mistake, it's not easy. It's physically demanding and it's emotionally demanding, and that's BEFORE you get to the start line!

But the fact that it's so demanding is what makes it so meaningful. Whenever I feel a little drained about my training, a little worried about injuries, a little daunted by the miles that lay ahead, a little shaken in my confidence; I just take a few minutes to think about Burlington. All I have to do is envision the start corral prior to the start, the sea of runners moving forward at the gun, finishing the race, or really any part of the race and I am ready to go.

With each shared long run together, my belief and confidence in our abilities grow. I can imagine what it's like to go through a season of practices on a team, developing that shared experience and working towards a shared goal together. As I look ahead to Burlington, I'm not just looking forward to RACE DAY. I'm looking forward to the journey, to each of the long runs between now and then, to all of the training milestones along the way, as we progress towards that day. I am filled with confidence about how we will run together in Burlington and I know that's going to grow with each passing week. It will not be easy and there will surely be ups and downs and setbacks along the way. Like anything else in life, there are no guarantees. With 18 weeks to go, a lot can happen.

Given that uncertainty, I've asked myself the question of how do I feel, how is my confidence at this early stage? It's a little difficult to answer. That's not because I don't know. Rather, it's because it's difficult to put into words how deep and fundamental my confidence is – in both of us. Our training between now and then will test us – repeatedly. And then, of course, RACE DAY will hold its own challenges. And, no I can't know for a fact what will happen. Joe Namath, I am not. But I do know that I could not possibly have greater confidence in myself or in my training partner. As always, I'm looking forward to our next long run on Sunday, and to the next step towards Burlington. Lots of challenges lie ahead, but at the end of the day, I keep on coming back to one thought. Man, this is fun.

This may have been my worst run of 2015. It was a tough run physically, I struggled over very tough terrain and in brutal conditions, and I did not run well. But more than that I really struggled emotionally. I was flat and down as this run went on and it got worse as I went. I just couldn't regroup from it. But, as happened throughout our training, I rebounded from a poor run to do much better in my next workout.

Rebounding, January 28, 2015

On Sunday, I had one of my worst runs ever. It was a tough 10 mile run, on snowy/slushy trails in the Blue Hills Reservation. My feet were a little cold and wet and sore from the uneven ground. The pace was kind of irrelevant under the conditions, it was more about getting the miles and the work done. This run was my weekly long run with Erika, which I usually look forward to all week.

This wasn't about the physical struggles on this run though. I was just psychologically and emotionally flat, tired, and unenthusiastic, with a low energy level. There is no blame here, no guilt, no beating myself up over it. And certainly no one else's fault. It just happens sometimes. And, while I could speculate, there really wasn't any particular reason for feeling this way. If I were on my own, I would just buckle down and focus on getting through the run. And, actually that's kind of what I did. But I was running with Erika, and that's just **not** how we run together. We talk together and we work together, and I just didn't do that well this time. She felt a little bad and I felt a little bad. But, in the end, I think I just have to chock it up as a poor run on my part.

What matters now is how I respond to it. I could dwell on it and churn through negative thoughts. Or, I could keep my thoughts constructive and positive and work towards a better run next time. And, at the same time, be better prepared should I feel similarly on another run this year. Of course, the positive, constructive course is really the only option. So here's what I've got:

I'm already feeling better. I had a good treadmill run today – the rebound run that I always get after a poor run. I also had my first core workout in nearly three weeks. I've been nursing a sore side and back that my trainer has told me is a strained hip flexor. I've been doing stretches for that and have assigned exercises that I'll be working on too. He told me to pick up core again, which I did yesterday – with good results so far.

And I've been looking forward to my next run with Erika this coming Sunday. Running over the coming weeks will require adjustments because of all the snow we've had, but I'm confident that we'll work through it together and have a great run on Sunday. One of the good pieces of advice that I've heard about life is that, when you are feeling down, one of the best things you can do is focus on helping and supporting someone else. It's amazing how often that can jolt you out of a rut. So, the next time I feel down like this on a run with Erika, I'm resolved to shift my thinking away from how I'm feeling to how Erika is doing and focus on supporting her. But, I don't expect that to happen often. Running, even in tough conditions, is just such a privilege, it's just tough to stay down about it, or during it. Plus, throw in a great, supportive running partner, and there's even more to feel good about.

As always, I'm looking forward to Sunday.

This not that exciting of a blog, but it's a good overview of our training plan and where we stood at the end of January.

Phase 1 Complete, January 31, 2015

When you run a marathon, one of the many pieces of advice you read is to divide the race into stages, as it's too much to focus on the whole 26.2 miles at once. That certainly also holds true, on a much larger scale, about marathon training. When you're training for a marathon, you always try to keep your eye on the prize. But, it's so far away, and it takes so long to get through, that I think milestones along the way are really important – both to have an interim short-term focus, and to recognize your progress as you go. I'm a check off the box kind of guy, and it's tough if you can't check off a box for 6 months!

In our marathon training, I'm thinking of this in four phases:

Phase 1 – Base Mileage – DONE

This began in late November and carried through December and January. During this period, we were typically running 20-25 miles a week, with a long run of between 6 and 10 miles. The goal here was to stay in shape and very slowly build the base for the next phases of our training. In my mind, this phase is now over. We each had some physical ups and downs during this stretch but I'd say, all in all, we emerged successful.

Phase 2- New Bedford Half Marathon – 6 weeks

Over the next six weeks, we will be building our long run and weekly mileage a little bit and adding in some faster tempo stages to our long runs. We'll get up to 14 mile long runs here and over 30 miles a week. The logical milestone here is the New Bedford Half Marathon in mid-March. That will be a chance to liven up our training with a race and push ourselves a bit together in a race environment. Other than a 5K we ran together back in December, this will be the first race that Erika and I have run together – and the first long one. Looking ahead to running Burlington together, I think this will be a really critical experience to race a long run together and develop that chemistry looking ahead towards Burlington.

Phase 3- The Long Runs – 7 weeks

Between mid-March and early May we will ramp up our miles – A LOT. This is the real heart of the marathon training, when we up our weekly mileage and raise our long run from about 14 miles to 22 miles. Hopefully, the weather and snow on the ground will be better by then and make these long runs a little easier. Depending on how you look at it, this is the really tough part – or the really fun part! This is when you start to stretch your limits and really approach marathon distance and pace. This is tough and I am so thankful to have Erika to keep me company through this stage this time.

Phase 4 – The Taper – 3 weeks

In some ways, this is the toughest part. This is the last three weeks prior to the race when we reduce our mileage and intensity. Between that and the potential pre-race nerves, this can be a very difficult time psychologically. We'll still be running a decent number of miles, but the reduction really feels pronounced – which is the idea. The idea is to get to the start line fresh and strong. We'll be needing that strength.

Ah, February. This was by far the most brutal month of running I have ever endured, by something like a factor of 50! This was probably the worst winter we've ever had and February was at the crosshairs of it. Erika and I had really, really tough runs together this month. And, while it was awful at the time, looking back on it, I feel a lot of pride in the character that both Erika and I showed through this stretch. It was not for the faint of heart, and thankfully we are not!

Embracing February, February 1, 2015

So, to start with, February is my least favorite month. It's in the heart of my least favorite season, and relatively late in the winter. Generally with February, I just want to outlast it and have it end. Perhaps the best thing that can be said about February is that it is only 28 days – most of the time anyway. And that was before I started distance running training through the winter. Running in snow and ice is unpleasant and just harder, both physically and mentally. And, after a mild start, this winter is now turning out to be a particularly tough one. But it will not beat me.

So there are two ways you can go with this. You can try to tolerate it and outlast it, and just hang in. But I've learned the hard way once this year that you've got to get up for these runs. You need to bring a little extra motivation, energy, and focus. You can't just wait for these runs to end – you've got to put your heart and soul into them. If you don't, you're in a for a long, long run. Trust me, I've been there, I know. Fortunately, I'm only running outside once a week these days. So it's not like I have to get charged up for this every day. Only for the weekly long run. Everything else can be on a treadmill until the snow subsides and after we get to daylight savings time in early March.

So that brings me to the second approach, which is to embrace February long runs. To me, embracing running in February is akin to embracing a cactus. Of course, they're different. Cacti are prickly and sharp and you get a lot of cuts and scars from embracing them. February running is bitter cold and wet. with uncertain footing and potential for injury that way. I know a lot more about running in February than embracing cacti, but I would call them roughly equally unpleasant. It requires a certain amount of mental fortitude to embrace something unpleasant like this. So here goes.

Each February mile is an opportunity and a gift. A chance to run that I will never get back again. Never. EVER. It's up to me to make the most of each of these gifts. Yes it will be unpleasant and it will hurt at times. Perhaps most of the time. The gift is the opportunity to overcome that adversity and emerge a stronger and better runner. And, I would also argue, a stronger and better person. It's a chance to realize and build the potential character and strength that lies within. To work, these words cannot be lip service. They need to be internalized and forged into an immutable core belief. It will be tested over and over and it must be rock solid to hold up. In a certain sense, the greater the adversity, the greater the opportunity.

So do I want to run in snow and ice? Well, all things being equal, no way! But it is here and it's not going anywhere. So it's up to me how I respond to it. And there's just one way to go. I will be fortifying myself mentally and emotionally for each winter long run that lies ahead. I will dive into this headlong (hopefully just figuratively) and take the opportunities for all they are worth. At the end of each run, I will commit to look myself in the mirror and know that I stared down February in all of its brutal glory and welcomed it. That I looked it square in the eye and embraced it physically, mentally and emotionally. And when I do that, I know I'll be better for it.

Seven more days until the next opportunity. Bring it.

This blog entry gives a good glimpse into how intense my training was in February. I was working so hard that I couldn't even look ahead to Race Day. I was just so immersed in the challenge of getting through each run and workout, on a day to day basis. I had to work so hard, which is why Burlington meant as much as it did.

Immersed in Every Moment, February 6, 2015

In my marathon training to date, I am constantly looking ahead to RACE DAY, thinking about the race itself often, and at length. This year is proving to be a little different. I still think about Burlington at some point almost every day, maybe even every day. But I'm finding that more and more often, my running thoughts are drawn to the moment at hand. I think this is driven by how demanding the training is this time around, combined with the effect of training together with Erika and following each other's runs, injuries, and successes – when we're not running together.

Now, rather than thinking of Burlington, I tend to be thinking no farther ahead than the next long run. The snow and ice has really been a big factor in this because it makes everything harder and more complicated. We can't just go out and run. We have to think about where and how we can run safely and reasonably well. That, combined with constantly tracking weather conditions, has weighed on me. The other thing that's been different this time around is that I've added regular core workouts to my training, so that I'm doing something every day. I will tweak that eventually to give myself one mental health day a week when I'm doing no training at all – maybe sooner rather than later at this point. That won't mean that I'll do less, just that I would combine a core workout and a light run on the same day. Eventually, when the miles pick up more, I'm planning to drop a core day.

It might be good advice to say, "Don't worry about it, just roll with it. It'll all work out." But that's not me. I'm a planner and I like to know what I'm doing, where I'm heading, when, etc. Of course, life doesn't always allow for that and sometimes one just has to adjust. And that's OK, I can adapt to that. But, one of the effects of all this has been to make my attention increasingly focused on the short term. I just updated my training schedule for Burlington but I just couldn't focus on it. Trying to think about a run in March right now, let alone May, seems almost surreal. I am finding now that it's difficult for me to look beyond Sunday each week, there's just so much packed into a week.

On my runs, as I've always tried to do, I keep my focus on the current mile. But now, my focus on long runs is sometimes even shorter than that. On these outdoor runs, I am finding that focusing on an entire mile is looking much too far ahead. What I really need to do is focus on my next steps, as I navigate the snow, slush and ice that I'm running around and through. Bottom line – training for a spring marathon in New England is hard.

This does not come as a surprise to me. I knew what I was getting into and knew it would be hard. But, like anything else in life, experiencing it firsthand is always more intense and, well, more real. So the focus now is the Sunday long run of 12 miles. After that, I can start thinking about the next week.

But the funny thing is that time keeps on marching on. Sometimes it seems far too slow. But then, before you know it, a week has gone by, then two. Then, before you know it, it's March, And then, some day, some month, the snow has melted. Maybe. And then, before you know it, you're at the start line in late May. Time is amazing that way. In the interim, I continue to immerse myself in each moment of my training, knowing what I've known all the way along. Marathon training takes heart, commitment, and focus. As I always have, I immerse myself in the training, in the work, believing in that leap of faith that all marathon runners take, believing in your training deep down. And knowing that when you bring that focus and effort, the results will follow.

The journey is not easy now. But it was never supposed to be.

This was a triumphant run for me and Erika, running a solid long run with tempo stretches in the snow in Bare Cove Park. These conditions were hard, they were uncomfortable and we worked very hard to hit these target splits. Every long run in February was tough for us, but time and time again we triumphed and beat the conditions. Always side by side. (Except when the cleared path was too narrow for that.)

Best Long Run of 2015?

Well, to be fair, it's not a long list nor a prestigious title at this point. But, I'd say that, so far, today's long run was our best so far in 2015. There are a few reasons for bestowing this minor, but still meaningful honor on today's run.

First of all, it's a study in contrasts. Two weeks ago I had a poor run and last week Erika struggled on our long run. So to have a run when we both felt good despite tough conditions feels really good right now and comes as a relief. Today we ran on packed snow in Bare Cove Park in our trusty Yak Trax. That was OK, but it still takes extra effort with each step. It doesn't seem like much but it adds up. Add in dodging and slowing down for a bunch of walkers and dogs and the conditions were challenging. It was also still cold today – not bitter cold – but in the mid 20s, cold enough to feel chilly and make breathing a little harder.

Today's run was 12 miles, our longest yet in this training schedule. It included 5 x five minute tempo intervals – which we nailed. (Erika, I'm pretty sure the first four were sub 7:30 pace. The last one was a little slower, but it was up that hill.) In spite of the challenges, and it was definitely not easy, we finished at an 8:09 pace overall, right about where we wanted to be.

So, it's early February and we've still got 15 weeks to go to Burlington, so it's no time to get carried away. But I can't help but feel good after today's run. We worked really hard and ran really well together. And, bottom line, we did exactly what we set out to do. Even better, we both felt decent at the end, despite running on snow and running around about 517 dogs. Right now, that is about all you can ask for from a 12 mile long run. As I've written recently, training for a spring marathon in New England is just – HARD. So when you accomplish a run like this, you've got to just sit back and smile and take another sip of your beer. Then repeat. This is good stuff, a run to build on, and a run to feel proud of.

Among a lot of really tough, grueling runs in snow and ice, I think this one was the toughest of all. This run crushed us in so many ways, but we pushed through it with the heart of marathoners. As Erika and I continued to train together through the spring, and even the summer, we kept on thinking back to runs like this one. If we could persevere through a run like this, we felt we could do just about anything. Runs like this also helped us bond together as a running team.

My Slowest Run - EVER, February 15, 2015

Well, at least since I've started recording times. This was my slowest run ever, slower even than my first 10 mile run, when I stopped and walked a few times. Yesterday, Erika and I ran 10 miles in 1:35:50. With apologies to those who run at a slower pace, these things are all relative. And, for us, this is slow. Historically slow.

Yet, when I look back on it, I am more proud of this run than just about any other run I've ever done. To understand why, to really truly understand, you had to be there. But I'll try to explain. For starters, I was fighting a cold and cough. And Erika was running for the fifth day in a row, But that is only a small part of the story. The story is the conditions that we ran in. We ran in Bare Cove Park for the second straight week. But, it was not cleared nearly as well as it was last week. We ended up being limited to a 1.2 mile loop, as that was the only area that was at all reasonable to run in. But, even then, it was tough. At best, we were running on packed snow. But, it was so narrow that we had to run single file. And, at times, we would run through pockets of deeper snow, slowing us down and making the footing even more slippery. The of course, we were dodging people and dogs on a path that was wide enough for about 1.5 people. And it was cold. Not single digits or anything. But mid 20s and dropping. And, after we were out there for a bit, the snow starting falling, blowing into our faces for much of the time. My water bottle began to freeze up late in the run, and I didn't even try to take my GU, knowing it would be a popsicle.

We talked about all of the ways the run could have been worse, and it's true. It could have been 35 degrees and raining, the snow could have been deeper, it might not have been plowed at all, the wind could have been worse. All true. But the story is this: We met the conditions head on, didn't flinch for a second, and just ran through them. Don't let the pace fool you, we were running with good, steady effort. This was just the best we had on this day and in these conditions.

The story of this run is so simple, yet so deep. We took on these conditions head on, ran our best through them, and came away with a feeling of great pride. This is the kind of run that we will look back on fondly in a few months – 14 weeks to be precise – when we run Burlington. It's runs like this that make you strong for a marathon. Not so much physically, but more psychologically. When you push through a run like this for 95 minutes, a marathon doesn't seem so tough after all.

Although Erika and I ran this run separately, I feel like this was one of our most important bonding runs together. Even though we each ran this on our own, it was a shared run in our training plan. And the fact that we both decided to do this one on the treadmill was important. This really emphasized that we were in this together and that we were fully bought in. So while we weren't side by side for this one, it was just as much a shared run as any of those that we did run side by side.

14 Miles on a Treadmill – Are You Nuts!?

A few years ago, I never would have even considered running 14 miles on a treadmill. The idea would have struck me as ludicrous. And, even yesterday morning, the idea struck me as a bit on the edge. But, when you establish a training plan as a distance runner, and you stick to it, you end up doing a lot of amazing things. And even though it's all laid out on paper for you, you end up surprising even yourself with what you can and do accomplish. That was the case yesterday.

Erika started it. Due to a combination of schedule commitments, the only way she could get in her long run this week was by doing it on Wednesday. And, the only really viable way to get it in, given the snow all around us, was on a treadmill. So she decided to do her 14 mile run on a treadmill yesterday. And, all in all, it turned out pretty well for her. When I heard that she was planning to run 14 on the treadmill, as I told her, I actually got a little envious. And due to a combination of moral support for her and just wanting to do such a crazy thing myself, I was tempted. But I told myself that was silly and set the idea aside.

But, as I thought about it more, in the twisted world of a marathon runner, it actually started to make sense. The alternative long run option for me this week was to run 14 miles back and forth on the Wompatuck Road, by myself, on Saturday. And that didn't sound that great. And you KNOW I am doing my 14 mile long run. So as I kept thinking about it, I convinced myself, and I think correctly, that it was the right choice. Once I decided I was going to do it, I knew I would succeed. Just knew it. But I was still a bit apprehensive. 14 miles on the treadmill is a long, long time. My previous long had been 8 miles. And that felt like an eternity. I don't use headphones, so it's pretty much just me and my thoughts – and the treadmill – for almost two hours.

This wasn't so much about the physical challenge, although this was my longest run since Chicago. It was most about the mental challenge. About hanging in and focusing on the run for nearly 2 hours – just running in place. It is mentally TOUGH. But that's part of the reason why this held so much appeal for me. When you're training for a marathon, there's of course a demanding physical component to it. But, at least as important is the mental strength to keep on going and going hard when you just don't feel it. You have to learn to set aside fatigue and negative thoughts and jettison them. Then, you just keep on going – always positive, always focusing on each moment, knowing that will bring you to your goal. Having faith in your training and in your own mental, emotional and physical strength. I've been down this road twice now and I know the work now will pay huge dividends.

The other new dynamic this time is going through this with a running partner. But not just any training partner. As I've written before, Erika and I are really well matched pace-wise so, even when one or the other of us is struggling, we can still run together. But we've also proved to be well matched for temperament. And, thank goodness, because this training has been brutal! Knowing that I have a training partner who is willing to go out on a limb and run 14 miles on a treadmill, for what also happened to be her longest run in 5 years, is POWERFUL. When you run with a training partner, you tend to feed off of each other when things are good and pick each other up when things are tough.

Erika asked me the other day, on one of our brutal runs, if I regretted signing up for Burlington. At the time, with snow freezing on my glasses, freezing cold hands, a frozen water bottle, and tired sore legs, I gave a somewhat unconvincing "no". But, throughout this training, deep down, I have not regretted my decision for an instant. It has been just as hard as I thought it would be, but even more rewarding. And, at times like this, when we both achieve concurrent victories, it is a simply awesome feeling. I'm flying high and looking ahead to Burlington with a feeling of great momentum, almost euphoria.

Why so excited? Well I knew this was a huge challenge and I knew I could do it. But knowing you can do something and actually going out and doing it are two very different things. And, when you succeed, along with your partner, passing with flying colors, you cannot help but feel STRONG – physically and mentally. It's that strength that will carry us through the finish line in Burlington – strong, confident, and positive throughout the training and the race. And, to think I get to do a long run every week. And most of the time together with Erika. Running like this is a privilege and a joy. And I can't wait until the next long run!

This time I was on my own outside and I felt it. I really missed Erika as a running partner for this run. And, to add to that, I had the start of what I eventually decided was plantar fasciitis. I was able to treat that successfully. But the combination of being on my own in the cold along with the injury was rough. I was able to push through this run and even hit my target splits pretty well.

A Tough Solo Run, February 22, 2015

First of all, let me just say, thank goodness I wasn't going 14 miles yesterday! I was running 7 miles, with the middle 5 at a tempo pace – shooting for around a 7:30 pace on those. This run was notable because it was a weekend run my own in winter conditions – something that I don't think I've ever (?) done before. Or, if so, very rarely. My running partner Erika was away for a few days and I missed her badly on this run.

I was running on the road in Wompatuck State Park, which is about 2.25 miles long. The conditions were actually pretty decent, all things considered. The temperature was in the upper 20s and the road was pretty well plowed. it was even sunny! And, best of all, the gate was closed, so there were NO cars! Although there were patches of snow and ice mixed with bare pavement, I decided to run sans Yak Trax and that worked out OK traction wise. I think this one is worth a mile by mile, blow by blow account – so here goes.

Mile 1 – 7:59 This was supposed to be an easy pace mile, but of course my adrenaline took me out really quickly. I settled down a bit and ended up at 7:59 for the first mile. I knew this run was going to be tough on my own so from the very first step I was pumping myself up for this run. I was actually under a 7:00 pace at first. Easy slugger....In this first mile, my right heel started to hurt a bit, something that would be with me off and on throughout this run, It didn't hurt much, but it bugged me that I felt it at all. Late in mile 1, there is a pair of climbs that take the wind out of your sails a bit.

Mile 2 – 7:30 This was when my tempo pace kicked in – while I was climbing a hill! Yup, a challenging run. But, again I was pushing myself on my run. Although my pace was up and down like a yo-yo, I hit this mile in 7:30, right on target. There were a few people out walking dogs and I think four other runners, running back and forth on the road like me.

Mile 3 – 7:47 I turned around early in this mile to head back. The terrain is rolling throughout the park, not a lot of flat ground here. For most of the run, you're either going uphill or downhill, so it was tough to stay on pace. I was warm, with probably one layer too many on. Last week, I had forgotten the running mittens that Erika gave me to wear over my running gloves, but I had them today, though I'm not sure I needed them. But, you know I was actually happy to be a little hot and sweaty.

Mile 4 – 7:37 My heel pain is a little more pronounced and consistent, so I'm focusing on quick, light strides, especially going downhill. My pace continues to be all over the map but, on balance, it is pretty good given the footing and the terrain. I'm pushing myself hard at this point, in my third tempo mile, and I'm feeling it. A treadmill may be boring, but you don't even have to think about pace. You just press a button and you hit the pace, automatically. I've been spoiled and am working really hard today to set my pace on my own,

Mile 5 – 7:44 Arrived back at the start just under 4.5 miles and I'm really feeling my heel now. So I stopped at the gate to do a few stretches. At this point, I was considering cutting my run short. But I did a good job stretching and tried out a loop around the entrance. Feeling better, I struck back out, reminding myself that I have only 2.5 miles left – 1.25 miles out and back. I'm no longer focusing on tempo, just focusing on running light and quick to minimize any pain. And, though I can still feel my heel a bit, it's really not painful and I'm hanging in, bolstered by the adrenaline of closing out a run.

Mile 6 – 8:01 This was supposed to be my last tempo mile, but is a bit slower. But, I'm running how I want to and am feeling decent about it. Just for my own satisfaction, I pushed my pace late in this mile and wrapped up mile 6 at just under a 7:30 pace, my target pace for this mile. So there!

Mile 7 – 8:03 This was supposed to be an easy mile, like 8:20 or 8:30 pace, but my competitive juices are flowing and I'm running an 8:00 pace. I'm a little ticked off about my heel and that I've missed some of my tempo paces. It's not that I'm feeling bad about the run, I know I've been working hard and that's all I can ask of myself. But this is the thing about me that makes me the runner I am. I do not want to back off on this mile, despite the hills, the packed snow and ice, my sore heel, and that I'm missing my running partner. Or maybe more that I don't want to back off BECAUSE of all those things.

So I finished strong, knowing now that I can look back on this run with pride. Knowing that I took on the challenges and adversity head on and did not back down. I knew going into this run that it would be hard. The run didn't disappoint. And neither did I.

116

I love this blog entry because I think it sums up the February experience so well. It was so tough and so punishing. But we persisted through it so strong, exactly the way I had wanted to when the month started. This was an inspiring month for each of us, but it was especially inspiring for Erika and me to work through this challenging month together. When it was all over, I knew I had a running partner I could count on!

A Month to Celebrate, February 27, 2015

I think it's safe to say that February was a pretty rough month for everyone in the Boston area. Most of us would say brutal. All of those big storms one after the other after the other after the other, and so on, made for a crazy amount of shoveling, roof raking, and ice chipping, along with all of the other hassles caused by all that snow, major commuting delays and so on.

Along with everything else, it was a tough month for marathon runners! We were pretty much running inside, or in brutal conditions on the few runs that we did outside. That, combined with all of the heavy lifting (literally) took a major toll on my body. I have never had such a parade of nagging injuries – one after the other – just like the snowstorms!

So, given what I've written so far, you may be wondering about the title. Am I just being ironic? No, actually I really mean it. Let me explain. No, there is too much, let me sum up. At the beginning of the month, I wrote a blog post titled "Embracing February." in that post, I looked ahead to how challenging a month this would be (though I didn't know it would be this challenging) and wrote about the need to embrace those challenges. In other earlier blog posts, I've written about how marathon training is a 100%, all in, endeavor. Of course, I have a family, a job, a house, and a dog, so I don't mean the 100% literally. But what I mean is that when you set out to train for a marathon, you need to be prepared to see it through and commit to your training plan all the way until race day. EVERY. SINGLE. RUN. EVERY. SINGLE. WORKOUT. So that was my mission.

In February, I ran 16 times for a total of 102 miles. In some cases, I did the runs on an elliptical machine instead of treadmill. And, I did a bunch of core workouts, though I gradually let shoveling, etc. replace those, as my core muscles got more and more extra work and became more and more sore. As I went and the nagging injuries piled up, my treatment time (heating, stretching, and icing) literally took longer than my workout time. Through it all, I brought it for every single run. I didn't just go through the motions. I poured my heart and soul into these runs. EVERY. SINGLE. RUN. This was my toughest month of running ever. Tougher than 150 mile months. Tougher than months when I ran a marathon. It's not even close in my mind. As a runner you spend a lot of time thinking about times, paces, and mile splits. And, from a stats perspective, these runs weren't that special. But, from an effort perspective, they were awesome.

So, when I look back on February, yeah it was a brutal month. But, what I will remember about my running in February goes a step beyond that. When I look back on this month, my heart swells with pride over the effort I put in and what I accomplished. Although running is a physical endeavor, emotional and psychological strength lies at the heart of it, especially for a distance runner. And I've come away feeling absolutely SPENT. Really spent and exhausted. But, at the same time, I have NEVER felt stronger. I am quite aware of my physical mortality and accepting of that, knowing that I may need to tweak my training to address these injuries that pop up. And I have already done that a bit along the way. And I'll do it more as I need to.

But when it comes down to a matter of will, of the heart and soul behind that will, my resolve has grown stronger and stronger. And, in a marathon, sooner or later, it does come down to that mental and psychological strength. To pure will. And I know now, more than ever before, that when I get to that stage, I will be strong. And I will not be beat by 26.2 miles. And that is really something to celebrate.

But there's even more. It's the month that just keeps on giving. Though Erika and I have only been running our long run together once a week, we keep in touch about every run along the way. And, along with my confidence in myself, my confidence in Erika as a training partner has continued to grow as we've worked through this adversity together. Of course, this has been just as hard on her. And she has been a pillar of strength. Should I ever falter, and I have, I know that she will be there. And I know that I will be there for her when she struggles.

118

So, yeah, it's been a rough month. I feel a bit like a phoenix rising from the ashes (though that's a completely opposite scenario for February.) But, you get my drift. Our next long run together will be in March. It will still be cold and the world around us will still be buried in heaps of snow. And I still have these nagging injuries to treat. But, I'm turning a corner mentally and emotionally. Just about 12 weeks to Burlington. Daylight savings time is on the way. Spring is on the way. And I have made it through the toughest running month of my life feeling stronger than ever. And, after missing my running partner for a week, we get to do a long run together on Sunday.

Like I said, a month to celebrate!

Just seeing the calendar turn to March provided a morale boost, as February had been so rough. There was still snow and ice all over, so we continued to run in Bare Cove Park. This blog entry also provides good insight into how important it was to have Erika as a training partner through these rough conditions.

Good Soreness, March 2, 2015

Wow, it's been a while. When you're a runner, there's not much of a better feeling than "good soreness." I mean the kind of muscle soreness after a hard run, the fatigue that comes from hard work. No joint soreness or stiffness, no real pain, just the soreness from muscles working hard. After today's run, that's exactly how I feel, and it feels great. No foot soreness, just minor back and hip soreness, mostly just the normal fatigue from a hard run.

Today's run was an 8 mile run with tempo intervals through Bare Cove Park. I'm not sure what it is about that place, but Erika and I are like snow magnets when we run there – it seems like it snows every time we go there. But, although the trails were snowy and icy, it was still much better than our last run there. Both better footing and a wider path. I had been looking forward to this run all day. It was kind of like Christmas morning, expect you have to wait until 3:30 in the afternoon to open your presents.

With that said, it was tough. I had the toughest time I've had breathing in a long time. Looking back, I think that was because I didn't bring water with me on the run, because it was "only" an 8 mile run. But, after some very slow easy pace miles, we hit our tempo parts of the run pretty well, especially given our typical Bare Cove obstacles of snowy, icy trails and people with their dogs. But, as with every run through this training, I stuck with it and worked through all of the tempo intervals well. I relied on Erika more for this run than perhaps any other run so far this year. And, after last week's tough solo run, it was great to be back with my running partner.

This was our last "short long run" until we taper for Burlington. I believe everything from here on in is 14 miles and up! And now we're only two weeks from our mid-point race, the New Bedford Half Marathon. Wow, how did that happen!? I really don't feel like I'm in racing shape quite yet, but this race feels as much like a means to an end, rather than an end in itself. It will be a good check on our fitness and an opportunity to push our pace under race conditions and see how we respond. Needless to say I'm looking forward to the challenge.

So it's March! Hallelujah! Next week's long run is 14 miles – just straight up even pace 14 miles. And now, all of that foundation that we've built through December, January, and February is beginning to take shape and look like something meaningful. These are rewarding times, times when you can take a step back every now and then and think, wow, I'm really getting somewhere.

Looking back later, I had forgotten how tough this training was on me. It really pounded me into the ground at times, both physically and mentally. With hindsight, I can see even more clearly how tough this winter was, how hard I worked, and how relentless I was in my training. But, as much as I struggled, as much as I hurt and questioned my abilities and strength, I never backed down. Even in the hardest stretches, I kept on pushing through. And that was the real story.

Confidence, March 5, 2015

Confidence is a funny thing. When you have it, it feels boundless and endless. You can't imagine not feeling confident. And confidence begets more confidence as you build off of it. But sometimes you lose it. There could be a good reason – like you perform poorly or make a bunch of mistakes. Or, sometimes it can fade away and you don't quite know why or how it happened. As you might have guessed, this is not a hypothetical situation. I've felt very confident in my running and training for quite a while now. As I've felt this way, I could of course find reasons to question my ability and my training, or cast seeds of doubt. But, when I'm feeling confident, all I see is the up side and reasons to feel good. The doubts are just cast off like drops of sweat. I've been on quite a run emotionally, for a long time, and I feel that has really helped my running – and the rest of my life too!

But recently, for a long list of reasons, my energy has flagged, I've felt a bit overwhelmed by life and by my running. I've felt tired, stressed, and, as a result, have not slept as well as I would like. I know, c'est la vie, right? But, the point to note here is not so much the challenges I'm facing (I'm going to skip right over those)but how I'm reacting to them. And, recently, they've been getting the better of me a bit. And, as these challenges have eroded my spirits a little bit, my confidence in turn has faded. And just like confidence begets confidence, turning around a lack of confidence can feel really tough. Rather than casting off those seeds of doubt like drops of sweat, they have clung to me like a soggy t-shirt. And, rather than focusing on the positive side of everything, I have slipped into negative thoughts, worries, and fears. Worrying about my injuries, wondering about whether my training plan is good enough, worrying that there's no way I'll be ready to run a half marathon in a week and a half. And so on. The substance of these worries is not the point – this is all about mental outlook and perspective.

So, just think positive right? Well, yeah, but when your mindset flips, it can be harder than it seems. Take a baseball analogy: you could have a .280 hitter who's, say 10 for his last 20, is ripping the cover off the ball and feels great. He's a .280 hitter, but feels like he's a .400 hitter. Then, you could have another .280 hitter who's 0 for his last 20, and feels like he's never going to get a hit again in his life. Both .280 hitters, but a totally different mindset. For the past few days, I've limited posting and writing about running to give myself a bit of a mental break. But sometimes writing can be therapeutic and help and that's what this blog is all about.

So I've thought about what I can do and the answer is pretty simple. Run. Backing away from my training at this point would not help and would only make my confidence dip further and my anxiety rise more. I've not missed a single run or workout during this stretch and I'm not planning to. What I need are solid runs. Runs that rebuild that strong mindset and confidence. Runs that make me feel good about myself. Tonight I did a 7 mile run on the elliptical and was aiming for just under 8:30 pace. But, as I went I felt good and without really pushing it, ended up doing the whole run at under an 8:00 pace. A nice step forward mentally. Coincidentally, or perhaps not, I took the same approach at work today. Rather than wallowing around about how far behind I am, I attacked my work today and got A TON done. Still behind at the end of the day, but it's about the progress and the mindset. And now that's a building block for tomorrow. Same with tonight's run. I'm not all the way back yet, but today was a good rebound day.

When I think back on 2015, in my mind, February was the toughest month. But, when I look back on my blogs, I realize that March may have been even tougher. I was running OK, but Erika was running much better and I was constantly down about my running. Perhaps more than I've ever been. You can see the emotional effort of trying to stay positive in my blogs, but I was hurting. And, while I tried again to look on the bright side of this race, it was really pretty brutal, and I was not feeling good about myself in this stretch. But I did not give in and I kept on working throughout, not missing a single run or workout.

10 Weeks to Go and All Systems Go, March 15, 2015

Today Erika and I ran the New Bedford Half Marathon. Although she ran much faster than I did today, for this race, I was focused more on how I ran than the result. And, while it was not the race I hoped for time wise, I was happy with the process and the way I ran the race. In particular, there were two points when I really slowed down – at the beginning for miles 3 and 4, and then later, in mile 11. But, in both cases, I was able to rebound and pick up my pace after those down miles. And, even more importantly,

I finished the race feeling healthy and in decent shape. That included a good strong finish.

So we're now at the 10 week marker and I'm feeling pretty good about my status looking ahead to Burlington. Knock on wood, I seem to be pretty much healthy and, although not running as fast as I would like, am feeling pretty good about how strong I'm running. Over the past few weeks, I have felt about as low about my running as I ever have. Nothing really bad, just drained and fatigued and trying to wrap up nagging injuries. So I really worked hard on my mindset this week looking ahead to New Bedford and I think it turned out well. I even resorted to leaving myself "psyche up" notes.

Now we're on to the real long runs, starting with 16 next week. But, with only 9 weeks in between now and Burlington, that means only nine long runs. And, given that the run the week before the race is only 10 miles, there are really only 8 true long runs remaining. They're going to go fast – at least I hope so!

I think this blog entry and this decision tells you all you need to know about how hard it was to train for Burlington. It was so hard that I had to switch to a four day work week to accommodate my training with the rest of my personal commitments. So I made a really important decision to make this all work together. And I believe that this was the perfect decision given where I was with all of my life commitments. This decision enabled me to meet my commitments effectively in all aspects of my life in March, April, and May.

Commitment, March 18, 2015

After quite a bit of thought, I made a big schedule decision this week. I did not take this lightly but, as soon as I made the decision, it felt right to me. To me, this is a watershed moment in my training. I've written before about marathon training being an "all-in" commitment for me – not something I choose to do halfway. Of course, like I've said before, I don't mean 100% literally. But, in the case of Burlington in particular, when I made the decision to train for and run Burlington together with my neighbor and running partner Erika, I knew it would be a top priority in my life from January – May. And I knew I would do what it takes to be successful in my training and to support Erika in her training.

But of course life's not that simple and I also have top priorities to spend quality time with my family, to take care of my other responsibilities at home, and to handle my work responsibilities. Sometimes the hours in the week and my energy for all of these priorities just don't add up. When that happens here and there, that's no big deal, you can work through that. But, when it happens day after day, week after week, something has gotta give. Looking back now, the decision seems simple to me, but it took me a while to arrive at it.

Eventually, I came up with the idea to take off from work every Friday between now and RACE DAY. As first, this sounded a little crazy to me but, as I turned it over in my mind, it began to make sense. I have more than enough vacation days to do this and we are not expecting to take a long vacation this summer, so the time was there. And, by doing this just one day/week in this sort of gradual way, I felt I could manage through my work this way. Friday is typically not a meeting day and I could squeeze in a little extra work on Mon-Thu. This wouldn't be without any impact, but as I thought through it, I thought of several ways I could better manage the work side of this. And, as long as I could manage that reasonably well from the work side, the personal side of the decision was a no-brainer. I'm also fortunate to work in a workplace that really respects personal and family commitments and, within reason, is very supportive of us as individuals.

So, I'm doing it. Taking the next 10 Fridays off from work. Basically in lieu of a long summer vacation. But I know deep down in my soul that I need this time NOW. So, here's the plan, and here's why it will make such a huge difference. As it stands now, I have some type of training scheduled 7 days/week, either a run, cross training, or a core workout. And, mentally, that's tough, really draining. It also allows very few quality blocks of time to do things together as a family, or for Anne and I as a couple. And that in turn, leaves me feeling further worn out and frayed at work. And so on…

Now, I will be able to switch my Saturday run to Friday (along with core), making Saturday a totally "training-free" day. An actual "rest day" and real weekend day! I will also have extra time to catch up on rest or work around home on Fridays, again making Saturday a true free day. That, in turn, will leave me much better prepared and rested for Sunday which is our LONG RUN DAY. Having the day before off will make me a little fresher for those long runs and ensure that I'm really ready for them. And, trust me, they are going to be tough and demanding! They will take all I've got and that's exactly what I plan to put into them! And then, after the Sunday long run is over, I can focus on rest and recovery.

When I get to the starting line in Burlington on May 24 and look back on my training, I will know that I truly laid myself on the line to train and prepare for this race. That I've given it all that I have. And, in the end, probably just a little bit more. But that's always been the appeal with running a marathon. Not just running 26.2 miles – but RACING 26.2 miles. And when I get through that finish line, that's the one thing that I HAVE TO KNOW; that I've done it all, that I have no regrets about my training or the race that I run.

After a pretty grueling winter, my spirits and energy are lifting and I am ready to dive into what I consider the third, and most significant phase of our marathon training. Just in time. (The first phase was building up base mileage of 20-25 miles/week and a long run of about 10 miles. Phase 2 was getting to the New Bedford Half Marathon this past Sunday and getting our long run up to 14 miles.) Now it gets real. This is the meat of the marathon training when the miles really build, as does the intensity. My training schedule is the most aggressive one I've ever had – by far. It's demanding, but with this schedule change, I am feeling ready for it. It's not just being accepting of it, but welcoming the challenge with open arms. Saying and believing that I want to run 18-22 miles at close to race pace. And then go out and run fast tempo miles two days later. And then run fast track intervals two days after that. Then go out and run the next day. And do core workouts and ride the bike in between. And repeat that over and over. You can't fake that. You can't muddle your way through it. You've got to live it. And, Erika, you know what I'll say when I'm done, right?

"I Lived."

I love this blog because this is when I attacked. I stopped feeling sorry for myself, stopped questioning my ability and just attacked. Since I ran the hills poorly in New Bedford, I went out and did a hard hills workout. And I did it well, with intensity and dedication. So I acknowledged the poor run, but did not bow to it.

Practicing Layups, March 20, 2015

When I ran the New Bedford 1/2 last week, I really struggled with the hills early in the race. I was able to pick things up on the easy part of the course after that, but the hills really did me in early. Normally, I do OK on hills and can run through them pretty well, so this bugged me.

When Kevin used to play JBL basketball, the kids on his team, being young, would inevitably go through stretches where they would miss a bunch of layups. I remember Kevin's coach turning around with a wry smile and saying, "Well I know what we'll be working on in practice this week." So, even during the race last week, I knew that I would be doing a focused hill workout this week. This was my version of practicing layups. When you struggle with something, it's like a spotlight showing you exactly what you need to work on.

My schedule this week got a bit mixed up. To start, I was making a regular switch, moving all of my Saturday runs (4 miles easy) to Fridays. But, I couldn't do my planned Thursday run last night, because I was going to an evening event at the high school. That was the hills workout I just did (though it had initially been planned to be a track interval workout and I chose to switch it to a hill workout.) I didn't want to move that one to Wednesday since I had just done a hard tempo run on Tuesday, so I moved that one to today (Friday) and then moved my easy 4 mile run from Friday to Wednesday. That way I could still have Saturday off. With me?

Anyway, I was doing hill repeats today. The plan was for 6 miles total – 1 mile easy to start, then 6 x 1/3 mile hill repeats, then 1 mile easy to end. For the hill repeats, I was aiming to do them at a 7:30 pace, so 2:30 per. Then, I would jog back down. With repeats like this, the goal is not to run every one as fast as you can, but rather to run them consistently. So that was the plan.

Here's how it went. I botched the timing on the first one, but estimated in the 2:25 – 2:30 range – I'm pretty confident about that estimate. The main goal here was not to do this first one too fast and I succeeded there. The approximate splits for the rest of the repeats were:

#2 – 2:32

#3 – 2:32

#4 – 2:28

#5 – 2:31

#6 – 2:31

So, in conclusion, I totally nailed this run! So there hills!

I believe this was the first long run after Erika had fallen on the ice while moving a washing machine and had it fall on her leg. Her leg was badly bruised and she was in a lot of pain. It's amazing to me that we started out with just 2 miles and ending up going 16! And that was with the pain building as we went. This was a very tough run emotionally but, as we went, my emotional pain kept being displaced – displaced by pride and admiration for Erika and what she was doing today. And hence the title of this blog.

Pride, March 22, 2015

Today's run with Erika would be called poor by just about any standard. It was a 16 mile run and it was slow. Very slow. Furthermore, Erika was recovering from injuries from slipping and falling on the ice and, at the same time, having a washing machine she was helping to carry fall on her leg. It was questionable whether she could run at all, let alone run 16 miles. She was in pain for the entire run, but especially in the last three miles after tweaking her lower back. So this was a struggle. From Erika's standpoint, it was a painful run and for me it was a run filled with concern and, at times, even fear.

When we started out, the deal was we would go 2 miles and evaluate how it was going. It was good enough, so Erika hung in mile after mile. And, ultimately finished the run, although there were times when that seemed doubtful. Midway through the run we settled in to a little bit better pace and the run was going decently. But late in the run it got tough. Really, really tough.

So thinking about the run afterwards, many words come to mind – slow, stressful, worrisome, and most of all, painful. But, most of all, the word and feeling that keeps on coming up for me is pride. Not pride in me so much as pride in Erika as a running partner, and us as a running team. I've always believed that character is best revealed in times of trouble and difficulty rather than when things are going great. And, man was I impressed today. I was worried that Erika would worsen her injuries by pushing as much as she did and as long as she did.

But in the end, in the bottom line, I was just so impressed. When you're a runner, you know you're going to run through pain sometimes If you don't want to do that, you might as well not bother. But there's pain and then there's PAIN. I already knew I have a great training partner. This does not come as news to me. After today, I'm still worried and concerned. But, most of all I'm PROUD of my training partner. Really proud. Now I'll be even more proud when she rests up and takes care of herself over the next few days!

The hard work of February and March was paying dividends now. As the intensity of my training increased, I was ready and nailed this tempo workout and interval workout. And I know it was thanks to all of the tough grueling runs in February and March that didn't look like March, but built my strength for these workouts.

Hitting My Paces!, March 26, 2015

This week I really started to ramp up the intensity of my mid-week runs. From now until when we taper for Burlington, each week I will be doing one hard tempo run, one hard interval run, one short easy run, and, my favorite, the long run. Plus a recovery bike ride on Monday and core three times/week. This week was the first week that I did the hard tempo and speed intervals together. And, through one week, it's been a huge success.

On Tuesday, I ran a tempo run along the Charles after work. My target paces were 2 x 8:20, 3 x 7:00, and 2×8:20, for 7 miles total. My goal was to hit these paces as closely as possible, including the easy ones (which I often run way too fast.) But now that the "hard" miles are so hard, it's important that the easy miles are really easy.

So I nailed the first two miles at 8:17 and 8:19. I felt great about that, but was a bit apprehensive about how I would do with the 3 at 7:00 pace. That's under 10K race pace for me, so it's pretty rigorous. But as I entered mile 3, I found that I accelerated really easily and got my pace under 7:00 almost right away. From then on, with help from my GPS watch, I found that I could easily hit a 7:00 pace and actually needed to moderate my pace to not go too fast. This is of course not literally true but, as I went, I felt like I could run virtually any pace I wanted for as long as I wanted. And the splits showed it. Miles 3, 4, and 5 were 6:55, 7:00, and 6:57.

At that point, I dropped my pace down to 8:20 and my main challenge was not to run the last two miles too fast. I hit mile 6 just right in 8:21. Mile 7 dropped to 8:30, although that was because my watch had showed some pace times that were a bit off, which made me think I had to slow down more than I actually needed to. Otherwise, I would have hit 8:20 easily.

On Wednesday, I ran my first track interval workout of the year. I had a tough workout planned – 12 x 400 m runs in 1:32 each, with recovery jogs in between. This one was daunting for me and I wasn't sure how well I would last through these. Plus I was running the day after my tempo run since it was forecast to rain Thursday night. My first 400 was at 1:25, and I said "whoa!". I settled down a little bit on the 2nd one, which I did in 1:29. After that, I really settled in, but was determined not to drop below 1:32. As a result, I ended up running every single lap under 1:32, and nine of the 12 were at either 1:30 or 1:31. This was really solid because my split times did not slide at all and because, after my initial fast start, I stayed so consistent through the whole workout. With my recovery laps, warm-up and cool-down, I ended up doing 7 miles total.

This was a great pair of runs, easily my two strongest runs all year. I was thrilled with how solid my splits were and how well I stayed on pace late in these runs. A great start to my first really intense training week!

This was a triumphant long run! It came on the heels of a brutal, pounding painful run for Erika the week before and it was so much better. And it was a great emotional relief for both of us. Perhaps the best way to evaluate this run, is that it would have been a solid, solid run even without rebounding from this injury. Under the circumstances though, it became a great run!

Relief! March 30, 2015

It's been a tough couple of weeks for Erika and me re: running. I should say, really it's been a tough couple of weeks for her. It's just been rough on me by extension. She's the one who's suffered through a lot of pain and worked really hard to recover from an injury. I've just watched, worried, hoped, and wished 'til my fingers (and toes) were twisted like pretzels! Yes, she's the one who's suffered. But, when you're a team, you take each other's setbacks and accomplishments to heart.

Last week, we went through a brutal run. She was courageous, but also overdid it, going 16 miles when her body was not ready to handle that. And she paid the price all week long. So this week was a recovery week, and a running-free week, for Erika. But she still worked really hard x-training in the pool and on the elliptical. Our planned run for today was 18 miles. But, after thinking it over and talking it through, we decided to start with a goal of just a 12 mile run, and HOPE that we could just do a DECENT 12 miles. That alone would have been a huge victory at that point. We figured then if everything was going great, we could head back out and run a bit longer, and maybe even up to 18. But I really didn't think that was gonna happen.

When we hit the first mile in 7:49, I knew this run would be a lot different than last week's. But I was still haunted about how Erika's body would hold up over a long run. Well our pace bounced around a little bit, but it never, ever dropped below 8:35, so we were running pretty steadily. We continued to plow along, with great conversation along the way, and it really felt like the miles were clicking by in the blink of an eye. This was a fun run. Just before we got to about 8.5 miles, and our planned turnoff for home off of 228, Erika said she was feeling good and wanted to go 18. Well, after last week, I was a bit hesitant and pushed a bit, but she was feeling legitimately strong, so we pushed ahead all the way down along 228 until 53, solid all the way. We stopped to stretch a couple of times, as well as removing a rock wedged in the sole of my shoe. But, otherwise, we were solid.

To make a long story short, we finished the 18 mile run in 2:28, at an 8:13 pace, exactly what we had planned in our training plan. But this run is about so much more than numbers. This run was huge for BOTH OF US from an emotional and psychological perspective. We're both feeling the effects of running 18 miles now but, at this point, this all seems like typical long run soreness and pain. Not totally out of the woods yet with Erika's injury, and continued rest and x-training are called for. But, more than anything else, we're feeling RELIEF!!

I guess the best way to describe how I'm feeling about this run is, that if you asked me how this run could have possibly gone any better under the circumstances, I'd think on a bit, scratch my head, and then think some more. Then I think I would have to say, "I've got nothing – there is no way that this run could possibly have gone any better." When you run 18 miles, it's hard and it's wearing. It's a long way to go and there is pain and discomfort – in a few places....And it will be worse tomorrow. But as I bask in the aftermath of today's run, about all I can do is shake my head and smile over a fantastic run. And think, hey we get to go 20 miles together next week. And 8 weeks until RACE DAY!

This was one of several blogs where I used an exclamation point in the title, a clear sign of how I was feeling. I was flying high now and, even on a run when I had nagging injuries and pain, was feeling so confident and strong. My confidence had rebounded and was now building in a positive direction, with each run seemingly making me feel better and stronger than the last.

Nailed It! (More or Less), March 31, 2015

Tonight's run was a tempo run on a nice night. It was almost 50, warm enough to run in shorts comfortably. So let's get right to it. This was a 7 mile tempo run – planned for 1 mile easy (8:15), 4 miles at 7:15 pace, and

2 miles easy to wrap up. I headed over towards Wompatuck – nice and simple – an out and back run. As is usually the case, my first mile was too fast at 7:52. That was in spite of some foot pain and left knee pain that lingered throughout the run. (I'm taking Advil and bonding with a bag of frozen peas now – my favorite frozen food for icing! I don't bother with icing and Advil for "normal long run soreness" because I want to get a true gauge of how I'm feeling, plus I know my body will recover on its own from that. This was a little different tonight though.) So, anyway, the first mile was a bit too fast even though I tried to slow my pace. In mile 2, I was all over the place with my pace – up and down like a yo-yo. I don't know if my watch showed my target pace of 7:15 once. Every time I sped up, I was too fast, every time I slowed down, I was too slow. But, for all of mile 2, I hit a 7:14 pace. Starting to feel like this could be my night! When I hit mile 3, my initial energy had worn off, and I was a little steadier. That one, by no coincidence at all, was 7:15 exactly. In mile 4, I turned around at the 3.5 mile mark and paused my watch to stretch my knee. Apparently it helped because I started back way too fast, finishing mile 4 in 7:05. Ooops. My last tempo mile, mile 5, was better and I finished that one in 7:12 – pretty close by my standards. From then on, it was two easy miles. Except they were really hard. I could not slow down for the life of me. I felt like I was nearly jogging and was still going sub 8:00 pace. Once you're flying along at 7:15 pace, unless you're really exhausted, which I was not, it's tough to slow down. Finally I got my pace to settle down and finished the last two miles in 8:11 and 8:08. Still a shade fast, but it was the best I could do... One thing I know for sure – when I next get to run a 10K, it's going to be a PR. I'm virtually hitting my PR 10K paces on my training runs now – comfortably! But, I'm getting ahead of myself. Focus John! It's all about Burlington now. 10K PRs can wait!

132

Erika and I decided to run on our own for this long run, and I felt a bit bad about that prior to this run. But the idea to run on our own for a week was a good one. We had run together so much, but it was also important to be prepared for a long run on our own. After all, we didn't know what Race Day would bring. I worked hard to get up for this run in my mind and ended up being very strong mentally on this run.

It, April 4, 2015

Erika and I had schedule conflicts this weekend and, combined with the fact that she wanted to get out for a solo long run at some point, we decided it made sense to do that this weekend. We made one switch to move a harder 20 mile run to do together next week and do an "easy" 17 mile run on our own this weekend. Solo long runs are no big deal for me, but I knew I was going to miss Erika on this run, so I worked a little harder to get pumped up ahead of the run. Although, as it turns out, she was really with me all the way.

Yesterday, I looked up my 17 mile PR (2:18:10), which I don't normally do for a training run. If I ran this run exactly as we had it scheduled, I would get 2:17 – so lined up for a PR. Then, I switched my GUs from raspberry and orange to 2 x strawberry banana (1 of my favorites) and a lemonade Roctane. I also wore my New Bedford Half Marathon shirt – with shorts! Since I was worried about my ears getting cold, I wore light ear muffs. Turns out all we're good choices. This all may seem like nothing, but it was all about my mindset as I headed out for this run. And my mindset was AWESOME.

Started out about 9:00, and though it was overcast, the earlier rain had faded. It was about 50 degrees, perfect running weather. The first two miles were intended to be easy (about 8:15), as I eased over to 228. I wanted everything today to be a shade fast, and the first two miles were perfect in 8:08 and 8:11. Not too fast and not too slow. Not much knee pain or foot pain – feeling good. In mile 3, I started to open it up and ran that one in 7:52. At this point, I was feeling really good and, as I ran mile 4, the sun started to poke out. Mile 4 was a shade slower in 8:02, but I was feeling so solid. The miles were starting to fall like dominoes, I felt so strong, and I was actually on the verge of shedding tears of gratitude, to be feeling this good and running this well on such a beautiful day. It was at that moment that I knew I had this run nailed.

The miles continued to fly by and my running was smooth as silk. At about 5.5 miles, I crossed over 3A in Cohasset , I think. Miles 5-7 were 7:53, 7:52, and 7:59. I was hitting these splits so smoothly and, at this point, felt like I could do this all day. But I reminded myself to stay in the moment, take that delicious GU, drink your water, and watch your form. Head up, quick and light. Right after mile 7, I hung a right onto Jerusalem Road and mile 8 was another solid mile in 7:50.

Miles 9 and 10 were the toughest miles of the run, as I was running on Atlantic Ave in Hull, I think. There was a strong head wind, followed by a hill, and it slowed my time a bit. But it didn't even dent my attitude and I ran solid splits of 8:05 and 8:02, despite the headwind. I was really proud of how I ran through this, didn't even bat an eye, stayed strong, and knew that everything was easier after this. Right before mile 10, I stopped at Tedeschi's for water and had to stretch out, as my knee started to tighten up. But, I thought it would loosen up as I got going again and it did.

Now I'm heading home! Back along Rockland Street and Summer Street into Hingham Harbor. Ran up a hill like it was nothing and miles 11 and 12 were 7:51 and 7:55. For mile 13, I'm heading back onto 3A on Lincoln Street. I'm still solid at 7:58. I can feel like I'm working a bit harder now, but I KNOW that I am 100% in control of this run. As I ran along 3A, I hit that pesky headwind again and my mile 14 split dropped to 8:02. But I was still running hard and running well. One thing I knew for sure at this point was that mile 15 would be sub 8:00, and it was in 7:50.

So, at this point, the scheduled run called for two easy miles, and I let my pace dip for a few minutes. But I wasn't quite done yet and I realized that I had the chance to finish the overall run below an 8:00 pace. And, on this day, I knew I could do what I wanted, So, I regrouped, picked up my pace and finished miles 16 and 17 (including a big climb in mile 17) in 8:03 and 8:07. On this solo run, I was not alone. I thought of Erika often, and certainly at every mile split, knowing that she would be smiling along with me about how great this run was.

So, I finished the entire run in 2:15:45, just under 8:00 pace overall, and a > 2 minute PR. So this brings me to my title. Some days, you just have "it". These days are rare, special, and to be treasured. Even on good runs, when I nail my paces, I don't usually feel like this. I don't know how to fully describe it, but I was in a running zone and was in complete control of my run. I was ticking off 8:00 miles, with very little effort, running smoothly, breathing smoothly, and feeling good. I found myself smiling as I went, I just felt so good. Even when I had to work a bit more late in the run, I had the energy for it and I knew it. Without a doubt.

This was an absolutely amazing track interval workout in awful conditions. I get proud and teary-eyed reading back on how well I ran. How I nailed these intervals and was so tough mentally during this workout. There were so many excuses I could have made, but I didn't give in to any of them. I worked through the whole workout so hard, always focused on my effort and performance. Days like these are magical days for a runner.

Some Days You Just Have to Suck It Up, April 9, 2015

OK, so it's not the most elegant title, but I think it fits. This week, I was facing a very challenging track speed interval run on my schedule. I needed to do this run on either Wednesday or Thursday, and some rain was forecast for both evenings. I briefly considered the idea of doing this run on the treadmill. But treadmill runs just aren't the same. For me at this point in my training, I really wanted to do this run out on the track. To make matters worse, it was cold, about 37 degrees out at the time of my run. In my hierarchy of running conditions, except for running in a natural disaster or in REALLY extreme temperatures, these chilly, rainy conditions rank firmly at the bottom. But I was doing this run and doing it outside. Hence the title.

But, I made up my mind firmly that, if I was going to go out there and suffer (and I knew I would) I was not going to just go through the motions and have a mediocre run. I made up my mind that I was going to nail this run in spite of the conditions. And, because of the conditions. I was a little late getting home Wednesday night and, given the overcast skies, I could have easily packed it in and said, it's getting too dark, I'll just do this run tomorrow. But I headed out because I was so ready to just do this. I had another chance, as I was absent-minded, forgot my running watch, and had to drive all the way back home from the high school to get it. But, now I was getting even more determined.

At that point, I got a break, as the baseball team was out practicing on the field, so the lights were on at the track. A sign perhaps? So here was the run: 3 sets of 2 x 1,200 m intervals at 4:47, aka, 6 1,200 m runs at 4:47 each, that's about a 6:23 mile pace. This is FAST for me. Although I can probably run a mile a bit faster than this now, the fastest mile time I've ever clocked is 6:06. Adding in recovery laps, warm up, and cool down running before and after, this was going to be an 8 mile run. So, all told, I was going to be out there a bit over an hour.

When I got there, it was raining, but lightly, so at least I wasn't getting soaked by a downpour. I ran my warm up in a windbreaker and rain pants, over ,my double long-sleeve running shirts and Under Armour tights. Also had my running hat and mittens. So, at least most of me was dry for my warm-up. But that wasn't going to do it for my speed intervals, so I took off that outer layer and started to get soggy. Before I was done, I literally felt water sloshing around in my shoes as I ran and my fingers were so cold and stiff that I could barely move them. Ironically, Kevin ran an intra-squad meet on that same track a few hours before and his hands were so cold that he ran his race with the shoelaces on his spikes untied as he couldn't tie them. For my part, I had a hard time getting the car key out and getting back into my car at the end.

But, back to the run. OK, 6x 1,200s at 4:47. The goal here was not to run these as fast as possible, but rather to come as close as possible to the target interval on all six. I'll spare you any further suspense – I was virtually PERFECT. EVERY SINGLE ONE was either 4:46 or 4:47. I can say without any doubt that this is the best set of intervals I've ever run. Not only were these really tough split targets to repeat, but I could not have possibly come any closer to my target splits. And the conditions were terrible, on a wet, soggy track.

So, going back to December, I will run about 100 runs to prepare for Burlington. Most of those will fade into the woodwork. A handful of them will stand out and be remembered for various reasons, either because they were so tough, perhaps because they were so good, or just memorable in some way. And, certain runs end up having greater meaning beyond that run. This run will stand out for all of these reasons.

As I've trained for Burlington, my confidence has flagged at times. It's not that I've been running poorly but, for a combination of reasons, I just haven't felt as positive as I would like. I think I know why and I've worked hard to change my mindset, but it's been slow in coming. But, as I hit my targets on one run after another, especially as they get tougher, my confidence continues to get rebuilt. I had this run mentally marked on my calendar as one of the tougher ones and, I was looking at this run as a barometer. The fact that I ran it under such difficult conditions made this an even more meaningful test. So, as I finished this run, and I finished it with a virtual sprint, I knew I had nailed it. And, as cold and soggy as I was, I felt invigorated. Or maybe that was just the tingling from the cold?

In addition to training your body, you also train your mind when you train for a Marathon. And, when you push hard late in runs like this, it trains your mind to push hard and fast late in the RACE, when your body and your mind have had it. To say forget about the fatigue, forget about the pain – just focus on light and quick strides. That's your whole world at that point. As I ran my last interval with water sloshing around inside my shoes, I did that. I just had one thought over and over – light, quick strides & cadence. I wasn't thinking about the cold. Wasn't thinking about the rain. I just kept on focusing on light and quick strides. And it paid off. And, the funny thing is, in the final analysis, yes the conditions were punishing. But that's not the part that sticks. The part that sticks in my mind, the thing I'll remember about this run, is how I absolutely nailed those target splits. And how, when I set my mind to hitting a pace, I can do it. As long as I need to.

Just need to remember this in 45 days!

This blog sums up the positive emotions of marathon training so nicely. There were so many tough runs and some down moments to get to this point. And there were more down moments to come too. But this blog captures the feelings of progress and accomplishment so nicely. It

captures the key set of emotions that course through my running –
gratitude, pride and joy.

Running Hard, April 12, 2015

As I reflected back on my week of running, I was struck by something. I mean really struck – like by a pile of bricks. I realized that this was my best week of running – ever. There were no PRs (though several were close) and it was not my highest mileage week ever. But I have never run harder or better over the course of a week. And I don't need to go back and check past training calendars because I know it's no contest.

As the week went by, I realized that each run was really, really strong. But it was something that Erika said on our long run today about all the hard runs I did this week that triggered this thought about the week as a whole. And, as I thought back on our long run today, which was good in its own right, this hit me.

On Monday, I ran a tempo run, 1 mile easy (like 8:15), 5 miles aiming for a 7:45 target pace, and 2 more miles easy. The goal for this run was not to run as fast as possible, but rather to come as close to the target pace as possible. Every tempo mile was under the target pace, but all within 6 seconds. And I felt in total control of my pace throughout the run. Just rock solid.

On Wednesday, I ran my best speed interval workout ever. it was 8 miles total, featuring 6 x 1,200 meter repeats, with a 4:47 target time for each. That's about a 6:23 mile pace – very fast for me! I ran this run in 37 degree rain on a wet track and still hit EVERY interval in 4:46 or 4:47. Basically a perfect workout, really could not possibly have been better. And, perhaps even better than the result is that, again, I felt in total control of the pace. I almost felt like I was driving a car set on cruise control.

On Friday, since I had Saturday off, I decided to make my 4 mile run another hard run – running 5 x 1/3 mile hill repeats with recovery downhill jogs. I was aiming for these to be in 2:40 each, for an 8:00 pace. So, not super-fast, but a good solid hill pace. Marathon race pace in fact. Turns out I ran them all too fast, averaging 2:35 per, or about a 7:45 pace. But they weren't ridiculously off, as 2:33 was the fastest. So, again, another hard and successful run, and the third run that I had conquered in 5 days.

So today, Sunday, was our long run day. My favorite run of the week. Again, we had a hard run planned, a 20 mile run including 2 x 10 minute tempo intervals at 7:30 pace and another three miles at 7:30 pace for miles 16-18 of the run! Very, very tough run. Plus, I planned a hills course which featured several hill sequences, including a really tough set of hills in Cohasset. And, yeah, we ran to Cohasset. This ended up being a really solid run, and I finished in 2:44:27, just 19 seconds off my PR. I think it's safe to say that we were both totally spent at the end of this run. As we bent over at the end, with most of our bodies wracked in pain, Erika and I were two very sore tired, people. Two very sore, tired people who had just conquered a 20 mile run. In my case, this was my longest run since Chicago. In Erika's case, it was her longest run in about 5 years or so.

If you've read some of my writing about running, you know that my emotions about my running are always right on the surface. This can be good and bad, but it's just me and the way I am. So, since this run was over, of course, emotions are coursing through me. First and foremost, there is gratitude. Gratitude to have such a great running partner, to have such a beautiful day here to run on, just to be able to run like this, and to have my family to support me though this challenging endeavor. Second, there is pride. Both pride in myself, and pride in Erika as a running partner. Pride in how we both are running these days, as we each face challenging training schedules that we're working to balance with the rest of our lives. And, as for me, pride that, yes, I did just have the best running week of my life – and I worked really hard to make that happen. Not just this week, but since December. That's what makes these accomplishments so gratifying. Because I know that my great runs this week are founded on our brutal February runs, when we battled snow and ice every Sunday. And pounded away on a treadmill throughout the week, and worked through core workouts in between. And we persisted every week without fail. And now, because of months of work, I am seeing the results of all that sweat, mixed with just a bit of blood and tears, and a lot of ice, Advil, heating, and stretching.

And that brings me my final emotion of the day – joy. When you train for a marathon, of course, the ultimate joy comes on RACE DAY. But it's

139

about so much more than RACE DAY. it's about the journey and all of the little accomplishments, building blocks, and progress along the way. And in the end, it's really so simple. It's about having the chance, the opportunity to work hard, really hard, for a long time and to see the results. And, for me, that's just PURE JOY.

I was running so well and so strong in my training at this point, I don't know if I've ever had such a consistent stretch of strong runs before. This run was just pure joy, letting myself go at 100% effort and loving it. It also shows how much training with Erika meant with me at this stage as she was right with me in my mind.

Oh What A Night!, April 16, 2015

It's a bit past my bedtime tonight, but I really want to write about tonight's run tonight, so I'm staying up a bit. So, the story of this run starts with yesterday when I had a really tough day at work. Nothing awful, but just grueling. I decided to get an early start this AM to really dive into work – with the attitude that I was going to have a great, super productive day today. And it worked! And I left work tonight on a real high.

What does that have to do with running you ask? Well, it's all me, the same body, the same mind, spirit, and emotions. So this laid the groundwork for a great high energy run tonight. Plus, it was a beautiful spring evening, an evening just made for running. And I was ready!

My planned run tonight was a tempo run, but a long one, 1 mile EZ, 10 @ 7:49 pace, and one mile EZ. I was heading over to 228, down to 53 and back, heading out on High Street and coming back on Ward Street – for those locally who know what I'm talking about. As I headed out, I had a lot of energy and my pace bounced around a bit as I tried to settle – 8:07 for the easy first mile, then 7:45, 7:53, and 7:43. In mile 5, I finally settled, and the next four were right on – 7:51, 7:49, 7:48, and 7:48.

So, in mile 9, I thought OK, I have four to go, and my thoughts drifted to Burlington. And that's when this run started to change. I thought of Erika and me running together in mile 23 in Burlington with 4 to go and my adrenaline surged a bit. I was still basically keeping on pace, and hit mile

9 in 7:46. But, the Burlington image stuck. And, you may think I'm nuts now but, as I thought of running that last stretch together, I actually moved over on the sidewalk as I pictured us running together. And my intensity continued to grow.

For months, every run I've done has been scripted. I've been running hard, but with discipline and with target paces set in advance for virtually every run. And I've pretty much nailed them. But I've never really just left the script and just took off. And I thought hey, my spirits are soaring, I'm feeling strong, I'm in the moment here, and I've only got two miles to go. How bad could it be? And I locked onto the Burlington image, mile 11 (aka mile 25), and I took off. I finished mile 11 in 7:26 and was running smooth and strong. I was feeling quite a bit of soreness and fatigue at this point and I thought, of course you're sore, you're in mile 25. But, forget that and run smooth, quick, and strong, and I did. Now, in my mind I'm in mile 26, with my favorite Chard Street hill looming to close the run out. Now I'm going pretty close to flat out, but still feeling strong and smooth. Yeah, three days after 20 miles, the tank is pretty full and I'm feeling strong. I close out mile 26 (mile 12 that is), in 7:12, a really great final mile.

All told, I finished the 12 mile run in 1:32:46. about a 4 minute PR, a 7:44 average pace, not far off my last half marathon RACE! Erika did great too. :)

I was now deep in the heart of training for Burlington and was continuing to run so well. Looking back, I'm particularly struck by how well I was running the interval workouts. Not just fast but right on target pace. I was just locked in and running so strong. And we were getting so close to the start line in Burlington and I could sense it!

Tic-Tac-Toe and Climbing the Mountain, April 17, 2015

When I started thinking about this blog, both of these titles came to mind. And I thought about writing two separate blogs. But I realized that one just kind of flows right into the other, so it just made sense to write one blog. But I liked both titles, so I'm going with a dual-titled blog.

I just completed my third run in a row – tic-tac-toe. I win. On Wednesday, I ran a hard 12 miles, followed by an easy 4 yesterday. Today was the real test, a 5 mile speed interval workout, running the third day in a row. And, once again, my track workout was run in a chilly rain. While it wasn't quite as cold this week as last week, I had forgotten my running gloves, so my hands felt just as cold. My target splits on this run were 1,000 meters in 3:56, 2,000 meters in 8:14, then another 1,000 meters in 3:56. And, has become almost routine for me these days, I nailed the splits in 3:57, 8:14, and 3:56. This is a really great result under duress and another solid step towards Burlington. Now I get the rest of today and tomorrow off to recover and regroup to run 22 on Sunday! And I definitely need that time right now.

I remember when Erika first sent me her training plan for Burlington, it was like it was a big mountain range off in the distance. Towering and impressive. And, in a certain sense, it looked so close, you could almost reach out and touch the peak. But, having climbed the marathon training mountain twice before, I knew those mountains are pretty tough once you get into them. Full of switchbacks, steep climbs, and rocky, slippery trails. And the climb looked quite daunting. But having done this climb twice before, I knew the key was to concentrate on the trail in front of you and just focus on the climb step by step.

From the foothills of December and January, we have been climbing for months now. And, it's funny how time passes and progress sometimes sneaks up on you. Make no mistake, it's been rough at times for both of us. And we're not done yet. But, looking back down on months of climbing, and all the ground we've covered, the view is pretty amazing right now. We're getting up pretty high right now and have got a few more hard stretches to climb. But, we're so close and I can sense the peak getting closer and closer.

Of course, once we crest this peak, there's one more climb left to go. That climb is 26.2 miles long and we'll be doing that one on May 24 in Burlington.

This blog entry captures one of the undeniable truths of marathon training – the ups and downs. We had both been running so well and, when you feel like that, it seems like it will continue forever. But inevitably, there are down days and you have to work through those as best you can. This was one of those days when we had to hang in through a grueling 22 mile run. But we did it and, eventually better days would return. Just not right away.

A Low Energy 22 Miles, April 20, 2015

Erika and I ran what I would call a low energy 22 mile run on Sunday. As for me, I was feeling flat from the beginning. From mile 1 I knew that I didn't have my legs that day. But I also knew I was doing this run, and that I was going to do my best to be there with Erika through this run. So I really buckled down and went into a kind of persistence/survival mode, where I just focused in on my running. As a result, I was pretty flat emotionally for much of the run.

Turns out Erika felt similarly. And, while she was bolstered by a friend of hers joining us for the middle 3rd of the run, by the time we got to mile 15 or so, it was clear that this was going to be a grind to finish for both of us. At that point, my mental and emotional outlook changed a bit. One of the best pieces of advice I've heard about life in general is that, when you're feeling down yourself, the best thing you can do is to try to be nice and supportive of someone else. So, I think it was around mile 15 or so, I started focusing on Erika and her running more than my own. After all, focusing on my running was not exactly inspiring, as I was just hanging in. At this stage, I focused my energy on supporting Erika and, in turn, I felt a whole lot better. Didn't do anything for my legs, but my spirits rose a lot. And we supported each other throughout those final miles, feeding off that tiny remaining kernel of shared energy.

As it turns out, this whole run was a grind, but the last 6-7 miles in particular were a real battle. When we look back on this run, without knowing the story of the run, it will look like a poor run. And, time-wise it was. But that's not the way I look at it in the final analysis. When you finish out a run like this, and we actually finished fairly strong, I think it is a huge character builder. Yeah, it looks like a crappy run on paper. But, having lived it, when I look back at this run, I see two people running through tremendous fatigue and not giving in – dedicated to finishing the run and to finishing it as strong as we could. It's runs like these when you demonstrate and hone your true character. And it's that character that you turn to in those tough moments during the marathon when you're on the ropes. And you do not give in then – even when you have absolutely nothing in the tank.

I'm no fortune teller, but we are scheduled to run 22 miles again in two Sundays from now. My prediction for that run is that we will both be a lot stronger and on that day, we will have the run that we both hoped for yesterday. And when that happens, the first thing I'll do is look back to the pain and fatigue from yesterday and smile. And I'll know that the brutal work of that run paid off.

But that's a story for 13 days from now.

This blog shows just how much training for Burlington meant to me. Erika and I had already been through so much together and it had become a very emotional experience for me. It was about to get a lot tougher too. Looking back later, this blog simply shows how much the shared experience meant to me.

30 Days 'Til Burlington, April 24, 2015

Sometimes it feels like Erika and I have been at this training forever. Other times it feels like just yesterday we started in on the first page of that training plan. But, however you look at it, we have been working very hard since the start of January to prepare for May 24 in Burlington. And now that's just 30 days away.

So how does it feel to be just a month away from the start line? Quite simply, very exciting. But that doesn't quite do the feeling justice. As we've gone through our training plans, through good runs and bad, I've checked off each long run and each week as we've gone, and each week has brought us one week closer to Burlington. And, when you measure time in weeks, and long runs, it goes really fast. Now we have only four more long runs left before Burlington. And after staring down this training calendar for so long, that feels like nothing. So I have this feeling of tremendous energy building up with each passing week. It's not just adrenaline, it's deeper, stronger, and steadier than that. It's a mix of adrenaline, determination, strength, and joy – all channeling towards 3 hours and 30 minutes of pure and absolute effort, beginning at 8:03 on May 24. All building towards that moment that I know will come, when I feel spent and dig into that reserve strength that I have been building through these months of training. That strength is as much mental as physical. Working on the ability to take that fatigue, set it aside, and just think "light and quick". Over and over – until I cross the finish line. I've practiced this in my mind over and over, getting ready for that moment. And getting ready to beat it.

Yes I am getting pretty psyched – and my energy level is really high right now. I have to say I'm glad that I have a couple more tough weeks of training left before I taper. Otherwise, I would turn into a raving lunatic. I may get there anyway, but at least it will be for a shorter time as I'll continue to pour my energy into my training over the next couple of weeks.

But the other emotion that's lingering out there is a little sadness. Sadness that this will all be over soon. While this has all been hard, this training with Erika has been just about the most fun and rewarding running experience that I have ever had. Especially our long runs together each week. This has been an incredibly meaningful experience and, while I've been looking forward to Burlington for so long, I also don't want this training to end. I will be signing up for more races soon so that I have something to look forward to once I cross that finish line. My short term plan is to run 5Ks and 10Ks, and perhaps a half. I know there are PRs waiting out there for me. And I know that Erika and I will continue to find chances to run together, including maybe running some of these races together. And, who knows, we may decide to do something longer together in the fall.

But, our training for Burlington will always be special for me. And, as we wind down our training and build towards RACE DAY, I have this curious mix of building energy and sentimentality. So how can I sum this all up? In the end I'm left with just one word:

Intense.

There really were so many great moments training for Burlington. And, at this stage, I was feeling very sentimental about all of those experiences. Marathon training really is about the journey, more than the destination. Yes, Race Day itself matters a lot to me. But, for me, the training is the part that means the most.

All of the Moments, April 26, 2015

When I'm training for a marathon, or any race for that matter, I spend a lot of time visualizing the final moments of a race – my final kick and crossing the finish line. And those are absolutely important and special moments and worth savoring. But, I would argue that the key moments in a race, the ones that determine success or failure, often happen much sooner than that. So, say I run a PR. The finish will always stick in my head. But the PR was really about much more than the finish. In fact, every moment of that race contributed to that PR. Of course you can't remember every moment. So, unless there's a memorable turning point in a race, the one that usually sticks in my mind is the finish. There are some races when I can pinpoint some of those mid-race moments that really mattered. But, even then, I'm taking away, at most, several moments in my head.

However, in the case of marathon training, I would take this one step further. I am looking forward to RACE DAY so much and, regardless of how I do, I expect to have some great moments from that race that I take away and savor. Those moments will mean a lot to me and I will always treasure them. But, with marathon training in general, and with Burlington in particular, there are so many more great moments along the way. And the marathon experience, I believe, is all about the journey. An odyssey really. And, in this case, a shared odyssey.

I looked back on a few of my blogs from January, February, and March last night. Man, have Erika and I been through a lot. This has been really tough at times. But, along the way, there have been so many fun moments and great runs. And the obstacles we have overcome make these all the more meaningful. Take today's run for example. It was an ordinary enough 14 mile run. But it was all about the shared experience together. And it was, quite simply, a lot of fun. So, the special moments of Burlington are a patchwork quilt of moments and memories. Taken individually they may not seem like much. But, woven together, they make for an amazing, rich, and rewarding experience.

So, when I look back on Burlington from May 24 on, I will always remember and cherish the key moments of RACE DAY. And I can't wait for that. But, even more than that, I will remember the journey. And all of the moments along the way. For me, that's why training for a marathon is such a rich experience. Because it's not just about a few key moments on RACE DAY. It's about hundreds, maybe even thousands of moments – all of them.

This was my toughest stretch of training for Burlington. I had to completely change my training plan to allow myself to recover from these tendon injuries. And I spent a huge amount of time going through physical therapy sessions. This was my most significant injury in my running career and it concerned me a lot. But I didn't panic and I kept my head up. I also was sure to get the medical treatment I needed to be sure that a minor injury didn't turn into a major one. I made all of the right decisions going with Plan B at that critical juncture.

Plan B, May 1, 2015

I think it's safe to say that, between the two of us, Erika and I have injured virtually every part of our legs at some point during this training schedule. But, fortunately all of these injuries have been things that we can treat, manage, and run through. My latest injury happened this past Sunday, just 4 weeks from Race Day. My achilles tendon started bugging me early in that 14 mile run, and never really stopped. But it wasn't that bad and I was able to run through it.

I kind of knew something was wrong and had an idea of it. Then this week, it continued to nag at me along with some swelling and clicking in the side of my ankle. Putting that all together, I got in to see an orthopedist at South Shore Orthopedics today. And I got my latest diagnosis – Achilles and peroneal tendonitis. The Achilles you know – the peroneal runs down the side of your lower leg into your ankle. So, inflamed and strained tendons – two of 'em.

So the key treatment is pretty simple – rest. But, rest is not on my list of options right now. My orthopedist tells me he's never seen a tendon tear just from running and that I should be OK to run Burlington. It may hurt and my times may be hampered, but I can run it. And that's all I need to hear right now. I am taking high doses of ibuprofen, icing after workouts, and will be beginning physical therapy, potentially including stretching, exercises, ultrasound, and massage, next week. I'll do that 2-3 times/week through and after the Marathon. I also saw my trainer, Matt, at Planet Fitness tonight. I just have to add that seeing a trainer 1 on 1 as part of a $10/month membership is pretty amazing. I've met with him three times and he is also readily available via text. So he gave me a customized workout to keep up my fitness, and do some stretching and strengthening to get me through the next three weeks. Running in general will aggravate this, but hill running and speed workouts are particularly bad right now. So, all of this leads me to plan B.

The training schedule I've had this whole time is over. And it's been replaced by something almost completely different. Speed interval and tempo workouts are out, replaced by intense cross-training workouts. Tonight I tried an Arc Trainer for the first time and I really liked it. I felt I could get the effort of a hard run, without any of the impact that will aggravate the Achilles. So resting the Achilles while working the rest of my body really hard – perfect. I also plan to do stationary bike and elliptical workouts as alternatives. As long as the pain is not too bad, I will keep one easy short run each week of 4-6 miles. I'm planning to do that one on the track, a nice smooth, flat, and forgiving surface. I'm also adding in some different stretches and complementary exercises. I will be trying to stick to our last three long runs of 22, 17, and 10 miles., but trying to do those on a nice flat course. One possibility is the Cape Cod Canal trail – although it's tough to add two more hours to a 3 hour + run. But we'll figure that out…

I know I will be able to run Burlington. I just don't know for sure how well. My hope is that all of this treatment and modified workouts will get me to Burlington fairly fresh and will enable at least partial recovery of my tendons. And I hope that all will be enough to allow me to push hard throughout the whole course. Then I can rest and fully recover.

Over the next 3 weeks, my training schedule will be turned upside down. And just about everything has changed. But there are a few pretty important things that have not changed – my will, my determination, and my belief in myself and Erika. The schedule will begin to taper soon, but I will continue to work hard through these next few weeks to be ready for

Burlington. While I'm working hard, I also plan to be smart about this – to take care of my body, to eat well, and to get good rest.

As I wrote to Erika earlier today, THIS WILL NOT STOP ME.

This was an important run for both of us, but it was a critical run for me. In my mind, at this time, this run enabled me to believe that I could run and finish Burlington. And maybe even run OK. Leading up to this run, I had a lot of doubt in my mind. But this run turned out great. After we were done, I felt a huge weight lifted, knowing that my tendons could hold up OK on a true long run. This run ranked high on my list of most meaningful runs in 2015. It was also one of my most meaningful runs ever.

A Beautiful Run on a Beautiful Day, May 3, 2015

Erika and I ran 22 miles today along the Cape Cod Canal. I'll get to why we ran there in a minute. Her whole family came along and her husband Mark rode along on his bike, carrying their two kids in a bike trailer – along with extra water – which was a huge help! As I was driving home, I had some time to think, and I kept on coming back to one thought – that this was my most meaningful run EVER. When I come up with superlatives like that, I tend to discount them as an emotional response after a great run. But I kept on turning this over in my head, and compared it to some of my other really meaningful runs. And, if it wasn't my most meaningful run ever, it was top 2 or 3.

The run itself was great. But to understand the meaning, you have to step back to realize the context of this run for me – and for Erika and me together. For me, this context is set in an injury that I've been battling and in comparing this run to three other prior runs this year. Let's start with the injury. On our long run last week (only 14 miles), my Achilles tendon and ankle bothered me the whole run. After two doctor's appointments this past week, I got the diagnosis that I expected more or less – Achilles (and also peroneal) tendonitis in my right ankle. (The peroneal tendon runs along the outside of your lower leg and around the ankle.) I was told I could run Burlington but in addition to Advil and physical therapy, I needed to totally rework my training. So tempo runs, speed intervals, and hills are out. And replaced by rigorous cross training.

I just hoped to keep my long runs, but I really didn't know how I would hold up. And, to be honest, I thought today's run was going to be brutal for me and I wasn't sure I could even make 22 miles. Because it's tough to find a truly flat course around here, we decided the extra driving was worth it and both drove down to the Cape Cod Canal,, where there's a great, flat, smooth, wide, paved path. It's seven miles long but, by tacking 4 miles onto each end, we were able to make it 22.

And this brings me to the other context – three other runs that are very important in comparison to today's run. First there was our other run along the Canal earlier this year, when we ran 14 miles. We went down there then because it was a paved trail and there was no decent place to run around here that was cleared of snow. We ran faster that day and, to be frank, Erika blew me away. That was our longest run of the season at that point, and it really crushed me. Today was a chance for me to get some redemption returning to the scene of a tough and mentally damaging run.

The second key run was our 22 mile run two weeks ago, when Erika and I both struggled. We both did well just to finish that run. I struggled throughout and we both struggled even worse late in the run. For Erika, more than me, that was not a great run confidence wise, and we needed to rebound. So that brings me to our 14 mile "recovery" long run last week. This was actually a pretty good run for both of us, except that was the run when my Achilles and ankle soreness kicked in. And that became a huge concern for me this week.

So, as we faced today's run, each of us, for varying reasons, had some things to overcome. Given that context, I was looking ahead to today's run with some trepidation. Both Erika and I invested in compression socks this week – the first time either of us had run with them. I tried them out on a short, slow track run on Friday and I liked them. But that was 4 miles, so I wasn't so sure about 22.

This is not a run to break down mile by mile, it is a run to be looked at and taken as a whole. On a beautiful, sunny day in the 50s, we both ran so steady and so strong throughout. And, my achilles and ankle felt fine the entire time. As each mile passed, I remember thinking, well it's great I feel so good, but it's early and I have a long way to go. But, my leg held up all the way through. I will never know if I may have been fine without the compression socks, but I really think they helped a lot. We ended up running 22 miles in a few seconds over 3 hours, not my fastest, but a really solid time for us for 22 miles. And, more importantly we both finished feeling good – both physically and mentally. Not only was it a really solid run, but it also was a really fun run. Under the circumstances, I don't think this possibly could have gone any better.

In many ways this was a dress rehearsal for Burlington. And, in that context, as well as the other context I explained above, it was a huge success. I'm not sure that I would say my mindset underwent a 180 degree turnaround, as I was working hard to keep my head up before this run. But, it was pretty close. And now, my worries and anxieties about Burlington have been replaced by confidence and anticipation.

So take this result and combine it with how both Erika and I felt leading up to this run. I've had several very meaningful runs in the past that come to mind when I think of meaningful runs. But, this is for certain my most meaningful run this year. And, as I circle back on my feelings before the run and now, the turnaround is really awesome.

This is not my first rodeo and I know I will have a lot of soreness over the next couple of days. And I know I need to continue to pay attention and be disciplined about my alternative training over the next three weeks. We are not quite there yet. But, with 21 days to go, all systems are go. And, every time I think of this run, a smile spreads across my face. It really was a beautiful run.

I like how I stepped back in this blog to gain a broader perspective about my running and my training. It's easy sometimes to get bogged down in the day to day and week to week routine of training and lose the bigger picture. While you have to focus on your training to be successful, I believe it's also important not to lose sight of the bigger picture. In my case it's been important for me to remember my progress as a runner over time, especially when I struggle and my confidence dips in the short term.

A Work in Progress, May 11, 2015

This blog is about both Kevin and me. While we are both at completely different points in our running careers, I believe the title fits for both of us.

I'll start with Kevin, since his running is front of mind for me right now. He had a great mile race yesterday, the latest in a long list of PRs for him. Today I was thinking back to when he started running track in 1st grade and cross country in 3rd grade. He has worked towards this time for so long. I can't remember Kevin ever wanting to skip a workout, skip a practice, or miss out on a race. Running is just in his heart and soul. And Anne and I have been there every step of the way, taking him to races, cheering him on, running races with him, taking him to practices, and helping to coach practices too. At this point, Kevin's running is in my heart and soul too. To look at his running today and to think how hard he has worked to get to this point is heartwarming and very emotional for me. Along the way, we've lost count of the PRs. But, all along the way, he has busted his butt to constantly get better. True, not every race is a PR, but his continual ascent has been a joy to watch. Every success and every setback is met with the same response. Continued steady hard work. Every day, every week, every month, every year.

But, even now, he is still early in his potential running career and his running continues to be a work in progress. And, I like to think, years from now he'll be plugging along and continuing to progress. And, I hope then we'll look back at his 5:03 mile from yesterday, and smile and think how far he's come. And, always, how hard he has worked to get there.

My situation is entirely different. But, in the final analysis, I think very similar. I didn't begin my running until I was 40, but I've continued to improve with each passing year. The spirit and joy of running also courses strongly through me. And, like Kevin, I've tried to meet each success and setback with more hard work. Never has that been more true than training for the Burlington (Vermont City) Marathon. Between Erika and me I, we've had all sorts of bumps and bruises along the way – pain, frustration, worry, and tears. And, as we've progressed, each of these has been met with the same steady response of hard work. Now, here we are, 14 days from Burlington and on the cusp of a great accomplishment.

As I look back on this training, overall, it has been a fantastic experience. It has been filled with a lot of fun, but I'm not sure that's the best word to describe the whole experience. Quite honestly, there's been a lot of suffering for both of us along the way. But, looking back on it now, the fact that we've overcome so many obstacles and setbacks makes our training even more meaningful. On May 23, the day before RACE DAY, I will take a few more moments to reflect back on the past six months. And, before I tear up I bit, I will smile, thinking of all the hard work, the perseverance, the pain, the suffering. And the fun. And as I close out these reflections and shift my focus to race day, I will treasure each and every moment, and treasure all the shared hard work that's in the rear view mirror.

When RACE DAY comes, I will be mentally ready. Of course I don't know what the day will bring. Except that I do know that Erika and I will each give our all. And, when it's over, I'll probably cry a bit more, either out of pain, emotion, or some combination. But then I'll settle a bit and smile, a big wide smile. And I'll think again that this is all still a work in progress. And while part of me will want to rest, the rest of me will already be looking forward to the next step.

I kept that broader, longer term perspective in this blog too. The take away point for me in this blog is how I kept my focus on the value and meaning of the entire experience, and not just Race Day. But, at the same time, I was fully immersed in the short term excitement building up to Race Day in Burlington.

Heating Up, May 11, 2015

Today was my second to last run prior to Burlington. Due to my injuries, I've curtailed my running, so I have just one more 10 mile run to go before Burlington. I'll have a few more cross-training workouts and PT sessions too. But, we are so, so close. Only 14 more days to go and they will go fast at this point.

It was warm and humid today, but could have been a lot worse. Thank goodness we ran at 6:00 AM. Today's run was "just 17" miles. Due to my Achilles tendonitis, I charted a course that was as flat as possible. But, even then, there were a few hills and I felt a little soreness and tightness in my Achilles. As always, Erika was patient as I stopped and stretched a couple of times, and that seemed to do the trick. Today's run was also nice because we ran through Webb Park and Bare Cove Park, which broke it up a little bit and gave a nice change of scene.

The other thing that I really liked about this run is that we didn't focus much on pace at all – we just ran. We ended up at an 8:08 pace overall, a little short of race pace, but not bad given that I was running cautiously on my ankle at times and had some cramping late in the run due to the heat and humidity. So, it turned out to be a solid run overall and another positive run as we get closer and closer to Burlington.

Now that it is so close, I am feeling three primary emotions. First, there is the mounting excitement and anticipation as RACE DAY nears. I've been feeling that for weeks now. Second, there is the sense of coming relief knowing that I will get to rest a bit after Burlington. I took very little time off after Chicago last October so have been training pretty hard and steady since last March. And, I'm definitely feeling it and can tell I need a break – physically and mentally.

The third emotion is the interesting one. When you run together as much as Erika and I have, you're either going to get sick of each other, or develop a bit of a rapport. Speaking for myself anyway, I'd say it's absolutely the latter. It's just a combination of little things, routines, running jokes (that is ongoing jokes...), familiarity with each other's running, cues, injuries, etc. I've come to look forward to these long runs so much as part of my weekend. And, as much as I really want a break and a rest, it's become hard to imagine a weekend without a long run with Erika.

When I look back at the whole Burlington experience, I hope to have awesome memories of Race Day, and I hope to have a great race to look back on and remember. But, I think it's safe to say that, however the race goes, this entire experience will always be first and foremost about the training together, and the chance to have such a great training partner.

My training for Burlington was so hard and draining. Even at this stage, in the supposedly easy taper phase, I was still struggling and working hard. I was both physically and emotionally worn. It was really a long, tough road. Both the injuries and the associated treatments were particularly draining.

Still Working Hard, May 15, 2015

We are solidly tapering now. In fact, I'm hardly running any miles at all. Really just our tapered long runs each Sunday. But I'm still doing cross training. And I'm also doing 3 hour marathon (almost literally) physical therapy/training sessions two times/week. Plus I've been sleeping poorly, while trying to keep up with work on a compressed schedule and keeping up with everything else. Speaking of which, it's time to mow the lawn again.

So I don't feel like I'm tapering and I don't feel rested. In fact I feel tired, especially mentally and emotionally. Compared to my past marathon training, this time continues to be a battle. Every. Single. Day. I'm constantly managing injuries and they're constantly weighing on my mind. I have to stretch before I get out of bed, heat before I do activities, ice after and over the course of the day, and so on. I keep on working hard, but it takes a toll.

155

I feel that there are two factors contributing to these injuries. One is that I'm running two marathons in eight months, with several other hard races in between. And second is that I really tried to step up my training for this one. Could be just some bad luck here, but the injuries I've been getting are overuse injuries. Doesn't take a rocket scientist here.

I've been working hard to keep my energy up, to keep my spirits up. But I'm tired. I'm tired, mentally and physically, of training for a marathon. My job over the next few days is to rest and relax and to build that energy that I have to have for race day. Race day always brings its own adrenaline. That's great for a 5K or 10K, but that's not good enough for a marathon, when you need to draw from a much deeper well.

So the mission for the next 8 days is to rest and relax so that, when we head to the start line, my mind will be filled with positive thoughts and energy and none of this angst over injuries, sleep, work, etc. Still plenty of time for this but time to get cracking. I started with a seemingly miraculous 7 hours of sleep last night followed by an AM nap. Sleep is going to be my priority every night (and some days) between now and race day. That, along with eating well. I'm still trying to drop two more pounds by race day so I'm cutting out all the junk – cookies, candy, alcohol, etc. May even reduce my coffee intake, though that's gonna be a tough one.

One thing is for sure. When this is all over, and I look back on it, I will never question the effort. Not for one instant. I have given this training my all and done everything I can possibly think of to be successful in this marathon and in the training. And I'm holding on tight to that thought, holding on that faith in myself and my training. Because I've always been a believer that, over the long run, if you work hard in your training and if you keep your nose to the grindstone, the results will follow. That work isn't always the workouts on paper. Sometimes it's the treatment in between workouts, or working on your mindset, or even just working on resting.

Less than 9 days to go. Time to get to work.

This blog wasn't so much about my running, but about how much of my time and energy I pour into my running. Inevitably, it eats into the rest of your life, especially when you're training for a marathon. Having a patient and supportive spouse is critical when you're going through this. But, at the same time, despite the intense devotion to my training, it was also important to me to ensure that I was also paying attention to the other critical parts of my life. And I made sure to do that, especially when I got late in the training.

My Wonderful Wife, May 17, 2015

I've written a bunch about how I've poured my heart and soul into training for Burlington. And I really have, over and over again. I've upped my training, both in intensity and time. I've run four days per week, added cross training, and done core three days per week. And I've spent countless additional hours planning runs, thinking about my running, and writing my blog. I have poured huge amounts of energy into my training.

As I've done this, Anne has been her usual incredible self. Every day I come home from work and head off to run, there's plenty of food, dinner is cooked, errands are run, kids get to where they need to go and so on. This is nothing new, I have always had a wonderful wife. Now, don't get me wrong, I strive to be a supportive husband and parent. That is hugely important to me and I care deeply about this.

But with my marathon training, there simply have not been enough hours in the day for all this. I've often eaten dinner at 8:00, while my family eats at 5:00, I have bags of frozen vegetables and a frozen water bottle purely dedicated to my icing, and I seemingly spend money on new running equipment and accessories every week. As Anne said once, this training is like my- having a second job, especially recently, as I've added hours and hours each week, and even more money, treating my injuries. Through this all, Anne has hung in with me, holding up more than her end of the bargain. You see, it's one thing for me to sacrifice myself to train for a marathon. But, inevitably, even with my best intentions and efforts, Anne has also had to sacrifice too. Through it all, she has kept up with everything with our daily lives. And she has kept supporting me.

157

A couple of months back, this all just no longer seemed sustainable and I knew something had to give. Fortunately I work in a workplace and for a boss who is hugely supportive of family commitments. So what ended up giving, just a bit, is my work. I ended up taking off the 10 Fridays before RACE DAY, basically my summer vacation. This has been huge and has made everything better. Now, Friday can be my day to do laundry, wash dishes, run errands, mow the lawn (recently), and still get my training done. That leaves time to actually have a bit of a life together beyond my training. And that has made me appreciate Anne even more. And, in the long run, I believe this balance has made me more effective across all of my commitments, from family, to running, to work.

When I decided to train for Burlington, I made the decision that I was going all in to this, putting everything into this training. And, when I look back on my training, I know deep down in my heart and soul, that I have held true to that promise to myself. I have laid my body, heart, and soul on the line, and I am hugely better for this experience. But what tends to get lost in this self-reflection is how I never could have done this without my wonderful wife. And, as I think back on all of the great things about training for Burlington, and there are many, one that springs to the top is how I love and appreciate Anne more than ever.

After all of the trials and tribulations of the past five months of training, after all of the injuries and the confidence dips, after all the triumphs and struggles, we were both ready to go one week out. And, at this point, that was all we could really ask for. This run was a bit of a test and we performed really well.

Last Run Before Burlington, May 17, 2015

Today was the last run for Erika and I together before the Vermont City Marathon in Burlington on next Sunday, May 24. And, for me, it was my last run prior to Burlington, period. I will have physical therapy/training sessions on Tuesday and Thursday and will do some slight cross training on Saturday. But this was an important milestone run in an incredible training adventure.

I thought a bit about how to write this blog, and some sentimental thoughts bubbled up for me. But, after entertaining those for a few minutes, I decided no. We're not done yet, and I need to keep this focused on the task at hand. I can write about those sentimental thoughts after the race is over, when I know my mind and heart will be filled with them.

It was a hot day today, about 80 degrees and humid, the hottest weather we've run in so far this year. Although it was only 10 miles, the heat did take a toll on us. Even after drinking 40 oz of water, I lost 2.5 pounds start to finish, in less than an hour and 1/2. The plan for this run was 2 miles easy, then two 10 minute tempo intervals at 7:30. Then the rest easy. I had wavered quite a bit about whether I should run these tempo segments leading up to this run. Eventually I decided I could handle it physically. And, I thought it would be good for me emotionally.

It turns out I was right on both counts. My Achilles felt OK and running with just that bit of speed helped me feel more energetic on the run and get me more mentally ready looking ahead to next Sunday. Even with the heat we both ended up running steady and strong throughout. And now I'm feeling ready.

Erika and I have shared hundreds of miles together over the past six months and run in everything from freezing runs on icy surfaces to warm, humid days like today. Along the way, we have battled one injury after another together. And we have come out of this so mentally strong both individually and as a team – I can really sense that now. Over the last couple of days, my emotional outlook has improved greatly. I did exactly what I needed to this weekend to get myself ready. Now with this last run behind us, I feel 100% ready.

Now I can focus on RACE DAY 100%. And I can see it so clearly now in my mind. The next six days will be all about visualizing the race and preparing my mindset. But now I know that all of the training has gotten me to where I need to be. I will be ready. And now there's really only one more thing left to do – RACE.

It was actually good and important to feel this way in the week leading up to the race. I had been a bit drained the past few weeks before this.

But this was race week, and it was important for my spirits and energy to be high at this stage. And thankfully I was ready. But I think I also had some nagging anxiety and was working to get myself psyched up and feeling positive.

Taper Madness Has Set in, May 18, 2015

A lot has changed since last Friday. At that time, I was feeling tired, worn down, a bit worried, and in need of inspiration. I was far from taper madness, I felt like I was just hanging on. I was confident I could turn that around before Burlington, but wasn't sure how long it would take. Turns out I had a great weekend, including some extra rest on Friday, Saturday, and Sunday and a nice, solid 10 mile run on Sunday. Now, three days later, things have turned around very nicely for me.

And now, for better or worse, I am firmly embroiled in taper madness! I am thinking about Burlington constantly and having a hard time focusing on anything else. I still have bits of anxiety crop up but, after Sunday's run, my thoughts and feelings are overwhelmingly positive My emotions are those of excitement, anticipation, confidence, and joy about the whole experience. I'm excited about all of it. I'm excited to have my Mom and Uncle Jack join me in Burlington; I'm excited to have Anne, Eliza and Kevin come up; I'm excited to drive the course, and to go to the Expo. And, most of all, after training hard since December I'm excited to run the Vermont City Marathon with my running partner Erika.

I'm actually glad it took me a bit long to get to this point, as it's tough. Although it's all part of the experience, and I wouldn't have it any other way! I'm trying to stay busy, to make the days pass, to stay focused on work, to distract myself with other things to pass the time. I got two Robert Parker books, a John Grisham book, and one of my favorite movies, Absolute Power, from the library. And I'll have physical therapy tomorrow night and probably Thursday too. Then my Mom comes into town and we're off to Burlington!

Right now, as Tom Petty said, the waiting is the hardest part.

This was a nice look back at all of the training leading up to Burlington.
I had worked hard at my mindset leading up to this race, and it was in a
great place. It's a good thing too, because man, was I going to need it
on Race Day!

Race Day Eve, May 24, 2015

This all began for me on October 21, 2014 when Erika and I registered for the Vermont City Marathon. But it really began way back in last July when Erika started talking about running this marathon. And, if you know me, waving a marathon in front of me is kind of like waving a nice juicy steak in front of a wolf. I have a hard time resisting!

So, ever since last October, I've been thinking about tomorrow. Laying out training plans, planning runs, running with Erika virtually every week, building up base miles in November and December, doing core workouts, and really picking up speed in January. We busted our butts through one of the worst winters ever – never missing a long run, no matter the conditions. We each battled a string of injuries along the way that we are still treating even now. And we each faced losing confidence along the way.

And now, here we are on the precipice. On Race Day Eve. And with all due respect to Christmas Eve this blows every Christmas Eve ever out of the water. I've never worked harder on training for a race and have given this race more thought than any I have ever done. This has been at the core of my life all year. I've already been rewarded with the most fun and gratifying running experiences of my life.

And now I am less than 12 hours away from an amazing gift, an awesome opportunity, the chance to lay it all on the line. And, not only that, the chance to run this together with my amazing running partner. And to do so with my family here watching and cheering me on. Yes, tomorrow is a gift, a treasure to be cherished. And I am so thankful for all of it.

With marathons, it's difficult to guarantee anything. They're just too long and there's too much that can happen to offer any certainty. But I know a few things for certain:

161

1. I will leave nothing in the tank. I am more inspired and driven by this marathon than any other. I also believe I am better prepared than ever. We will be going out at a measured pace that we hope to be able to sustain throughout the race. (8:00 miles). But I know that if we can push it more, we will.

2. I will savor the moments in this race, all of them. Before, during, and after. This has been a special experience and I know this is a gift. And I plan to embrace it fully.

3. Whatever happens tomorrow, I am proud of myself and am proud of Erika as my running partner. And I know that, out of the thousands of people out there tomorrow, I have the best running partner!

It's hard to know how to close this, in part because I really don't want to close this chapter. Kind of like when you're reading a great book and you can't put it down. And you can't wait for the end. And then, when it's over you wish it weren't. But now I have tomorrow. And it's gonna be a great day. And one that I can remember and "re-read" forever. Time to race!

There's no point in sugar coating it. Burlington was a tough race for me and a tough day. Even today, my first feeling when I think of Burlington is pain. Not the physical pain though there was plenty of that, but the emotional pain and disappointment of not being able to finish the race the way I wanted to, with Erika. And that will always be there. But, it is always joined by pride, pride in how hard I worked despite a brutal race physically and pride in my running partner. It is also joined by joy, joy about how well we ran together for much of the race. And joy in spending a wonderful weekend with my family, including my Mom and Uncle Jack.

It's Just What We Do, May 26, 2015

I did not want to write my post-Burlington blog right away, as my emotions were too raw and I needed to let them settle down a bit before I could write well at all. Once I was ready to write, I thought of a number of titles for this blog. Ultimately it was a post-race email from Erika that led to this title. And, one thing I knew for sure about this blog, is that I would be saying "we" early and often.

Burlington is now in the rear-view mirror. I will always have a bit of a twinge of disappointment about my time there. But, more and more, that is being displaced by a great deal of pride. I am so proud of how I ran through the adversity late in this race, adversity that would have brought many to a halt. But I knew I was finishing, and I knew I was going to finish as hard as I could. And I absolutely did that, just absolutely busting it at the end of the race. Laying it all on the line. And in the end, I know I ran this race with the spirit of a marathoner. I'm a marathoner, it's just what we do.

Erika ran a great race in Burlington, getting the time she wanted and feeling good in the process. She hung with the 3:30 pacers like a magnet and beat 3:30. And, while I could not keep up after mile 19, I know I would have if I didn't have these digestive and cramping issues. My legs were otherwise strong at that point and I know I would have hung on in different circumstances. But Erika did hang on and she ran the whole marathon with strength, determination and great will. After all, she's a marathoner, it's what we do.

As we ran the first 19 miles together, we shared a lot of smiles, a lot of laughs, a lot of fun, and a lot of support together. We were always positive, always focused in the moment, and just enjoying the experience and the challenge of running a marathon together. We absolutely crushed the big hill on the course and stayed strong over and past the hill. Even after we separated, we thought of each other often in the last 7 miles or so. We're marathoners, it's just what we do.

And now, as we work through the recovery phase, both physical and emotional, I find we are approaching recovery with the same discipline, energy and focus as our training. And just two days after the marathon, I'm already thinking about and looking forward to my upcoming races. I just can't help myself, it's in me. It's in my spirit, my heart, my soul. We are marathoners. It's just what we do.

This was a wonderful, cheerful, and uplifting blog to write. I had already come so far from how sad I felt at the finish line, physically and emotionally. It would still be a few more days before I was physically ready to run again. But mentally and emotionally I was ready to go, and that was the key.

Five Days Along Recovery Road, May 29, 2015

On Sunday, in Burlington, I was a mess – in more ways than one. I could barely walk, had a terrible time going up and down stairs, my digestive system was a shambles, and my emotions were raw. I barely slept at all that night I was so frayed emotionally. But, as is typically the case with marathon recoveries, each day is better than the last. I gradually improved a bit each day. I was able to do a slow walk on Monday, then ride the stationary bike without pain on Tuesday and Wednesday. And I got great support from my co-workers when I returned to work on Wednesday!

Thursday, day 4 of my recovery, was the breakthrough day for me. I saw my physical therapist, Jake, in the AM. He did an evaluation, including my knee, which was a new injury bothering me, and pronounced everything OK. Just that was a relief. Then they gave me some treatment and set me to work! I did a hard 30 minute elliptical workout followed by lifting, And then, after they iced me down with electrical stimulation, my legs felt great. That was the first time since Burlington that my legs felt decent, and I could walk without any pain. When you've been through a few rough days, that's a great feeling. Jake advised me against running for the next five days or so and to check back with him first next week. But what he said next was like music to my ears. He said, "You can do whatever you want on the elliptical because that won't stress your joints and tendons like running. You can do speed intervals, tempo, endurance, anything you want." I asked him to repeat that just to make sure I got it right. And he said, yes absolutely, in fact it will help your recovery. And I thought later, how about if I do a speed interval, tempo, and endurance workout all wrapped up together!? Then, my emotional recovery was further boosted that evening when I got to visit with Heike Tuplin, Kevin's former youth track coach, at their practice, and had a chance to debrief with her. After all, she's kind of a coach for me too by extension and an important part of my running support system. Just a great day for me.

The thing about Burlington is I left that race hungry. Not hungry in the sense of food – I could barely handle my lunch that day. But, hungry in terms of the will to run again. And to run better and faster. So, today, I took another step along recovery road, going to Planet Fitness and really airing it out on the elliptical – going hard. And did some strength exercises too. And I felt good. Really good. I'll write more about my upcoming races soon. I'm allowing a month between Burlington and my next race, but then I'm planning to do a bunch. And that will, that competitive fire that fuels my running, is burning stronger than ever.

My summer of racing was not great overall. I ran some poor races and just wasn't strong. But, this decision turned out to be a great one! As the summer went on and I returned to marathon training mode, I ran so, so well. And, though I had no idea right then, Philadelphia would turn out to be the most special race I've ever run.

What do you do when a good time comes to an end? Find Another!, May 31, 2015

This was the tag line for a Twix commercial a long time ago and it always resonated with me. And, while I like to think I've matured a bit along the way, I still have some of this little kid in me, combined with the spirit of a marathoner. I know, a dangerous combination.

Right after Burlington, Erika came up with the idea of running a 2nd marathon within three weeks or so. The idea here is that the 26.2 is just another extended long run. After all, we run a long run the week after running 22, why not 26.2 three weeks after running 26.2? So, after training for 6-7 months, it would be great to run two marathons out of that instead of one. We were both conceptually bought into this, but the scheduling didn't work.

But, the idea didn't die there. The next thought was what about a "double" in the fall or spring? We went around about this a lot and there's an epic email chain or two behind this. I gave this a ton of thought, talked with Anne about it a lot, and went to my PT guy Jake for advice too. Jake was positive about running a fall marathon, and also about the 2 for 1 idea.

Well, Erika and I have taken the first step, signing up for the Philadelphia Marathon in November! We're still thinking about a second fall marathon. When Anne and I make decisions in life, we sometimes ponder them forever. But when we finally decide, we often decide in an instant. And, after I make a decision, I usually can tell right away whether I feel good about it. This one was hard and I thought it through a lot. If you've known me for a while, you know that stuff like this always appeals to me and, more than that, really hooks me. But now that it's done, and the registration is submitted, I feel that feeling of a well-chosen decision.

Of course, this won't be easy, but it will be different from Burlington – for both of us. Our Burlington training was really intense, and we focused like a laser on that 3:30 goal. Our dedication to our training plan was absolute. While we will still train hard for Philly, the dynamic will be a little different, a little looser. I'm modifying my training plan to do a little less running, a little more cross training, and a lesser overall time commitment. But the training runs will be intense and hard. Kind of a more with less mentality to this training.

So don't get me wrong. I'm serious about this. It's still a big time commitment and I'm still driven to run hard and fast and I'm taking the training seriously. For now, I will be focused on shorter races – running my first track meet at the end of June, running the Hingham 4th of July race, and running two 10Ks in July. I'm going PR hunting on those. I think these races will be really important because they will shift my mindset away from marathon training for a while and I won't feel like I'm constantly training for a marathon. Then, when I start to pick up distance in August, I expect my marathon spirit to feel fresh and renewed. And I'll be ready for another good time.

This was an ordinary enough run, but it was important as my first run since Burlington. And, for that reason, this was an important run to do with Erika. Under the circumstances, it went well and I think was all we could ask for. When I first run after a marathon, I always feel a bit skittish to start. After all, the last time I ran, I was exhausted and in great pain. So it's a big leap mentally.

Back In the Saddle, June 7, 2015

After American Pharaoh's historic performance in the Belmont Stakes yesterday, I knew I had to go with a horse racing themed title for today's blog. Of course, the similarity between his performance yesterday and ours today ends with the title. But that's OK. We weren't trying to blow anyone away with a beastly kick down the homestretch.

This was my first run since Burlington and I'll admit that, for whatever reason, I was a bit nervous about how my body would respond. And, as we said at the end, it felt good, even though it didn't feel that good. Erika and I were going 8 miles today, plain and simple, without any real pace target. Just trying to run kind of steady. And, given that goal, this was a successful run. We both felt flat, a little sore, and slow. But, in the end, we ran the 8 at an 8:13 pace, so we were OK. But it was one of those runs when I just didn't feel that surge; I just never kicked into high gear.

But it was a beautiful morning. One of those days when you realize it's a privilege just to be able to be out there and to have the chance to run. And, as a runner, that's the simple take away from today's run. I got to run today and that alone makes today a great day. And now that I've got this one under my belt, it's time to get back on a regular training schedule. I am three weeks away from my first ever track meet, so there's work to be done. And, you know, I wouldn't have it any other way. It sure feels good to be back in the saddle.

This was the beginning of a very tough time in my training. I didn't know it yet, but I was going to struggle over the next couple of months. Although the track meet turned out to be a great success, the rest of this training turned out to be a bit more than I could handle. I was trying to train for too many different distances at once and I learned an important lesson from my great enthusiasm.

From a Marathon to a Track Meet, June 13, 2015

Yes, literally. On May 24, I ran the Vermont City Marathon. Just 34 days later I'll be competing in a track meet. But, not just any track meet; the first track meet that I've ever competed in. So I'll be going from running (and training for) 26.2 miles to running and training for a 5K, mile, and 800 meter. And, if I get really carried away, maybe even the 400 meter or 200 meter. Of course, I never get really carried away. But, at this meet, I get to compete in five events for the registration fee. I'm not sure it's a good idea to run in five races on the same day. But, it's kind of like if someone said you can buy one donut and get four free. Having five donuts may seem like a bad idea. But, if they're handed to you for free, it's kind of hard to refuse. You know what I mean?

So I'm balancing recovery training for my marathon, combined with training for a track meet. Makes for an interesting combination. For example, I'm not doing any track intervals to train for the track meet because I don't want to risk injury doing those so soon after the marathon. So, instead I'm doing medium length tempo runs, long runs, and doing my speed work on the elliptical. But, so far I feel like it's going OK and my legs are gradually feeling stronger and healthier.

But then, to make things a little more complicated, I'll be running a 4.5 mile race and then two 10Ks in the three weeks after the track meet. So I'm training for 10Ks at the same time as I'm training for my track meet. That's where the tempo runs will become really valuable. So my training plan feels like kind of a hodge-podge, a little of this, a little of that. This is made even more complex, as I am reducing my running to 3 runs per week to limit the impact on my legs.

But there's more, I'm also in the early stages of training for my next marathon in Philadelphia in November. So I'm trying to build up the mileage on my weekend long run (one of my 3 weekly runs), yes, while training for a track meet at the same time. For the planner in me, this is a bit of a nightmare. I kind of like things neat and clear, and this is a bit chaotic. It makes my head spin a bit trying to figure out how to blend this all together.

But, for the runner in me, this is an embarrassment of riches. And I find that the idea of running shorter races after having trained so long for a marathon is refreshing and invigorating. So, I admit it's a bit unorthodox. But it sure is fun!

This was a tough, strong, and gutty run on this day. I still had not fully regained my strength and speed since Burlington. But, in spite of that I set a PR for a 15 mile training run by nearly 3 minutes. I still wasn't back, but today gave me a glimpse of the promise that lay ahead.

A Father's Day Treat, June 21, 2015

Today's run was an unusual run for me in a bunch of ways. To start with, I was running on my own after running with both Erika and Kevin last week. And running nearly every long run this year with Erika. And, since the charger for my GPS watch isn't working, I was running with just a regular stop watch, rather than my GPS watch. On top of that, I was running a different route through Braintree and South Weymouth that I had never run before. I felt kind of lost and naked out there (mentally that is.) I had very little idea of my pace and splits as I went, though I did at least check the 5 and 10 mile marks on my mapped route so I had some idea of how I was doing. But, sometimes, maybe running that way can be a good thing because I didn't think much and just ran.

I had a 15 mile run planned, and was hoping to run it at an 8:00 pace, But I'm still just 4 weeks out from Burlington and still don't feel quite 100% yet. On shorter, faster runs, I've really struggled with my pacing. So I wasn't exactly brimming with confidence. Early on, I had some left knee and left Achilles soreness, which ended up sticking around off and on throughout the entire run. But, it was familiar soreness, and didn't trouble me, so I felt I could run through it. I also had some lower abdomen soreness from an extended core workout on Saturday which bothered me more, but there wasn't much to be done about that. I did stop and stretch out my knee and Achilles at my water stop and a couple other times, as it really tightened up as I went. But I was able to manage through it OK and just ignore it and run through it for the most part.

So, as I went, I didn't have a great sense of how I was doing, though I knew I was at least ahead of 8:00 pace at the 5 mile mark. But, I was hurting, and wasn't sure how I would hold up. After my water stop and stretching at about the 6 mile mark, I felt like I had opened it up a bit and, by the time I got to the 10 mile mark, I was nearly 3 minutes ahead of the 8:00 pace. At that point, although I didn't remember my PR precisely, I was pretty sure I was well ahead of PR pace. So I just decided to go all out for the last 5 miles – almost like running a race. As I went, I was thrilled that I was able to draw on speed and endurance that, frankly, I wasn't sure I had at this point. But I did have it, deep down I was strong. I was running hard and I was running with heart, running through steady pain, just ignoring the pain. And, even though I wasn't sure about my PR, I had a pretty good idea I was going to crush it.

Turns out I finished in 1:56:15, an average pace of 7:45, and beating my previous PR of 1:58:58, by 2 minutes and 43 seconds! And that despite nearly constant pain on the entire run. Some runs you run great and just feel great doing it. This was not one of those days. On today's run, it was a battle the entire time. I knew I was strong, but I had to really work for this one.

In the aftermath, I lost 3.5 pounds and was so sore in so many places, that it was too much to ice. So I started with a cold bath. After a bottle of GU recovery brew and then a dinner of pizza and beer, I'm feeling kinda human again. Time to ice some more before bed, where to begin? And then some more water.

You might ask, with all that pain, was it worth it? Oh yeah! This is what running is all about for me. Those days when you can dig deep, exceed your own expectations, and just crush a run. There's just nothing like it. I can't even tell you how satisfying this feels. And the pain is far from over. But this is one of my most satisfying runs ever, and the joy of this run will last a whole lot longer than the pain! Happy Father's Day to me!

This training plan turned out to be a very good fit for me over the course of the summer and fall, and I am continuing to use it in 2016. It turns out that my July races were too soon to see the results of this training, but it sure paid off later. I liked the combination of limiting my runs and miles, while making every run and workout tough. This approach seems to work very well for me.

3+2=PRs?, June 21, 2015

As I trained for Burlington this year, I really stepped up the intensity of my training. I kept to running four days per week, but made the runs more intense, running a tempo run and a speed interval run every week. And, I also added 2-3 days of core workouts per week, along with a cross training day thrown in sometimes. This training was going pretty well for me for a while (after we got past the brutal winter weather that is.) I was running some great track workouts in particular. But I think that, in the end, it may have been a bit much for my body. Maybe it was just bad luck, but it seemed like I just went from one injury to another and just never could get healthy.

So, this time around, I'm training almost straight from "Run Less, Run Faster", a book by Runner's World. The basic training plan here is just three runs per week, plus two cross-training workouts per week. The runs are a tempo run, a speed interval run, and a long run. When I used to do cross training, it was often easy, just to loosen up my legs. But this cross training is all hard, either tempo or interval workouts on a stationary bike or elliptical. The hard elliptical workouts are also informed by advice from my physical therapist Jake, who encouraged me to do hard elliptical workouts in lieu of hard track workouts while I get ready for my track meet and try to recover from Burlington at the same time. And then I'm trying to stick with two core workouts per week too.

One of the themes here is quality, not quantity. Every run and workout is hard and purposeful. There are two reasons I'm following this approach – to reduce the cumulative wear and tear on my legs, and to also reduce the time commitment, so that I can have a bit more time with my family. It's much too early to look at results, but I feel like I'm off to a good start. As I go, if I'm feeling too much wear and tear, I may periodically switch a run for an elliptical workout to further reduce the stress on my legs. Time will tell how this works out, and I'm trying to keep my eyes wide open as I go. I want to stick with this and be consistent, but I'm also trying to pay attention to my body and what it's telling me.

Some of the other guidelines I'm trying to follow are:

– do not run two consecutive days

– try to keep at least one weekend day/week fully off, or with just a quick workout at least

– modify the days where I can to enable running with Erika when it works.

The next four weekends are race weekends for me, so I'll get to see the early results pretty clearly. I already have my typical extra energy that I feel as a race nears – just a bit on edge, and beginning to chomp at the bit a little bit. In fact, the next race is less than 6 days away. I have to get through a crazy week before then, but will be inspired all week long looking ahead to race day Saturday.

Although I've watched Kevin run in countless track meets, competing in one myself was an entirely new adventure for me. I went into it with eyes wide open, ready to fully immerse myself in the experience. It turned out to be one of my best running experiences of 2015, full of excitement, fun, and adventure. It was quite a shift from running a marathon, but just as much fun.

A Marathon Track Meet, June 27, 2015

When I left home this morning at 5:00, it was beautiful out. Beautiful in the unique way of early morning. The light was soft and the air was cool, but the light over the horizon promised a bright day full of energy and hope. I hoped the gorgeous early start to the day was a sign of a special day ahead. The forecast was excellent for running, starting in the mid 50s and topping out around 70.

I stopped at the South Shore Plaza to pick up my carpoolers, my co-worker Mike and his former co-worker Steve. We were bound for South Portland, ME to compete in the Maine Corporate Track Association Regional

172

Meet. Mike and Steve were competing for the Texas Instruments team, as they both used to work there. I was running "unattached", just as an individual. But Mike and Steve were part of my extended support team on this day. I was kind of an honorary Texas Instruments track team member – in spirit anyway.

This was a special day for me — my first ever track meet. I had a busy day planned. The event registration allowed you to compete in 5 events. Since I was doing this for the experience, I was determined to get my money's worth – even if it left me a slobbering, quivering wretch at the end of the day. So, at a minimum, I planned to run the 5K, the 800 meter, the 400 meter, and the 1,600 meter. And I was thinking about the 200 meter too. If you've ever competed in a track meet before, you know that's a little nuts. And it's certainly no way to get great times. But I wanted to suck up this experience, every bit of it. So I dove in head first.

The 5K – We were blessed with great weather, especially at the start of the day. It was probably about 55 degrees and sunny at 8:00 – about the best running weather you could ask for in late June. It was a small race, maybe 30 people? The course was easy, started and finished on the track and flat except for a couple of easy hills. My limited speed workouts leading up to this meet were not good. I felt like I was still recovering from Burlington and could not run with any consistent speed at all. While I felt pretty good today, I really didn't know what to expect. I went out a bit cautious, running the first mile in 6:45. Not fast, but I felt really good and strong at this pace and felt my confidence starting to grow. So I worked to pick it up in mile 2, which I ran in 6:30. I could feel the fatigue building but I knew I was on track for at least a good time, so I kept on pushing myself and focused on my leg turnover. And I finished mile 3 well in 6:38, as I circled the track for the finish lap. I started my kick gradually but it built as I circled the track and I finished really fast, finishing the race in 20:28, just 7 seconds off my PR. While I was a bit disappointed to come so close and fall short, this was an awesome race under the circumstances and was a great way to start the day. Perhaps most important to me was how strong I finished, which was encouraging for the rest of the day and my other upcoming races.

The 800 meter: We got a break now, as the rest of the running events didn't start until 9:30, and the 800 probably didn't run until almost 10:00. So I drank water, grabbed a GU, and worked on staying loose, stretching, jogging, etc. As I talked with Mike prior to the 800, he asked what I wanted and I said, "Honestly, I have no idea, just want to get under 3:00." We talked about 400M intervals we've run and decided that 2:50 would be a good goal to shoot for. I started off easy, first because my hamstrings were a bit tight and I didn't want to pull a muscle, but also because I really wasn't sure about pace. The first lap ended up at 1:24 – not bad. The cool part is what happened next. I started picking up my pace a bit and I felt so, so strong. I pushed through the whole 2nd lap, and ended that in 1:21, and 2:45 for the full 800. This was a great race for me and I was left feeling that I could have done even better!

The 400 meter: This one came very soon after the 800, and I really wasn't recovered fully. (Well I wasn't recovered fully for any of these but I really wasn't for the 400.) I was stretching a lot and doing a lot of calisthenics because the back of my knee and hamstring was bothering me increasingly – really feeling tight. But I was able to keep it at least loose enough to keep from getting worse. What can I say? This race nearly killed me. I don't know that I've ever run so hard in my life. With the coaching of one of my TI "teammates", I focused on pumping my arms and keeping my leg turnover up, but I think I was spent by like 150 meters. And then I just hung on with shear, desperate effort. I was very proud to finish in 1:09, a great time for me. But this one hurt.

The 1,600 meter: Again, this came up really fast. When they made the first call for this, my first thought was, "UGH, you've got to be kidding me!" It felt really soon. But I rallied and went through another round of jogging, stretching, calisthenics, jogging, stretching, etc. trying to stay loose. As I headed to the start line for the 1,600, I felt gassed, like I had nothing in the tank. But I really wanted 6:00 for this one, so I made myself focus. I don't have my exact splits for this race, but they were really even. But unfortunately, they were just a hair shy of what I wanted and I finished in 6:03. A good time for me, but I just didn't have that extra gear in this race. But I was really proud of how well I ran, smooth, hard and focused. Just didn't have enough left in the tank. That 6:00 mile will just have to wait until the next track meet. And you know there will be a next one!

The 200 meter: This immediately followed the 1,600. I mean immediately. I probably had literally 10 minutes in-between races. But like I said, I was going all in today. So I said to myself, "Why not?" It's only 200 meters. Well, I had absolutely nothing left for this race. I felt like I was almost jogging the last 50 meters. But, in spite of that, I ran it in :32.6 seconds. So I know I can run a 200 under 30 seconds now.

The Wrap Up: This was an awesome, epic day! One of the most fun running events I've ever done. All in all, I ran 5 events in about 3.5 hours. And 4 events in just 2 hours! I know that I've got more track meets ahead in my future. And based on today, I actually think, at least for my age, I can be decent in some of these events. Just so much fun to race on a track too. The camaraderie was awesome among all the competitors – just a really cool event and a lot of fun. Today really came as a revelation for me. I went in very excited about this meet, and came away feeling even more excited. I don't have any new track meets planned, but I can't wait until the next one.

Just as long as I get a couple days off.

This turned out to be a really great interval workout on kind of a downer of a day. Running can be helpful that way in lifting your spirits and clearing your mind during stressful times. Although I would have many tough and disappointing runs in July and my legs still weren't fully back, this run showed me that I can still be fast and strong.

A Therapeutic Run, July 2, 2015

My runs are almost always meaningful to me, but rarely does the meaning extend beyond the run. I value each run for the inherent challenges and accomplishments (even the bad ones), but every now and then, a run takes on a little bigger meaning or value to me. That was the case tonight.

Yesterday was a very tough day for us at the state Department of Environmental Protection, where I work. I believe 111 of our about 740 staff retired, including 12 people within our bureau. One of those is someone who works for me and has been at DEP for 31 years. And there are several others who I work with closely who retired after very long careers. On top of that, I had coffee with a friend (and one of my favorite coffee partners) for the last time before she moves to San Diego. And I had to do a wrap up interview with an intern who has worked for us for 9 months and is leaving now. There were four retirement events over the course of the day and it was a very emotional and sad day for all of us. In the wake of that, today felt like an emotional hangover. I was completely drained emotionally today and felt very flat all day long.

As a result, I've been looking forward to tonight's run from the moment I woke up today. I really thought this could be a therapeutic run for me, a chance to clear my thoughts and emotions and reset a bit. A chance to just throw my energy into a run and lose myself in the run. And that's just what I did tonight. I ran at the Hingham track, running 4 x 1 mile intervals with a mile warm up and cool down, stretching, calisthenics, etc. I was aiming for 6:40 mile splits. It was warm when I started, I think in the upper 70s, and I could tell I was going to work hard tonight!

My first warm up mile was 8:11, about where I wanted to be, and fast enough to get nice and warmed up. My first mile interval was a bit fast, in 6:35, and I eased up to get that. But I expected that to start – I was just so jazzed up – but this wasn't terribly far off. Mile interval # 2 was just about right in 6:37. By the time I got to my 3rd fast mile, the heat was beginning to catch up to me, and my time slipped to 6:46. But I was happy that I ran the last lap in 1:40, right on my target pace. So, at least I didn't fade late in the mile.

I decided the 4th mile interval (and 5th mile of the run) was going to be the "make it or break it" mile of this run for me. No pressure. I didn't mind so much that I faded on the 3rd interval, but I wanted to finish strong. So I walked a full recovery lap to make sure I got my breath back. As I worked through that final mile interval, I was a second behind pace entering the last lap and I was struggling a bit. So I turned to what I always try to do in tough times – focus on short quick strides and fast leg turnover. Turns out I still had some left in the tank, as I ran my last lap in 1:36 and finished that final mile under my target pace at 6:37. In the "make it or break it" mile, I made it! Then just a cool down mile to finish in 43:16 overall for 6 miles.

This was a great satisfying run and gave me just what I needed mentally and emotionally. So, not only was it a great run, it was an important part of my healing process. And a great way to close out a tough, tough day. Now I feel ready to get back to work tomorrow and not just hang in, but to attack my work with the attitude that I should bring every day. And I know the run helped get my mindset back on course.

I don't think there was a lot I could have done better on this day, as I was battling a lower abdominal strain and it was tough to run through. I faded badly and did not get the time I wanted to. But, at the same time, it was kind of a cool, rewarding race. The last time I had run this distance was this race in 2011, and I beat that time by more than 6:30! It was gratifying to see how far I had come in four years, when even a disappointing race was so much faster.

You've Come a Long Way Baby, July 4, 2015

Today I ran the Hingham 4th of July Road Race – to varying degrees with my running partners Erika and Mike. And, Kevin was there too, though I can't say that I ran with him! It was a nice cool morning, though more humid than I realized at first. But still a great summer morning to run, and it was a lot of fun. It was also a lot of fun to see a bunch of other runners and spectators I know along the way.

There are two ways for me to view this race. I'll start with the narrow, critical approach. I did not meet my goal, and that is always disappointing when that happens. And I ran positive splits through the whole race, i.e., each mile was slower than the last. And THAT is NOT the way to run a race and I am never satisfied with positive splits on any run. There was a reason for this though, as I've had this nagging lower abdominal strain that keeps on cropping up. During the race I thought it was cramps, but know I realize it's a muscle strain that needs treatment. I was really batting this the second half of the race. So I don't fault my effort, but wanted to do at least a little bit better than this. However, I hung in and didn't collapse and THAT I am proud of.

But the real story of this race, and the really cool part, is comparing today to the last time I ran this race – way back in 2011. And, since 4.5 miles (or 4.47 miles) is a unique distance, that was also the last time I ran that distance. So, four years ago, back when I was youngster at 41. I was in shape back then from playing Ultimate, but not in running shape and up to that point, this was my longest race. I finished in 37:08, about an 8:15 pace, and I remember at the time thinking that was pretty good.

Fast forward four years (and four years older might I add) and I COMPLETELY BLEW AWAY that time. I'm talking a PR by 6:30 in a 4.5 mile race, nearly 1:30 faster per mile!!! That is a MASSIVE difference. So on a day when I didn't even run my best, I just crushed this PR. You know how as your kids grow up, and you see them every day, you don't even realize how fast they're growing? And then you look at a picture for a year ago and you think, "WOW!"

This was just like that. In the day to day, week to week, and month to month view of training, sometimes progress gets lost. You can't see the improvement because your focus is on each run as you go. But when you have a chance like today to compare an apples to apples comparison four years apart, the progress is stunning. My running history and career is unusual compared to many and has allowed me to capture PRs and to continue to improve at the age of 45. I am extremely proud of this success and that is my primary takeaway from today.

So race PR #1 for 2015 is under my belt and that's a good feeling. Over the next two weeks, I'll be running two 10Ks and will be seeking another PR in those races. And that will be a chance to shake off that bit of disappointment from today and gain yet another PR. This would be besting a PR from last May, even more exciting that I can continue to improve from 44 to 45. I know my days of setting PRs will not be infinite, so I'm enjoying and appreciating this time. But even more than that, I'm enjoying the journey, the chance to challenge myself by whatever standard I choose. For me, that's really what this is all about and what drives me. Today was a nice chance to look back at my improvement over the past four years and enjoy how far I've come. At the same time, I'm already looking forward to the next step and the next challenge.

Some of my favorite memories of running in 2015 were these super early AM runs with Erika. It was a bit crazy, but it made a lot of sense in the summer. And runs like these were a lot of fun and really helped bond our running partnership. Let's face it, running in the dark, at 4:00 AM, is a bonding experience.

A Little Crazy, July 6, 2015

OK, I'll freely admit this right off the bat – getting up at 3:30 AM to run at 4:00 AM is a little crazy. Especially when you really don't have to. But Erika was running then and this was a chance to run together – which are sometimes hard to come by these days given race and other schedule commitments.

So you might say, "So John, if Erika were to jump off a bridge, would you too?" And I'd say, "Of course not, don't be silly. But, just out of curiosity, how high is the bridge?"

I'm not sure I can explain it in a way that makes sense. I was off from work today, so I could go back to bed later this AM. But then, you might say, "That's even worse, you got up at 3:30 to run on your day off?" And I'd say sheepishly, "Well yeah, but…" You see, in the end, it just comes down to a life adventure. And when you get to be an adult, you get to make your own decisions and do stuff like this.

It was a beautiful morning out. A bit humid, but still cool and a nice time to run. It was still dark out and just getting light late in our run. We ended up having a very good run too – 5 miles at about a 7:40 pace – a quality run. It was my third day running in a row, which is unusual these days, and outside of my training plan. But, while I'm icing my foot, ankle and knee a bit, overall I actually feel pretty good. There's something about getting up and running early that feels really good, especially when it's over!

So yeah, a little crazy, I know. If you're gonna get out there at 4:00 AM, it sure helps to have good company and support. And a running partner who's a little crazy too. And I mean that as a compliment. Now I get to rest and am off from running until my next race on Saturday. Between now and then, I just have a hard elliptical workout planned on

Wednesday. Plenty of time to rest, recover and get ready to run a great race. Unless I decide to sneak in another early morning run? Nah, just kidding. I'm just a little bit crazy.

Looking back, with hindsight, this was too intense a workout two days prior to Race Day. I was running a 10K race two days later, a race when I ran very poorly. Looking back now, I would have made this elliptical workout an easy one. I was just a little too aggressive and I believe it hurt my stamina on Race Day. But you live and learn.

98% Effort, July 9, 2015

Yesterday I stayed home from work and skipped my workout due to a cold, allergies or something along those lines. Not so much the regular sneezing and runny nose, but more what's usually the back end symptoms for me, sore throat, a bit of a cough, and a headache. I was hoping to nip this in the bud by staying home, and hopefully I did, though I still didn't feel quite right today. But it didn't seem like it was getting worse, so I figured I better get back to work – and to working out.

Given that I skipped working out yesterday, I was determined to work really hard tonight, even if my breathing was a little strained. Turns out I hung in pretty well and didn't really cough until I was done. Tonight I had an elliptical workout planned at Planet Fitness, one of my favorite workouts: 1 warm up mile, 3 @ 7:30 pace, 2 @ 7:00 pace, 1 all out, and then 1 cool down mile (with 2 minute recovery intervals between the hard stuff.) Although the elliptical pace doesn't translate exactly (I think it's a bit easier), this is still a hard aggressive workout for me. But I was especially charged up tonight, and really pushed it on that "all out" mile "running it in 5:25! Now, 5:25 miles are not part of my skill set, so that's not really a 5:25 mile, but it was pretty close to 100% effort. It was hard and it was fast. I really like this workout because it simulates what I need to do on race day – to push my hardest when I'm the most fatigued. It's not the same as running these paces, but the relative effort is a pretty good match.

But I wasn't quite done. Saturday's 10K will feature a steep hill (twice) including right before the finish. So I wanted to tack on a hills workout at the end – again to simulate climbing the hill late in the race. So I tacked on a 15 minute "Pike's Peak" hills workout on the Arc Trainer – and it was TOUGH – almost like climbing stairs. And, in the "easy "cool down" stretch, I "sprinted", again mimicking the race on Saturday AM. Then, for good measure, I did my hip lifting exercises after that.

So how do I feel after all that? Well, a bit drained to be truthful. I really need a good night's sleep tonight to help my body recover. But the workout also felt really good. After a kind of lazy day and a half, it felt good to work HARD. I don't think I could call this a 100% effort but, for a training run, it was pretty close; hence this blog title – 98% Effort. Now I just have a tempo bike workout and upper body stuff tomorrow night, an off day Friday, and then RACE DAY! Tonight's workout was an important one, both in helping to build fitness but, at least as importantly, to build my mindset for Saturday. And, chances are, that's what it's going to come down to. When I get to that point, when it's late in the race and I'm tired, I'm looking to exceed 98% effort. And if I can do that, I know I will meet my goals.

This was a hugely disappointing run for me. As I mentioned with the last entry, I don't think I did a great job of planning my pre-race training. And, not to make excuses, but it was hot! I was still very disappointed in how I ran and it was a poor race. But as with my July 4th race, there was a pretty cool silver lining here. I ended up finishing 2nd in my age group and getting a trophy. So, out of 57 other people in my age group, I beat 56 of them. Not bad for a hugely disappointing race!

A Lost Run, July 11, 2015

When I left the house today, I had this surge of adrenaline and I thought, "I just know I'm going to run well today." My base goal today was to beat my 10K PR of 44:59, which felt like a slam dunk. The second goal was to run at a 7:00 pace (about 43:24) and the third goal was to finish under 42 minutes. I had been up four or five nights in a row coughing, but I felt good and I felt that energy that I always look for on race mornings. Everything felt great. But man was I wrong.

I was running at Stonehill College in Easton. I've never run this 10K there before but have run a half there twice. Interestingly enough, for some reason, my times there were poor both times. I can't explain it because the course is not that tough, but I haven't run well there in the past. But I really felt today would be different.

Getting to the race was smooth and, as I warmed up I felt good – all systems go. I went through a bottle of water while I was warming up, but had decided not to carry a bottle with me during the race. After all I was just running a 10K today. Looking back, I think that was a mistake, as I stopped for all four water stops (which slowed me down) and still felt dehydrated.

As I finished warming up, I could feel the heat already and was a bit concerned. I grabbed a small cup of water and chugged that down. I could really feel the heat building as I stepped into the starting corral. The forecast was for low 70s and maybe it was, but it sure felt a lot hotter than that.

The first mile was good at 6:37, but I faded quickly, running the 2nd mile in 6:58. My mouth felt dry and I could feel the heat draining me from the very beginning. There wasn't much shade on the course and it felt really hot. From there, basically everything went downhill. My pace continued to drop, I continued to try to push my pace, and it just wasn't there. In the end, I finished in a disappointing time of 45:50, well over my PR and failing to meet any of my goals for this race. And I found myself just shaking my head and thinking, "How did that just happen?"

I gave up my two free beer passes – just wasn't in the mood for that any longer. (Probably a wise decision in the end as I'm still battling this cough after the race.) Fortunately I decided to pause and check the results before I left, and was shocked to discover that I finished 2nd in my age group (out of 58) and won a trophy. While I was picking up my trophy, I talked with the guy who won the race and he said he also had a really hard time with the heat. He said everyone around him did and he thought he lost at least two minutes off his time because of the heat. So if he lost two minutes, that's more like three minutes for me, which would have put me right in the zone where I wanted to be.

So this made me feel a bit better. But I still found myself looking back at my time and my race and shaking my head. I think I was actually in a bit of a state of shock over it, as I thought I would definitely PR today. Yeah, it was hot and yes, I was probably a bit drained from being sick this week. But I expected a better result and I can't help but feel disappointed in myself and almost ashamed with the result.

When I got home, I did something that I never do. I assigned myself a punishment run. This was purely an emotional reaction, but the logic behind it, to the extent there was any, was, OK if the heat is so tough and you can't handle it, then you need to get out and run in the heat So I tacked on four more miles when I got home when it was in the mid 80s. And I hung in through it pretty well.

So I've got 8 days until my next race, also a 10K. The key between now and then will be rebuilding my mindset and getting my mind and heart back in the right place. Today was a demoralizing race for me and I'm struggling to come to terms with it. My job between now and next Sunday is to get my head back on straight and get mentally ready to race again. One thing I know for sure – I do not want to feel like this again.

I struggled a lot with my running in July, but I still had a number of nice runs. This was a really nice run, not for the time, but for how I felt emotionally. In the end, I work so hard with my running and put so much into it, that it's important to enjoy runs like this. Running is such a special opportunity and this run brought out one of themes of my running this year – gratitude. In this case, not gratitude to anyone in particular, but just feeling grateful for this opportunity and these moments.

Chicken Soup For A Runner's Soul, July 15, 2015

My Garmin watch leaped to life almost instantaneously. Yes it's old and weathered (just like me Erika), and it was a little before 4:00 AM, but it was ready to go. And, at least today, so was I. I was planning on running 15 miles today and the only way I could make this work was to go at 4:00

AM. I've been putting a bit too much pressure on myself recently so I was looking for a healing run today. I didn't care much about pace or time, just wanted to immerse myself into the run. To remind myself that I am a runner and to rediscover that part of my soul. As it turned out, it was a slow run for me, but that didn't bother me today.

It was a soupy morning as I stepped out into the dark. The road was still wet from rain last night (or earlier this morning) and the air was thick with humidity. The water sprayed up onto my calves as I ran and it felt good. It wasn't hot, but I knew I was in for a challenging run today. There's something about getting up and out at 4:00 AM. Yeah the getting up part is tough. But once you get out there, it is my absolute favorite time of day to run. It's so quiet, calm, and peaceful. I headed through Jackson Square going towards 228. There were a few cars out, but not many. I mostly ran in the road, as it was too dark to see the dips and bumps in the sidewalk. Plus I didn't have my normal bodyguard Erika with me today, so I was a bit skittish about running along the dark wooded areas. Along High Street, I saw a deer, a doe, standing still right in front of me. It finally hopped off to the side a few feet, but didn't run away. And I thought, I'm with you buddy, it's a great morning to stand and eat grass along the road. Or to run.

By 4:30, I could see the sky lightening, and I almost didn't want it to. I was enjoying the peace of the darkness so much. I hung a left on to 228, then took Main Street down into Hingham Center. From there, I turned down Lincoln Street, headed out to 3A. I passed by a marshy area, with fog rising up from the marsh, with the sun beginning to light clouds behind the marsh. Something about that moment was just so beautiful. As I did many times throughout this run, I thought about how grateful I am to be able to run like this and to be able to be out there to enjoy that moment.

As I reached 3A, I greeted the clerk opening the Tedeschi's store at 5:00 AM and grabbed a water. As I left the air conditioning of Tedeschi's, the warm soupy air felt like I had just stepped into a steam bath. And another frequent emotion of this run came to mind – pride. Not pride in how I was running – I was slow today. But pride in being a runner and being dedicated enough to be out there at this time. I felt that again as I passed by Planet Fitness as people began to show up at 5:00 AM, when it opens. And I thought of how I had already been out there running for over an hour.

The traffic along 3A interrupted the peace of my run for a bit, but then I turned off to head out to Webb Park. Again, this is a beautiful spot in the early morning. As I headed into the park, the sun was long since up, but was rising above some low clouds; another just stunning view. The humidity had been affecting me for a while now and I was going slow but steady. I was sweating like a fountain now, losing water quicker than I could drink it. So, on my way back from Webb Park, I hit McDonald's for another water. (My normal CVS water stop wasn't open yet.)

I knew I had the Commercial Street hill ahead of me and knew I was going to struggle there. But I had made up my mind that I was at least going to run it, and I did. Most of my body felt done, but my legs kept churning relentlessly. I did a little back and forth segment along Middle Street to get the mileage right and, bingo 15 miles done!

Physically I am exhausted and spent. I lost 4 pounds on this run and that's after three bottles of water, two GU gels, and a cliff bar. But it's the emotional part that counts. And this run was a huge success emotionally. This run restored the runner in my soul, the pride, the satisfaction, and the sheer joy of running. Just me and my Garmin. Both ready to go.

This decision to run two marathons only four weeks apart in the fall felt a bit crazy, but also really exciting. Looking back, it ended up being a great decision for me. Those two races turned out to be my two most meaningful races of the year and, perhaps of my entire running career!

My Next Great Running Adventure, July 18, 2015

My next race is a 10K in DW Field Park in Brockton on Sunday. Although the bulk of the course is flat and fast, there is a short, steep hill that gets repeated three times that makes the otherwise fast, easy course a bit challenging. I've run parts of this course probably a dozen times with Kevin. And, in fact, Kevin will be running this one with me on Sunday. It's a beautiful park, I know the course well, and I like it a lot. But it's not to be underestimated. While I will be fully focused on this race (like every race I run), my next great running adventure is just over the horizon.

As my running has progressed and I've gotten increasingly into racing, I always like to have my next race planned each time I race. I never look past a race, but I always like to have something to look forward to after I finish a race. It can be something really exciting like a marathon or my first track meet, or a simple 5K. Over the years, I've had a lot of running "firsts" – my first 5K; my first 10K; my first half; my first marathon; a mile, 5K, and half all in one day; and my first track meet. These have each been exciting milestones and great adventures, and each has meant a lot to me.

The other thing that's changed over the past few years is that I've become more and more aggressive about planning races. As Anne knows all too well, I've rarely seen a race that doesn't appeal to me. Sticking a calendar of races in front of me is a bit like plopping me down in front of a breakfast buffet. I just want to feast. In the past year alone, I've run at least one race at each of these distances:

200 meter

400 meter

800 meter

1600 meter (and mile)

5K

4.5 miles (actually 4.47)

5 miles

10K

1/2 marathon, and

marathon.

But, with all that, I think my next running adventure may top those all. After Burlington, Erika and I got to talking and writing about "what next." And I have to say, "She started it." But I mean that as a compliment. She came up with this 2 for 1 marathon idea. That is, we spend so much time training for a marathon, why not run two marathons for your training dollar? After all, we run a marathon just three weeks after running 22 miles. And the actual race is only four miles longer. It kind of made sense, and there are certainly a lot of people out there who have done this. Initially we explored a race soon after Burlington, but that didn't work out.

But I'm pleased to say that I have a running partner who's just as willing to dive into crazy running adventures as I am. So the idea didn't die there. For Erika, this was driven in part by striving towards running a full or half marathon in all 50 states and crossing more Northeast states off of that list. For me, 10 years older, and with fewer races under my belt, I'm not thinking about that. But I was drawn by the adventure, the audacity, and the camaraderie of the idea. And while I'll admit I felt some trepidation (and still do) once I got it into my head, it was tough to shake it. For me, this was also driven by the fact that we may not be next door neighbors forever and I wanted to take the chance to train together while I know we can.

We made the ultimate decision in phases. We began by deciding that we could at least commit to running one fall marathon together and both signed up for the Philadelphia Marathon in November. Then we took our time deciding on whether to run a second. This was not an easy decision to make given the life commitments we each have. But the allure of doing this was pretty strong. So, a week ago today, we ultimately decided to go for it and signed up for the Loco Marathon in Newmarket, NH. Four weeks earlier than Philly to the day. I know, a fitting name.

This is not just a whim. We've got a training plan and, while neither of us have done THIS before, we're not novices here and we know what we're doing. So I feel confident we will be smart and strategic about the training. But, more important than that, I think this will be an incredible running and life experience. Running 26.2 miles once is a big deal and a big accomplishment. The challenge of doing it twice in a four week span draws in my spirit almost like a tractor beam. If you've known me for a while, you know how I am about stuff like this. I'm looking forward to my biggest running challenge yet perhaps more than any other. I know it will be grueling. I know how my body feels in the weeks following a marathon and I know this is asking a lot. But I also feel confident that this is quite doable and that we can both handle this.

This is not something that I would have done on my own. I'm fortunate enough to have a running partner in Erika who lives right next door, trains at the same pace, and has the drive and dedication to take on a challenge like this. And, at the same time, provides great support around every turn. When you put all of that together, it feels like a pretty short leap of faith. What seems like an almost overwhelming challenge on my own, seems completely feasible as a team. And not only that, but a whole lot of fun. No really, it will be fun. At least in the twisted world of marathon runners anyway. And however we do in these marathons, it is sure to be a great adventure.

Looking back, I have absolutely zero regrets about how I ran in this race. It was a hot day and a tough course, with a steep hill repeated three times. I failed to get the PR I was seeking again. But, looking back, I was running better and stronger than I gave myself credit for at the time. The result was disappointing, but the effort was right where it needed to be.

A Tough Race, July 19, 2015

Kevin and I had a tough race in Brockton today. It was hot, about 80 degrees at race start, and this course featured a tough, steep hill that got repeated three times. I have to say I think I did everything right today, and it just didn't happen for me. I can point to the hills and the heat and they were absolutely factors. But I also know I'm just not running as well as I'd like to right now. But, in the final analysis, I gave all I had, I had the right mindset going into the race, and I prepared well. My body just isn't there right now. And Kevin had an equally tough race today. Both of us faded consistently over the course of the race and just couldn't hold on.

I'm a firm believer that character is illuminated most brightly in times of failure, in times of struggle, under the test of adversity. Granted, this is just running, this is not real life adversity. But, in the microcosm of my running world, I am being tested right now. And, after a discouraging race like today's my resolve is only heightened. This is not about going all out and running myself into the ground. In fact, I'm going to back off my training a little bit this week, as my body is clearly sending me a message. But my mindset and emotional outlook about my running remains as strong, aggressive, and positive as it has ever been. I will not be racing next week for sure, but I am eyeing two more races in August. And, in the meantime, my marathon training with Erika will continue to progress. And, when I have my next great race, I will look back to this time and now that my strength and my success flows directly from getting my butt kicked today.

No journey worth taking is without adversity, without dead ends, without struggle. Today was but another step in my odyssey as a runner. And as I emerge from today's struggle, my head is held high. And I know better than ever that I am a runner. And I am not to be stopped. I will take this discouragement and this disappointment and use it to feed my future success. As always, it's about the journey. And I can't wait until the next step.

Looking back in hindsight again I can see that I was really running pretty well. But rebound runs are as much about the emotional rebound as the physical rebound. In this case, it was another really tough run due to the heat and humidity. But this time I felt great about both the effort and the result.

The Rebound Run, July 22, 2015

One of the silver linings of a poor run is that, 9 times out of 10, the next one is much better. Such was the case tonight, as I had a great rebound run. It was hot tonight, about 88 degrees when I started running. Really hot. And humid too I ran from Hingham High, where I dropped Kevin off to help coach South Shore Fireboltz. My legs didn't feel sore from my Sunday 10K, but they felt flat and weary, just kind of dead and low energy. The plan tonight was to run 1 mile easy, 5 @ 7:45 pace, then 1 easy cool down mile. This was actually a little tougher than my original planned run which was 5 @ 8:00 pace, but I wanted to push the pace a tiny bit.

My first mile wasn't that slow, at 7:50, and I had a good feeling about tonight. Miles 2 and 3 were 7:35 and 7:34 respectively. I was running through some rolling hills and flying through my water. As I neared the end of mile 4, I was starting to worry a bit. I was fading a little bit, but also feeling like I needed to pay attention to make sure I didn't get dehydrated and pass out. I was losing a lot of fluids! That mile split was 7:58. So I decided to treat this kind of like an interval and walked for two minutes and drank a lot before I picked back up. Then, shortly after, I stopped for water at that general store/convenience store on Main Street because I was almost out. I had no money, but I was desperate and the guy just gave me a bottle of water. I think I looked like I was in dire straits. After the water, I rebounded a bit and ran 7:50 and 7:47 for the last two 7:45 miles – not bad. In fact, those miles 5 and 6 were faster than my 5th and 6th miles in my 10K race on Sunday! Then I just had my cool down mile and I was done.

I was totally spent at the end, but felt really good about the way I hung in and kept my splits pretty steady on a very hot night! This was exactly the run I was hoping for tonight – a cleansing run. By the way, I did stop back by the store on the way home and paid for the water! After bike and core tomorrow, my next test will be 800 m intervals on Thursday, but it should be a bit cooler by then, so those should go well.

Running partnership was a key to my running year, most of all with Erika. But now I had an additional running colleague in Mike and this support continued to be very valuable in down times, and fun in good times. My 2015 running year really revolved around my running partnership with Erika, even on the days when we weren't running together. Not only was Erika really helpful and supportive, but also just a lot of fun!

With A Little Help From My Friends, July 31, 2015

I've been in a running slump recently. I'm working hard. Really hard. I've changed my diet – cutting out junk food, desserts, and beer. I've lost 8 pounds compared with my peak weight earlier this spring/summer. I've cut back coffee to sleep better. I've worked hard at running, cross training, and core. I've never worked harder. But nothing is coming easily. And I'm fading on a lot of my runs. Sometimes just a bit, sometimes dramatically. This culminated with another disappointing run on Thursday AM. I was trying to hit some aggressive splits as kind of a dress rehearsal for a 5K on Saturday. If I ran well on Thursday, I was planning to sign up for the 5K on Saturday. Well, I won't be running that race. To be fair, my overall times weren't that bad. But, for the times I was trying to hit, it was awful. And hugely disappointing to me.

I've got a pretty good sense of my strengths and weaknesses. What I do well and what my limitations are. When I set goals, I take that all into account. So, while this may sound a bit snooty, when I set a goal, I know what I'm doing and I expect to meet it. Maybe not right away. And it may be really tough, but I expect to meet it. And, when I don't, I can be very hard on myself. That's where I was at yesterday.

When a hitter is in a slump in baseball, it can feel like they'll never get another hit again. Of course they will, but sometimes it's hard to see that in the depths of a slump. You take extra batting practice, you look at video, you work for hours, you do everything you can think of, and nothing gets better. Even when you hit a hard line drive, it gets caught. At times like that, you just need a break. A little bloop single. A "ground ball with eyes." A 45 foot chopper down the third base line. Anything just to get you back on track. That's me with my running right now. I just need a bloop hit. Doesn't have to be anything special, just a good solid run. A win of sorts where I meet my goals for a run and run a solid run.

Along the way, in addition to all of my own training, I've gained an excellent running support system. That's been a lot of fun along the way and added a lot of enjoyment to my running journey. But it's perhaps most important at times like this. When you're struggling and need a boost to get back on track. So yesterday, I reached out to my two most important running partners – Erika and Mike. From Erika, I got an awesome, thoughtful email about how things are going, providing great perspective and thoughts about how to get back on track. I'm not just talking about a simple pat on the back, it will get better message. This was meaningful and thorough. And, her latest inspirational writing on my front walk, which I'll post along with this on FB. From Mike, who is recovering from his own Achilles tendon injury, I got a suggested alternative course to run

– both for a change of scene and a different running surface. Plus an offer to run together when his Achilles heals sufficiently. Earlier this year, a change of scene helped me a lot, and I'm thinking it can again.

Now, with this support, I'm no longer hanging my head, but rather looking ahead with positive anticipation. Does this mean I'm magically running well? Well, no, not yet. But, with running, next to staying injury free and healthy, a positive mindset is the most important thing you can have. And now, thanks to my running friends, I've got a more positive vision and thought process. I'm not out of my slump yet. But I'm just one bloop hit away. And thanks to great friends and running partners, I've been reminded that I can do this. And I'm already looking forward to my next run – with spirit, with heart, and with a smile.

This was the start of a very strong month of running for me, and the start of a marathon PR. This was a pretty typical long run for Erika and me – strong, steady, and enjoyable. July was a wearing month for me tinged with some disappointment, but a run like this really helped me feel back on track!

Now That's More Like It!, August 2, 2015

This morning's run was great! While there may be a handful of factors that contributed to this success, I think it comes down to three keys:

1. I was well rested.

2. It was a beautiful, cool, lower humidity morning.

3. I was back running with Erika.

Although the past couple of days were wearing ones at Kevin's track meet, I was not running, nor doing any workouts, And I made a real point to stay hydrated and stay in the shade for a lot of the time. I think those two days really helped my weary legs to recover and feel strong again. While today wasn't an especially fast run, the pace was decent, it was steady and

I felt strong all the way through the last mile. We went 14 miles at an average 8:10 pace – pretty solid run for us.

It was nice and cool this morning – in the 60s – and that felt great. Clearly running in the 80s, or even upper 70s, saps a lot more energy than running in this beautiful weather. And, as Anne pointed out when I got home, that definitely affected these runs when I've struggled. Running in these cooler temperatures made that really clear, as I felt great out there. Just solid and strong throughout.

Then, as always is the case, running with Erika made a big difference. Having someone who just matches your pace is great to begin with. It's a steadying influence and, while we weren't locked into a pace, you find that you don't have to think about it so much. And, at least as importantly, having someone to talk with for nearly two hours makes the time pass a lot quicker and keeps your mind from wandering to how you're feeling and questioning how you're doing. And that made a big difference mentally and really made the miles fly by.

A wonderful run on a wonderful morning. And this run reminded me of how much I love running, and why I think the Long Run will always be my favorite. There's something about just getting out there and going and going for hours at a time. It's different than short and medium distance runs and there's something very cathartic about it. I've gotten to the point where I can't imagine a weekend without a long run. And today's run was one of the better ones. What a great way to start the day!

I absolutely love this blog entry. It captures the spirit and energy of my marathon training so well. My mindset at this point was excellent, right where it needed to be. And my running was improving to match my mindset. This tempo run that I wrote about was so strong and it was founded on my awesome mindset. This also reflects all of the great support that Erika provided along the way, support that meant a great deal to me, both then and now.

A Sprouting Seed, August 4, 2015

Over the past few weeks I've passed on a few races that I've considered, which is unusual for me. Most recently I decided to skip the Surftown 1/2 in Rhode Island in September, and have also passed on a 5K and another track meet. On the surface, you might think that's an indicator of my enthusiasm for races dropping; a sign of my running passion and drive dipping a bit. In fact, nothing could be further from the truth.

Erika and I are signed up for a 5K on August 22, which I am looking forward to. And, I am doing speed work in addition to my long runs over the next three weeks to get ready for that race. But, to be honest, I'm already looking past that. Well, not so much looking past it, but focusing more on my marathon training now, rather than the 5K race. The way that I've run races recently that I've been tightly focused on, I think this may be a good thing for me. I may do better going into that race with a more casual attitude, and perhaps run more relaxed and free.

But, for better or worse, my mind is increasingly focused on our October marathon. Not so much the marathon itself actually, but the marathon training. More than any other race for me, a marathon is more about the journey, rather than the destination. The race itself means a great deal to me, and I take it to heart. But, when I look back on my marathons to date and think of them, the part that brings me the most pride, satisfaction and joy is reflecting back on my training. Not just individual runs, but the whole process and the entire marathon journey. In fact, the journey itself really is the destination. In that sense, I've already arrived. This one kind of snuck up on me a bit, as I was focused on so many other races post-Burlington. But, after last weekend, I feel like I am now fully immersed in marathon training. That our journey has begun. And this is the part that gets really cool, when the miles build, the momentum builds, and the energy grows. Don't get me wrong, it's exhausting, it's painful and there are always ups and downs. But if it were easy, it wouldn't mean as much as it does.

When I'm excited to write a blog, I find that the title either leaps immediately to mind OR I come up with four or five titles that I like and I have a hard time deciding. This is an example of the latter case. I went through several titles until I arrived at this one. Last week, when I was really down about my runs, Erika wrote a message on our front walk that read, "Every seed know it's time – all in good time." – Russian Proverb Then she added, "Keep Watering." And I have. I've continued to plug away with my running despite feeling down and I can sense things turning for me now. The seed is sprouting! On Sunday, we had a nice, solid 14 mile run. Then, last night, I did a 45 minute Arc Trainer workout with 30 minutes of hill repeats – grueling. Then, tonight I went out and ran a challenging 9 mile run (1 mile easy, 2 between 7:00 and 7:15 pace), 1 easy, 1 more @ 7:00 – 7:15, 1 easy, 2 more @ 7:00 – 7:15, then one last easy mile. I included a 2 minute walking recovery (on the clock) as part of my easy miles. This is a hard workout for me, but I felt optimistic.

I had originally planned to do this run in Boston and Cambridge along the Charles, which would have been awesome, but due to changes in my work schedule, I ended up doing it from home. I did a route through Bare Cove Park, then back on 3A. My first two hard miles were at 7:15 and 7:19 pace and I felt good about this. After my recovery mile, I just knew I was going to run a solid 5th mile and did – finishing that one through Bare Cove in 7:09. I was out on 3A then and took a break at CVS to fill up on water. The 7th and 8th miles would be my last fast ones. I could feel the fatigue in my legs and knew I would have to work very hard to hit my target splits for those miles. But, despite my fatigue, I felt confident and strong. I finished mile 7, coming back on Evans Street in 7:10. While I felt good about that, I was exhausted and felt like I had nothing left in the tank. But, unlike last week when I felt that way and faded, tonight I rejected the fatigue. I just refused to give in and pushed harder than ever in that 8th mile. I was working very hard, just about pushing myself to the limit. When I finished the mile and my trusty Garmin beeped, I looked down and saw 7:04 for the 8th mile.

Nice seedling, huh?

Another week, and another strong long run. I was rolling now, physically, emotionally, and mentally. I was feeling confident and strong, and I had good reason to feel that way. Yes, this one was tough at times, but I persevered through it strongly. I wasn't just strong mentally, I was relaxed. And this turned out to be a mindset that would be very important for me in Newmarket.

Despite It All, August 9, 2015

This morning's run came after three days of hearty eating and drinking for me, including an evening beer pong event last night. It was two miles longer than last week's run. And it was one of our hilliest runs ever. Despite all that, it was faster than last week, and Erika and I ran strong throughout the entire run. Not an easy run, but an excellent run. Strong and solid, and really pretty fast.

Although our route today was hilly, it was picturesque, heading out all the way to the tip of Worlds' End and back. This was our first run out there together, and it was really nice. The one flaw in the route I mapped for today was the lack of a timely water stop but, fortunately we were able to fill our water bottles at a fountain at the entrance to World's End. There were a lot of hills on this run, both in World's End, but also outside the park. These were tough and wearing, but we both ran THROUGH those hills with good pace and kept our speed up nicely.

As we got later in the run, I started to feel my stomach a bit more and took a Pepto Bismol that I carry in my water bottle holder. Once bitten, twice shy, you know. But I was hanging in pretty well despite that. Just before the last mile, I had to stop and fight off a bit of nausea. We paused for a minute, I caught my breath and we picked right back up. I started to feel some pain in my knee, which was actually welcome, as it distracted me from my upset stomach. When you become a marathoner, it's amazing how you think sometimes. We finished the last mile, including a steep hill up Chard Street, in 8:04, just below our average pace of 8:06 (or 8:05 if you use Erika's speedy watch.) And I didn't even throw up.

So we finished strong, despite it all. And now, with 11 weeks to go until our next marathon, I'm feeling strong, fast, and confident. I worked through my slump and feel like we're right on track. We're both running well, running fast, and running strong. In fact, I think we may be in a better place than we were at the same point in our Burlington training. And, as I always feel when I'm running well, I can't wait until the next long run. I might even have to have a beer or two the night before.

Next to the long run, my favorite run of all is a "bonus run". Bonus runs are extra, unplanned runs that just work out. And, when they do, they're often the most fun of all. Especially when I get to do them with my running buddy!

A Bonus Run, August 10, 2015

When I have vacation time, I always like to take one more extra day at the end to stay home, relax, and gather myself. So after a really fun weekend with my Mom, my brother and his family visiting, I took today as an extra day off before I return to work.

Erika had a run planned today, so we took the opportunity to get out for a bonus run together. It was a nice day, sunny and warm, but nice and clear and manageable. We were running a 5 mile loop through Bare Cove Park with enough hills to keep things interesting. I believe the last time I ran there, we were running through a narrow tunnel of snow, single file most of the time. Ah the good ole days.

This run came the day after a 16 mile run for both of us, so it was intended to be an easy pace run. Turns out the "easy pace" run was at marathon race pace. Still only 5 miles, but I took it as an encouraging sign that the easy pace we defaulted to was our marathon race pace. We also had the added bonus of pushing Erika's son Carter in their running stroller. Not really a bonus for Erika as she does that all the time, but it was for me! Extra work! I took over pushing in mile 3 and got a little carried away, running a 7:38 mile! I was trying so hard not to slow down that I ended up going a lot faster than I intended. But my legs were also a lot stronger than I thought they would be the day after 16 miles and I was running strong again. In fact, I've only had one day off from running and cross training since last Saturday – I've been working really hard with two "bonus runs" in the past four days.

After that fast third mile we settled back into a more even 8:00 pace for the last two miles and, since I was having so much fun, I pushed the stroller the rest of the way. I was pretty worn out by the end. But the important thing is that my legs and body feel really strong. I did an upper body workout when I got home to keep up with my core work. Tomorrow will feature a track workout – mile repeats. That's a hard workout, but I'm feeling ready for it – both physically and mentally. And for now, just appreciating the fact that I got another bonus run today.

This was a cool race – a mid-week race with Kevin, which was a lot of fun. I was very sore warming up and had trouble running at all, let alone racing. But I warmed up through the soreness and ended up running a really strong race. I was able to run most of it with Kevin. And while it was shy of PR pace, given how I was feeling, this was really an excellent effort.

An Ego Boost, August 12, 2015

Today Kevin and I went down to Abington to run in a Colonial Road Runners Fun Run. It was a 3.28 mile race (totally random distance) and only $2. But it was timed with a clock and measured so it made for a good practice race in lieu of my mile intervals on the track tonight.

To set the stage, my hamstrings were sore all day today. I had run 16 miles on Sunday, then 5 more on Monday and run or done cross training for 9 of the last 10 days. I have been working very hard and my body was feeling the effects today. I hurt every time I stood up from my desk and walked. But I decided to give it a whirl and go down there and see what I could do. We were fortunate to dodge the rain tonight, only a tiny bit of sprinkles at the very end. But it was soupy!

Warming up was brutal. I mean I could barely run at all. In my first warm up lap around the school where the race was, I was stiff and every step hurt. And I thought well, at least I only paid $2 for this. But then the 2nd lap was a bit better. Then I did calisthenics, then stretching, then another lap and I started to feel almost decent. Then some more stretching. I decided that if I was going to run this race, I might as well get serious, so I did a couple of strides, gradually building to close to a full sprint before easing off. And, while they were painful, and I was still a bit stiff, the speed was there behind the pain. And I thought, hey maybe I can race tonight after all.

When we stepped to the line, a loosely defined area of the school parking lot, I honestly didn't expect much. But then, a funny thing happened. They started the race, and I went out nice and easy, 3rd behind Kevin and another high school kid – I think. So here I am going nice and easy and wondering where everyone is. I mean it was a small race and not super competitive, but I figure I'm in the upper 7:00s – got to be somebody around me. I look down at my watch and I'm running around 6:15 – 6:20 pace – no pain – and it felt like about 7:45! Yikes, where did this come from. I don't even feel winded to start.

So I figure I might as well try to pace Kevin. He had already run this morning and it turns out he was having shin pain, so he wasn't having his best night and I was able to pass the other kid and catch up with Kevin. At the end of the first mile, my watch read 6:45, but Kevin had it at 6:38 at the mile marker, which is probably more accurate. And I'm thinking, wow, I'm hanging with Kevin in mile 2! Yeah, he wasn't having his best race, but the pace wasn't bad and, running together, we started to pick it up in the 2nd mile, getting the pace down to an even 6:00 at times, and finishing that 2nd mile at 6:24. By that point the humidity and the fatigue was catching up with both of us and we both began to fade – me more than Kevin. My 3rd mile was in 7:13 – Kevin's was probably about 10 seconds faster. I glanced at my watch and I was at 21:02 at the 5K mark, only 41 seconds off my PR on a night when I wasn't even sure if I could run even decently. And there wasn't even a finishing kick there, so a really solid 5K time for tonight. I finished the race in 22:19, 2nd behind Kevin, and well ahead of the 3rd place runner – like a solid minute or so. Since it was a 3.28 mile race, we ran a 0.72 mile cool down. I'm serious, I hate these random distance numbers.

This was a great race on a tough night, when my legs felt like they had virtually nothing. And I passed this challenge with flying colors. At the end, I was being recruited to join the Colonial Road Runners. Like I said, a nice ego boost. This is the 2nd race that Kevin and I have run together where we ran most of the race together and ended up finishing 1-2 – with Kevin of course being 1st! I thought those days were over, so this was an added bonus for me tonight to be able to run a good part of this race together. A really, really fun race and a night when I totally shattered my own expectations.

This was a birthday run for me, and it was a treat to do a long run with Kevin on my birthday. What I didn't realize beforehand was that, not only would this be Kevin's longest run to date, it would also be the first time he had run a half marathon distance! Very cool! Note: Although this was written on my birthday on August 15, I didn't post the blog until August 18 and I've used the actual blog posting date here.

Kevin's First Half, August 18, 2015

Today, Kevin and I were running in Blairstown, NJ, where we're visiting my Dad. That's out in Western New Jersey, by the Delaware Water Gap. It was nice and cool this AM, in the low 60s. It was sunny, but there was a lot of shade on the trail, so it was cool. We were running on a nice flat rail trail called the Paulinskill Valley Trail. It was a dirt trail and, every now and then, we had to dodge some muddy spots, or horse poop, but it was a pretty easy, smooth surface to run on.

Oh, and it's my birthday today too! I can't think of a better way to start it than going on a long run with Kevin. So we were planning on 12 today, which would tie Kevin's longest run ever. We were shooting for an even 8:00 pace on this run. We were planning on an out and back run – 6 miles out and 6 miles back. When we got to the 5 mile mark, I was feeling good and asked Kevin if he wanted to add a mile – which would really be adding two miles. Of course, he agreed – that's like asking Napoleon whether he wants an extra dog biscuit.

When we got to the 7 mile mark, we were at 56:17, just over pace, but pretty close. I decided we should take a short break – 1 minute walking – off the clock. That paid immediate dividends, as we hit mile 8 in 7:33, and every mile the rest of the way was under 8:00. When we got to mile 10, Kevin asked if I could let him know when we hit 13.1. And then it hit me, that Kevin would be running his first half today. Not a race, but still running 13.1. Pretty cool. So we kept on flying along with great pace and finished our half in 1:43:10! Congratulations Kevin!!

From there, we ran a cool down pace the rest of that mile, but still finished the whole run in 1:51:06, at a 7:56 pace. We both had sore knees, were soaked in sweat and had mud splattered all over our legs. My GU flask was empty, my water bottle was empty, and my calf behind my knee was throbbing with pain. But I was there for Kevin's 1st half, and his longest run to date! Just a great morning run. Overall, our 2nd 7 miles was 54:49, compared to 56:17 for our first seven. Now that is a quality run!

After we got back, I jumped into my Dad's pond, which was nice and cool and felt great on my aching legs! I'll have to take another dip later. But for now, I'm relishing my morning coffee and the afterglow of a wonderful birthday morning run. And, as I often do when I run, I'm feeling grateful for ALL the wonderful people and the joy in my life. Happy Birthday to me!

My awesome mindset continued through this 5K today. Being in the right place mentally and emotionally is so important as a runner, and I was doing great now! And, while it didn't pay off today, it would in a couple of months.

A Phoenix Rising from Disappointment, August 22, 2015

I've had a number of races this summer that have finished with disappointing results for me. Most recently, Erika and I ran a 5K today in which neither of us met our goals for the race. It was very humid, but when you lay yourself out there, you're not interested in excuses. When you train as hard as we've trained, you want the bottom line result in your race time. And anything less than that feels disappointing, regardless of all the other circumstances. It's a legitimate emotion and, I believe, properly played, is a beneficial one.

Earlier in the summer, I felt anger and frustration mixed with my post-race disappointment. It was a bad way to feel, but it took me a little while to get past it. This was not a matter of throwing up my hands and saying "Oh well, that's OK." It was not that simple. I am competitive, fueled by drive and passion, and you can't just say that and not worry. I was helped out a lot by great support from my running support system – particularly my running partner Erika. And I emerged from that disappointment stronger and better in every way – like a phoenix rising from the ashes. While I didn't get the 5K PR I was seeking today, and I faded late in the humidity, I know that I am running better and stronger than I was a month ago. And I know that PR, and more, are just around the bend.

The difference is that my mind and spirit were flooded by confidence and pride, which washed away the anger and frustration. The disappointment in my race results is still there, but my emotions are overwhelmingly positive. I'm ready to run in every way, my running spirits are soaring, and I just want to go. I am strong physically, emotionally, and psychologically. Rather than dragging me down, my disappointment only fuels me now. It's not so much that I think I'm going to get a PR. I KNOW I will. And not just one. I can't say when for sure, but I know it will happen.

When I think about running, I often think about means and ends. Typically the training is the means and the race results are the end. I do feel that way to a great degree. I really care about how I race when I'm really going all out. That matters to me a lot. And I will always consider races to be a bottom line result for me.

But I realized something else today. This spirit; this emotional cocktail of disappointment, pride, confidence, determination, and will; training so hard with Erika and running these races together; laying my heart and soul on the line only to rebound stronger; that's IT. That's both the journey and destination – all wrapped up together in a neat bundle.

So yeah I didn't get the race result I wanted today. And that matters. But I am not defeated. I am not beaten. I will rise from this better and stronger than before. I am a runner and I am strong – in body, mind and spirit. I have arrived and yet my journey continues. The road ahead is not an easy one. Just the way I like it. Today was an important reminder for me that, even though I didn't meet my goal today, I can do anything I set my mind to. And my mind is set. And the pile of ashes is now a distant speck in the rear view mirror.

This was one of our toughest runs of the year, a character run. The fact that we decided to extend this run from 12 to 18 miles, the day after running a 5K race speaks volumes about Erika and me. It ended up being an ugly run late, but it was a strong run both physically and mentally.

Relentless, August 23, 2015

Two hundred and seven people ran the Jamie Fund 5K Race in Mansfield yesterday. I'm going to go out on a limb and guess that only two of them ran 18 miles this morning. I think you can guess who.

This run had been in my plan all along but both Erika and I questioned doing 18 miles the day after a 5K race. So we actually structured this run as a 12 mile run first, with the idea that we would reevaluate after running the 12. We could then decide to stop at 12, or do any other increment up to 18.

It was drizzling from the moment we started and between that and the humidity (which actually kind of seemed like one and the same) we were wet pretty quickly. We started out at a pretty decent pace around 8:00 or so, but we were both feeling yesterday's race in our legs from the very beginning today. And while we were running OK, I think we both had doubts about doing the full 18. We were doing a nice 12 mile route today – out to Webb Park and back through Bare Cove Park. But it wasn't too scenic today with the rain and hazy weather. Plus my glasses were covered with rain drops and fogged over for most of the run. We both hung in pretty well for the 12 mile stretch, but were definitely tired and feeling a lot of fatigue in our legs after finishing the 12.

At home after the 12, we had a choice to make. There would have been no shame in stopping at 12 miles – that in itself was a good, hard demanding run today. But, the decision seemed like an easy one. And, fortunately I have a running partner who's just as relentless as I am. So we filled up our water bottles and off we went. We agreed that the last six miles would be at a slower pace and it absolutely was. But this was not about speed at this point. This was about endurance, determination and will.

When you're a runner and accomplish goals that you set for yourself that's extremely rewarding. But some of my greatest moments in running are when I've accomplished things that I just didn't think I could do. Today's run was on the verge of this category. It's one thing to write it on paper in a training plan. It's entirely different to go out and DO IT. While our last six miles were ugly from a pace standpoint, they were beautiful miles in terms of will and determination. We set out to do a very challenging run and absolutely nailed it. And when you complete a run like that, somehow all the pain and exhaustion feels worth it.

In the wake of the run, I lost five pounds, the skin on my fingers is like prunes, and my legs are absolutely drained. I may be relentless, but I am not foolish. This run was by design, but I know I put my body through a lot today. And I will be focused on recovery today – rehydrating, refueling, icing, rolling and heating, getting ready for the next run.

While the long run is typically my favorite, this particular run is probably the most fun I've ever had on a training run. Running intervals with Erika was great to begin with, but the bonus intervals at the end are what made this workout so much fun and so special. Every time I think back to this workout, I smile. Fun, just so much fun!

Gluttons for Punishment, August 25, 2015

I am pretty sure today was the first track workout I've ever done together with Erika. Normally our schedules don't work out to afford this, but it worked for once today, so it was a great opportunity. This was my planned workout today — 6 x 800 meter repeats at 3:10 each, with a mile warm up and cool down. These are fast, as intervals are, but not that fast for us for 800 m repeats. The real challenge with all of these is to run them relatively consistently. I was really looking forward to having company for track intervals for a change – in particular Erika – whom I knew could match these splits at a nice steady pace. I knew that would help me a lot – and hopefully vice versa too.

It was cool enough, but still humid out. We headed over at 6:00 AM and it must have been close to 6:30 when we started in earnest. I don't have all the splits, but I believe they were all between 3:03 and 3:11. And the 3:03 was the last one, when Erika decided to kick the final 100 meters – just for fun. Of course I joined in, how could I resist a finishing kick? We were doing 200 m walking recovery intervals after each interval so, after that recovery for the last lap I got ready to line up to cool down. But Erika lined up to start another 800m and said let's do one more. I looked over long enough to see whether she was actually serious and realized yes, in fact she was.

Well there's really only one response to that, so I lined up for interval #7 and off we went. And we nailed it, finishing it in 3:04. So we walked our recovery interval and Erika asked what I wanted to do for the cool down. I responded, "A mile", then grinned, and said, "But it's not time for that yet." It was her turn to gauge if I was serious – which of course I was. I mean here we were with an odd number of intervals and an extra 1/2 mile sticking out there, and that would never do. So we lined up for interval #8 and nailed that one too in 3:07.

At this point, we really were done, and ran our mile cool down to wrap up the full 6 mile workout. I've got to say that was one of the most fun runs I've had in a long time. Running intervals doesn't give the same chance for chatting as long runs do, but the run itself was so much fun. And I know that, in the end, running this workout together helped both of us run faster, steadier, and farther than we would have on our own. And the two extra 800s? I'd say those were the most fun of all!

I was 100% focused on my marathon training now and I was running great. Erika and I did a number of these early AM training runs last summer and I really appreciated them. Not many people are willing to get up and run HARD at 5:00 AM and I valued that a lot. Marathon training is such a demanding and rewarding experience and I was neck deep in it now.

Working Hard (& Lovin' Every Minute of It), August 27, 2015

When you run marathons, every once in a while, someone will ask you, "Why?" The basic answer to this is simple. It's about taking on a great challenge, working hard towards a goal, and realizing the great satisfaction that comes from that. But that kind of simple answer doesn't come anywhere near explaining the depth and richness of the marathon experience. And, honestly, I don't think you can ever fully get it unless you train for and run a marathon yourself.

In some ways, running a marathon is like anything else that you work towards over a long period – a big project at work, a college or grad school thesis, or a big landscaping or home renovation project. But, unlike a marathon, all of these things have their own benefits and purposes. But when you finish a marathon, that's it. That's the reward, the benefit. There's really nothing else. So you better really want to run and train for that marathon! The other difference with a marathon (or other similar athletic endurance events) is that they combine a unique set of emotional, mental, and physical challenges to overcome. So, to be successful, you need to be emotionally strong, mentally strong, and physically strong.

Races are what got me hooked on running. And I still get really amped up for races and feed off of that energy and motivation. But I also have come to really enjoy training for races, and sinking myself into training plans. In the case of marathons, while the races themselves hold great meaning for me, I find the training odyssey to be the most meaningful part of the marathon experience. It is so long and so extensive, brings you through so many highs and lows, and tests you in so many different ways. That was certainly true when I trained for my first two marathons on my own. Now that I am running with Erika and we are going through this training odyssey together, the shared training experience is even richer.

In a sense, I have been in marathon training mode for about 2 and 1/2 months now. But, because I ran several other races along the way, I wasn't 100% focused on marathon training. I still had one eye on these shorter races. But, when Erika and I completed our 5K last Saturday, that was the last remaining race prior to our first fall marathon on October 25 in Newmarket, NH.

Now a switch has been flipped inside of me. And, seemingly all of a sudden, I am 100% in marathon training mode – physically, mentally, and emotionally. I am locked in. This week, following a 5K race on Saturday, I will be running 60 miles in 7 days (counting 8 hard elliptical miles.) And all are tough miles. On Tuesday, Erika and I ran a hard 6 mile track workout. That was followed by a very hard 8 mile elliptical workout on Wednesday night. Then, Erika and I got up to run another 8 miles at 5:00 AM today! And that run tells you all you need to know right now.

I was very tired after last night's elliptical workout. And getting up at 4:15 AM was tough. Our planned run was 1 easy mile, 6 miles at a 7:45 pace, and then an easy cool down mile. I was concerned I was going to fade on this run so, once we got to the tempo portion, I really worked hard to sustain my pace. And Erika was running equally strong. Our first tempo mile was 7:41, a good start. Turns out that was the slowest tempo mile of the whole run and we ended up averaging a 7:34 pace, for the tempo portion, including the last mile in 7:28! This was an aggressive run and a strong run. It was not easy for me to sustain my pace, but I worked hard throughout to make sure I didn't fade.

In the wake of the run, my legs are tired, I have some soreness, and I desperately need a day off. We will be moving our long run up to Saturday this week and that will be 20 miles – my first 20 miler of this training session. So I'm moving my planned bike workout for tomorrow to

Sunday, and will make that a post long run recovery workout. And I'll "just do core" on Friday.

So I'm tired, sore, and kind of beat, But I'm also elated! This is the depth and richness of the experience I referred to earlier. The experience of getting up and running in the dark at 5:00 AM, pushing through sleepiness and fatigue, pushing myself mentally and physically to stick the pace, and absolutely nailing the run. And then, after a day's rest, getting back out there and running 20 miles. This is the part I love the most – the meat of the marathon training. When you work so hard day after day, week after week, and you see the results. Of course, you don't always get this on every run. Some runs are brutal, discouraging, painful, and disappointing. But then you have runs like these and it's difficult to describe how great it feels. And how you can't wait to get out there again. To run hard, to push your mind, work your body, rest. and then do it again. These days I'm focusing just as much on my rest, recovery, diet, and hydration, as I am on my running.

I am in full-fledged marathon training mode and it's a great place to be. I'm sinking myself into the work, the fatigue, the soreness, the intensity of the marathon odyssey. It's hard work and I'm loving every minute of it!

This blog pretty much speaks for itself. I love long runs in general but, when you get up to 20 plus miles, those are a bit different. They're just so long that they really test you, even when you're in great shape and running great. This one was awesome and, despite all the soreness, I knew I was right where I needed to be. And, once again, this run was highlighted by Erika's companionship, support, and toughness. Yes, I was running great, but we were also running great as a team!

A Strong 18 – No Wait 20 – Mile Run, August 29, 2015

I have a clear hierarchy against which I evaluate every run I do. I generally have a positive mindset about my running, so most of my runs end up in the upper portions of that hierarchy. Recently I've had a streak of very good runs that rank very high on my running hierarchy. In short, this has been an awesome running week. This week was particularly cool because Erika and I had the unique opportunity to run together five times in eight days. That won't happen again for a very long time. I suppose it's only fitting that, in this awesome week of running together, that we closed it out with the best run of all. In fact, I'd say that this week included two of my favorite runs ever – quite a week!

I had this run slated for 20 miles on my schedule, but Erika was wavering between 20 and 18 miles, so we initially planned this as an 18 mile run, with the plan that we would figure out the last two at the end. It's a beautiful morning here. It's probably in the low 70s now, but it was 60 degrees when we started, clear, pretty dry, and very comfortable. Super running weather! We headed out through Jackson Square and got off to a fast start, running our first "easy" mile in 7:48. That was a sign of good things to come! We were headed to Wompatuck, where we ran through the park to the Whitney-Thayer Woods Trail and out to Cohasset. Though we slowed a bit from that first mile, we were consistently hitting splits just over, or sometimes just under, 8:00, a really strong pace for us for a long run. This is one of my favorite stretches to run, and I was enjoying it today. Just a beautiful day with great company, and we were running strong and steady. This was one of the many runs we have when I just feel so grateful – for the ability to run like this, to have such a great day, and to have such a great running partner.

After that trail, we crossed 3A and turned onto East Street, headed over to 228. Then we went almost to Hull, before we turned back towards Hingham Harbor. Right around mile 9, we hit the first real challenge of the run for me, after we stopped for water at Tedeschi's. After we got our water, we headed back out and my legs and back felt very stiff, sore, and tight. Even on a great, great run, it's not easy. But I loosened up after a bit. A good thing too, because soon after that, around mile 10, we fit our first real hill of the run. Of course we crushed it.

From there, we turned through Downtown Hingham and then took Lincoln Street back out to 3A. Still running strong and steady throughout – just nailing this run mile after mile after mile after mile after mile. Well, you get the idea. Right after mile 14, we made our second water stop at CVS. Getting started back up was even harder this time. But we did it of course. At about 14.5, we reached the intersection of 3A and Green Street. I won't trouble you with our advanced math, but Erika decided she definitely did want to go 20 miles today and, given all that advanced math, this was a good time to make that decision. So we hung a right on Neck Street, headed out to Webb Park to add some miles. Gluttons for punishment, you know? And still, so strong and steady. EVERY. SINGLE. MILE.

I was sore pretty much everywhere now, including my knee, my back, my hips, my butt, my calves, and intestinal cramps. But we are crushing this run, I know it, and I'm loving it! For whatever reason, our GPS watches seemed a bit slow today, so the out and back distance that we thought would give us the 20 miles was coming up a bit short. But, no matter, we could run more! Coming home on Green Street, in mile 19, we were both pretty much spent. And we had the biggest hill of the run, coming up Commercial Street, in mile 20. But we were not just having a great 18 mile run today, we were having a great 20 mile run!

I'm not going to lie – that hill was brutal – but we beat it, as we knew we would. We still had to add a bit more distance, so we tacked on a loop through Legion Field, where we were thrilled to see the sprinklers going. And we took full advantage of those. From there, it was a bit tedious, stretching out the run to get the full 20 miles, even on my watch, which was running behind Erika's. We finished the 20 mile run in about 2:42:15 – probably a bit quicker on Erika's watch. 8:06 pace.

So here we are, 8 weeks out – running 20 miles at an 8:06 pace – just over target race pace. This was such a strong, strong run and leaves us at a great place in our training. This is the kind of run where I get back, go through all the various recovery work, feel the pain, the soreness, the stiffness, and the fatigue. And I just can't help but smile. Because I know I just reached the very top of my running hierarchy. This is the kind of run that sticks in your psyche for a long, long time. In fact, I'd be willing to bet that I think about this run on RACE DAY on October 25. Because I know how strong we are. Not just for 18 miles. And not just for 20 miles either. I know that we are strong for 26.2 miles.

This blog summarizes August perfectly and really requires no further introduction.

A Month to Be Proud Of, August 31, 2015

In the month of August, I ran 141 miles. And, when adding in equivalent miles from treadmill and bike workouts, "ran" a total of 178 miles. And, virtually every single workout was tough in some way, either due to speed intervals, tempo, or distance. But what stands out for me most about August was how hard I worked – in every single way.

July was a bit of a disappointing month for me, especially in terms of my races. I realize now that I was asking and expecting my body to do things that it just wasn't ready for. I hadn't recovered fully from the combination of the Burlington Marathon on Memorial Day weekend and my punishing track meet in late June. And my legs and body just didn't have any oomph. I was working hard, but it was like beating my head against the wall. It just wasn't there for me. I can see that now, but that was tough to come to terms with in the moment.

But later in July and when the calendar turned to August all that hard work began to pay off and I began to turn the corner. And I continued to work hard – every single day. I wasn't just running hard. I was doing tough cross training and core workouts. And, while I gave myself a bit of a break for a couple of family visits and vacations, I really tightened up my diet and focused on getting better sleep – at the expense of other free time. And, in the end, I believe August of 2015 may be the most rigorous, intense, disciplined, and determined month of training that I've ever had.

All that effort, discipline, determination and running spirit paid off in the results I saw in my training runs. I've run faster before, but I don't know if I've ever run better nor trained better. While the highlight of this month will always be the great eight day stretch when Erika and I got in five runs together, I've also had some great solo runs and workouts.

I entered August beginning to rise from a down stretch. And now I'm running perhaps stronger and surer than I ever have. And as I look back at how I ran through and conquered adversity and disappointment, I am filled with confidence, joy and pride. But, perhaps most important of all, as our marathon training enters the peak stage, my determination and will is stronger than ever. And as September lies just hours away, I can't wait to continue to pour myself into my training. Looking back with just a tiny amount of hindsight, I really do think that I've never worked harder than I worked in August of 2015. But that's only because September hasn't started yet.

This track workout showed just how strong and fast I had become as a runner. I beat these target splits by a lot and it came pretty easily for me. That wouldn't be such a big deal if it were just 3 or 4 400s, but do to that for 12 straight is pretty impressive. And, yet again, my mindset was strong.

Poor Willpower, September 2, 2015

My planned run tonight was a track workout. I headed over to Weymouth High to run, but there was a football scrimmage and there were people all over the track. So that wasn't going to work. A bit annoyed, I turned around and headed over to the Hingham track with my fingers crossed. And fortunately the Hingham track was wide open.

My scheduled workout was 12 x 400 meters at 1:34 each. Now I wasn't sure how I was going to run because I was a bit out of sync and frustrated and that's not how I like to run. I worked at settling down in my warm up mile and actually didn't feel that fast at first. But I still finished my warm-up at just about 8:00.

I was off from the very beginning tonight. I just couldn't hit my target splits for the life of me. I actually tried for the first four or so, but I wasn't watching my watch as I ran and I kept on missing my splits by more as I went. So after the first four, I basically gave up and just ran how I felt.

If you haven't guessed this already, I'm being tongue in cheek here. I ran all of these 400s WAY too fast! And I'm actually kind of serious about the poor willpower. There's a reason that I was planning to run these at 1:34 each and I basically blew off the planned paces as I went. And, generally speaking, that's a bad idea. But, tonight I was just flying and I couldn't hold myself back. So eventually I just let go of the reins and let it fly. In the end, I ran virtually negative splits throughout the entire workout – crazy, crazy, crazy:

1 – 1:29

2 – 1:29

3 – 1:27

4 – 1:27

5 – 1:25

6 – 1:24

7 – 1:21

8 – 1:22

9 – 1:21

10 – 1:22

11 – 1:21

12 – 1:16

This was just a nutty, silly run. The only one of these 400s that I actually tried to run really fast was the last one in 1:16. Otherwise I was just running them how I felt. I should definitely not make a habit out of this, but I let myself have this one. I think sometimes when you work so hard over an extended period, it's important to keep it fun, just ignore the pace targets every once in a while, and just run. And, I've got to say it was a blast to run like this. Smooth, quick, and light, efficient – I felt great out there. And while I let my willpower slip tonight, it sure was fun!

This was one of my toughest runs in a while and I was right on target in this blog. A couple of months ago, I would have folded like a tent. But I was stronger now, both physically and mentally and I pushed through when I was tired and sore with stomach pain.

A Punishing Run, September 4, 2015

Today, I decided to run after work along the Charles River in Boston. This was the hottest, most humid weather I've run in for a long time. I had initially planned to run 6 miles tonight with 3 of them fast at a 7:15 pace. But I dealt with some particularly unpleasant, draining topics at work today and had a long and tiring work day, so I decided I wanted a longer, extended run tonight just to clear my head. So I decided to switch to an 8 mile run, with 4 miles at a 7:30 pace. From a training standpoint, this also kind of made sense because the ratio of my long run to my weekly mileage is pretty high right now. So a little bit longer mid-week run kind of made sense. But, because I had initially planned on only 6, I didn't have a water bottle and wasn't fully prepared for this.

So the plan was 2 easy, 4 at the fast tempo and then 2 easy. I started out with an easy 8:37 first mile, which I was fine with. A bit slow and just what I wanted tonight. But as I entered the second mile, I was already feeling drained, and I thought "uh oh, this is not good." But I had a treat and a morale boost shortly after when I saw my sister-in-law's sister Cori running and she joined me for a minute. Soon after that, my stomach began rebelling a bit. Either I had eaten too much too close to the run, or not the best stuff, but I was treated to stomach discomfort and cramping off and on through the rest of the run. Nothing worse than that, but it was still uncomfortable. Throughout all that, I hit mile 2 in 7:55. I was nearly across the Mass Ave Bridge at that point, heading over to run along Memorial Drive in Cambridge.

As I picked up my pace in mile 3, I was working so hard, sweat pouring off me, stomach aching a bit, just grinding out this run. In mile 3. Not a good place to be. But the pace came to me, and I realized what would become even more clear to me throughout this run – I am in very strong running shape. I can take a punishing run and absorb the punishment. And I did, nailing mile 3 in 7:26. Shortly after that, I saw a former teammate of Kevin's who is now running at BU, and was out running with his teammates. And we said hi quickly in passing.

It's mile 4 now and I'm feeling like I'm in mile 20. Just exhausted – but pushing through it anyway. I ended up slowing a bit in mile 4, with my pace dropping to 7:39, but that's not bad. I paused briefly at the turnaround point at mile 4, took a deep breath and plunged into mile 5. I noticed a water fountain that I had missed on the way out and stopped to get a quick, desperately needed drink. There were several runners lined up for drinks there. Also hit a couple other water fountains later in the run, which I think was critical. I hung in in mile 5, at 7:38 and told myself – just one more hard mile to go. I was approaching the Mass Ave Bridge again, and my spirits were buoyed by the fact that I had just one more tough mile and was "heading home". And I dug deep, drawing from all the tough training that I've been doing, drawing from that inner strength and endurance, and drawing from my running spirit. And I crushed mile 6, in 7:27.

Part of the reason this is so gratifying for me is that I know I couldn't have done this 8 weeks ago. I would have dropped like a stone back then. But I'm a different, stronger and better runner now. And I pushed through the pain, the exhaustion, and the adversity and ended my last tempo mile strong. After so many grinding, draining runs this summer, I can see the results right in front of me and that's an awesome feeling!

The pain, discomfort and exhaustion of this run will be with me for a couple of days. I was badly dehydrated on the way home, and still am a bit, my stomach is still not quite right, and the leg soreness will kick in soon. Yes, it was a punishing run and there's no denying that. But I will have the next two days off from both running and cross training. And I will re-hydrate, refuel, and recover. But the satisfaction and confidence earned from this run will last much, much longer. And I can sit back with pride and know that I took the punishment, sucked it up, and beat this run.

I will always remember this run as the "failed water stop run." But it also happened to be a very strong 22 mile run at a key point in our training.

A Comedy of Errors, September 6, 2015

Today's run was a completely different route for Erika and me. That was kind of cool in a lot of ways but, sometimes when you venture into unfamiliar territory and you don't know routes quite as well, you run into a few surprises. And that's how it went today. I had spent a lot of time mapping it out and thought I had everything figured out, but sometimes little details crop up that you just don't anticipate. I'll get to the comedy of errors part in a little bit.

It was a nice morning here – about 60 degrees and it felt cool out. We headed out through Jackson Square and down Pleasant Street to South Weymouth, past the high school and through Columbian Square. Erika had had some knee pain but we were off to a pretty good start. We were running well – not crazy fast, but just over an 8:00 pace. We got to Route

18 just after mile 4 and turned into Southfield just after mile 5. There was a long stretch of this run without a good water stop, so I had asked Eliza to drive out and bring us an extra set of water bottles. She and Anne got to us a bit earlier than I had expected (my first error of the day), so they went and got coffee (Eliza's payment) and then met us a bit farther along about mile 6 or so.

This was an entirely new place for both of us to run. We ran through Southfield all the way up until mile 9, and were continuing to run steady and strong. In fact, we hit sub-8:00 miles in miles 7-9. Shortly after that, we crossed under Route 3 and then wound our way along Gardner Street across Route 53. We made a bathroom stop at the Dunkin Donuts there and starting up again was tough for both of us. As a footnote, and some obvious foreshadowing, we could have easily gotten water there. But I had our next water stop all planned out – so no worries there. You know?

We continued to run well here though. We slowed a bit in miles 12 and 13, as we crossed Main Street and headed towards Wompatuck on South Pleasant Street. The planned water stop was the Wompatuck Visitors Center, just after mile 15, which I was sure would be open with all the activity in the park. After all, they had opened up the park gates, so surely the visitors center would be open. Nope. Oops, mistake #2. We could have easily backtracked to the campground or the spring for water, but that would have been kind of boring and uninspiring to run "backwards", plus the hills are tough. So I decided a better option would be the small general store on Main Street and I could fix the miles from there. After all, it was after 8:00, that's bound to open, right? Well, apparently, that store doesn't open until at least 9:00 on Sunday AM. I tried texting my friend Mike who lives nearby in the hope that he would be up, checking messages, and respond, but that didn't work either. We tried stopping at the Hingham Fire Station, but couldn't find anybody around and decided against ringing their bell to ask for water. Our odyssey finally ended at the Atlantic Bagel and Coffee Company on Main Street, at mile 18, when the woman there very graciously agreed to fill our water bottles with ICE WATER. Hallelujah!!

217

In the meantime, we were continuing to churn out one steady mile after another, very much like our 20 mile long run last week. We talked about this on the run and how we BOTH feel stronger than we did during our Burlington training. Our long runs now are consistently a bit faster. But more importantly is how steady and consistent the miles are and how steady and strong we are late in runs. We've each got our share of aches and pains, but we are running exactly how we want to right now.

Armed with our ICE WATER, and with 4 miles remaining, I felt a lot better morale-wise. Physically, aches and pains were spreading throughout my body, but I still felt strong and I knew we had this run in control. We slowed a bit in miles 20 and 21, each at an 8:16 pace, but this wasn't bad and we were still running steady. When we reached Jackson Square we had to stop at a light to wait for traffic. Not good! Somehow, someway, we managed to start up again, but I was incredibly sore and stiff. It was tough to just put one foot in front of the other and run at all. And this is the point for me when a great run turned into a glorious run. The way the miles ended up working on this crazy mixed-up run, we would be ending just after the top of a steep hill going up Chard Street from Broad Street. But we kept on pushing, relentlessly, and charged up that hill. I mean we really flew up the hill. And when we got to mile 22, and finished that last mile, my watch showed an 8:07 mile split. What an incredibly strong finish to a 22 mile run!

We saw Anne heading out for her run, and laughed at the fact that, while we were out there, Anne and Eliza had driven to Boston and back, Anne and Kevin had gone to church, and who knows what else. Our final time was 2:58:50 but, with all our stopping and starting, I think we were gone for about 3 and 1/2 hours! So our final pace for 22 miles was 8:08. So, so strong and we've still got 7 weeks to go until Race Day.

So, in the wake of a somewhat chaotic run, I am quite sore and stiff, but feeling on top of the world. I am so grateful for Eliza and Anne hand-delivering water bottles to us. I am thankful to have a running partner who is strong mentally and physically, and who is great company. After all, 3 and 1/2 hours is a long time to spend together! And I am filled with pride for how we ran today. It would have been easy to get frustrated, but we kept our heads up, kept charging forward and finished a fantastic run strong. And despite all of these setbacks, or maybe because off of them, this ended up being a memorable and, in a sort of twisted way, a really fun run.

This is the story of one of my very few rough runs in this training period. It was bound to happen eventually, to have a long run when I really struggled. But I persisted through it, actually finishing in a decent time, despite all my struggles. I didn't feel good afterwards, in any way. But I was able to rebound, in every way, with a great elliptical workout the very next day.

A Courageous Run, September 15, 2015

I've always written this blog honestly, to give an accurate portrayal of my experiences as a runner. Often, those experiences are great, but I've had down times too and I've never shied away from writing about them. Yesterday was one of those days. Erika and I had a 16 mile long run planned, a shorter long run for us, but with 8 miles of steady tempo to push us a bit. Prior the run, I thought no big deal. But this run tested me to the very core.

I was never right from the start, didn't feel strong, didn't feel fast. And, along the way I stopped for dizziness, needing to go the bathroom (very badly), back tightness, and, at the very end, Achilles and calf soreness. But all of that is only the tip of the iceberg. As much as I struggled physically, I struggled more mentally and emotionally. And that's unusual for me. Every mile was a struggle for me, a battle, almost a war. I fought hard throughout this whole run and, as much as I struggled, we hit every target split along the way – most by a good margin. And, in the end, the time ended up being very good, in fact just 2 seconds off of my PR for a 16 mile run.

But yet I felt awful afterwards – physically, mentally, and emotionally – this run really crushed me. That feeling lasted all night, and I had a really bad night's sleep as a result. As much as my brain would tell me, it was a good run, my heart just didn't listen, just wouldn't accept that. Yesterday was one of the rare days when I had no interest in writing about a run afterwards – I just didn't have anything in me, but raw negative emotions. I needed time to get some degree of insight and perspective on this run.

The human capacity for resilience is amazing. I feel like as today wore on, I gradually gained that insight and perspective, and began emerging from my funk. And, while I never will look back on this run as a fun run (it just wasn't), I am gradually getting to the point when I can look back on it with pride. To realize how well I battled on a day when I just had nothing from the start. And how hard I fought all through the run and never gave up – just battled with absolutely nothing in my arsenal. And just kept going. Throughout the run. With just pure determination. Determination and energy drawn from deep in my soul that left me absolutely crushed in the end. But I won every battle along the way.

After all those difficulties, the only one that really poses any concern to me is the left Achilles and calf soreness. Oh and my compression sock removal injury when I strained something in my right ankle. Yeah, really, I'm serious. It was that kind of day. But I'm icing both of those, and cutting out my track workout this week in favor of a second elliptical workout to help my Achilles recover.

And that brings me to tonight. I had a very hard, aggressive 9 mile elliptical workout planned for tonight. I could have gone several ways with this. I could have said, "Hey I worked really, really hard yesterday, I'm clearly drained, I'm going to give myself a rest day." Or, I could have said, "Well I'll do it, but I'll make it a bit shorter and easier." Or I could have thrown myself into this workout 110%. In the end it was an easy decision for me. I knew what my heart and soul needed tonight. I needed to do this workout, do it hard, in fact absolutely CRUSH IT. And that's just what I did. With easy stretches at the beginning and end, and recovery intervals in between, I did 3 miles at a 7:00 pace, 2 miles at a 6:30 pace, and then 1 all out mile. While this pace doesn't quite equate to running pace, I did that all out mile in 5 minutes! I have never done that on the elliptical before – don't think I've come close in fact. I really was going all out, and it was just what my heart and soul needed to rebound from yesterday.

And, after I finished my cool down and did my lifting for my hips, a kind of cool thing happened. A smile spread across my face – naturally and easily. My soul was refilled with pride and energy. Ironically, it just took an all-out workout to get there. And that's life in the twisted world of a marathoner.

This was another great, strong run in hot and humid conditions. I estimated I lost 7 pounds on a 12 mile run, which is a lot! This run would have been good in most conditions, but to do it in 86 degree temperatures is really noteworthy.

Now That Is A Run!!, September 18, 2015

Tuesday night, I emailed Erika and wrote that I thought I needed to take a bit of time away from writing and posting about running. I wrote that I planned to keep up with all my workouts but that I was feeling a bit drained emotionally and mentally and needed to regain my energy. This is in part about my running, but also due to the fact that I've taken on a major new responsibility at work – and it's all the same me. I did say I wasn't sure for how long I could resist and we already ended up exchanging a few emails yesterday, including my latest long run idea.

Today I was off from work to take Eliza to a visit at Clark in Worcester and it was a really great break for me. I liked Clark a lot (Eliza did too) and it was a fun trip with Eliza. And, after having some rough nights of sleep, I had two pretty decent nights of sleep in a row, So I felt a bit renewed and refreshed today. My planned run today was 12 miles, an easy mile at the beginning and end, and then 10 at an 8:00 pace in the middle. This is my longest mid-week run to date and, to compound that, it was hot here. I waited until 4:45, but didn't want to finish this run too late, so started out then, despite the 86 degree temperatures.

I warned myself from the start that it was hot and not to worry too much if my pace flagged. My goal was just to try to run steady, even if it was a bit slower than my target pace. I don't think I've run in weather this hot in a while and I was very aware of the heat to start. My first mile was supposed to be easy, and I was thinking:8:15 – 8:30. But I finished that first mile in 7:54. And I was actually a little annoyed with myself – thinking, "don't you remember how I just thought so much about the heat and how I want to run a measured pace today!?" But something felt different on this run. I felt strong. Not necessarily super-fast, but strong. I hit mile 2 in 7:36 and mile 3 in 7:28 and I thought, "OK, this is really getting silly now."

Miles 4 and 5 turned out to be a bit of a mess for me. I had turned right from High Street onto 228 and I stopped my watch just before I reached mile 4 to cross 228 to stay on the sidewalk (it was very busy) and then didn't start it up again for roughly a 1/2 mile after that. When I realized that, I stopped again to try to figure out how to proceed. And, by instinct, I pressed the stop button on my watch, except it was already stopped, so I started it while I was standing still, so I ran about 30 seconds of time standing there while I was trying to figure out what to do. So, my watch said 8:11 for mile 4, but I think it was actually about 7:41. And, in the meantime, I had run an extra 1/2 mile off of the clock. Jiminy Cricket! I figured I would just ignore that extra 1/2 mile, consider it a "bonus" off the clock and keep going as if it had never happened. This meant I would have to tack on an extra 1/2 mile on the end, as my 12 mile run would actually be a 12.5 mile run, but I was OK with that. But I did subtract the 30 seconds.

So, my head was spinning a bit now, but I started back up in spite of that and tried to regain my momentum in mile 5. It was not easy and I was further stymied when I had to stop while a car pulled into a side street in front of me. Then, some dopey high school kid yelled some stupid comment out his car window. Meanwhile I am working much harder than

I want to try to regain my stride and pace in mile 5. In spite of all that, I finished mile 5 in 7:48. But I know I am working so hard, really too hard, losing so much water, salt, etc., and flying through my water quicker than I expected. At the turnaround point on route 53 the sunshine was bright, it was hot, and I was really pushing. It wasn't so much that I was trying to keep running so far ahead of pace. But I didn't want to back off too much because I was afraid if I backed off mentally, I would have a precipitous drop in pace and then not be able to regain my momentum. So I kept on pushing, just trying to run smooth, with quick light strides. And it felt a bit easier. It turns out I hit mile 6 in 7:36 and I'm just kind of shaking my head now in a bit of disbelief.

Meanwhile I'm working on my mindset, telling myself that all of the little up-hills I just did would be down-hills now and I could coast on those. I know I'm working really hard, I'm losing a lot of fluids, but my legs still feel good and strong. But, water is starting to become a concern. I hit mile 7 in 7:51, which feels about right at this stage, but my water is getting VERY LOW now.

This next part is going to sound like deja vu Erika. I stopped at a fire station on 228 thinking perhaps this one will have water. But there's not a sign of life there and I don't see any hose or anything. And I'm thinking to myself,. no, no, no, not again! So I go next to the elementary school next door, where some parents are picking up kids from an afterschool program and, eventually, I make my way to the cafeteria entrance where school teachers are still there and one of them said she couldn't let me in, but could take my water bottle and fill it for me. I could have hugged her, but she probably wouldn't have appreciated that so much. So I just told her she had made my night instead – and indeed she had.

Ok, deep breath now, time to regroup and finish strong. I finished up mile 8 in 7:43 and then mile 9 in 7:54. These are still great mile split times for me at this point in the run and I'm feeling great about this run. But as I began to run through mile 10, I could feel the fatigue building in my calf muscles and Achilles. It wasn't pain but given that I've already had some warning signs about this, I took stock and decided I had already accomplished all I wanted to and more from this run. So in mile 10, I began easing up and finished mile 10 a bit slower in 8:09. Still pretty close to the target split. Then, in mile 11, I gave myself permission to ease up a bit more and ran that mile in 8:34. That was my last "hard" mile and the last one was supposed to be easy. Given how hard I had already run tonight, the conditions, and how my legs were feeling, I took a 2-minute walking break "on the clock" to start mile 12. No need to try to be heroic here – my goal was to finish this run strong and healthy. After that, I "jogged" the rest of mile 12, actually at a decent pace, as I finished in 10:02, including 2 minutes of walking.

Overall, I finished below my target time for the run, even after backing off in the last three miles and walking 2 minutes in the last mile. And all this in 86 degree heat and after a really rocky time in the 4th and 5th miles. And even throwing in a bonus 1/2 mile off the clock. I didn't do a "weigh in" before, but I estimated I lost 7 pounds over the 12 mile run, actually what I consider a dangerous amount of weight loss for that time. So tonight is all about recovery, rehydrating, eating, icing, and, soon, working on settling back down to aim for yet another good night's sleep. A very well deserved good night's sleep!!

Erika and I supported each other constantly over the course of our marathon training. This run was especially tough for Erika and I worked hard to support her on this run when she needed it. It was a tough, tough run, but Erika was so resilient and so tough. After all that happened on this run, I was so proud of both of us that we ran it at an 8:06 pace.

A Character Test, September 20, 2015

Today Erika and I went for a change of scene and did our 22 mile run along the Charles in Cambridge and Boston . We left home at 5:00 AM and started at 5:30 or so. It was cool enough, in the upper 60s, but it was pretty humid throughout the run. It was still dark when we started out and it was a bit tough to find my footfalls when there were little dips or rises in the path. It was kind of neat that the city was all lit up, it was a pretty nice view to start.

We started at the start of Memorial Drive in Cambridge running up the Charles. As we passed by some of the boathouses, all the crew teams were assembling to head out on the river. Our turnaround point was around mile 4, as we crossed the Eliot Bridge. We headed past the Harvard athletic facilities on our right, heading east and then south. Our pace was good and strong, despite some leg fatigue and I was feeling pretty good about this run. I think our first water stop was around mile 7 or so, as it turns out the first of many.

We continued along the Esplanade, past the Hatch Shell, and under the Longfellow Bridge. We hung a left and headed past the Museum of Science, still going strong. Just past mile 10, we passed the car and headed out on our 2nd loop of the run. The Marathon that we are running in Newmarket, NH on October 25 is a double loop course so, as practice for that, we decided to make this a double loop route. So we headed past the car and kept right on going into our 2nd loop.

I think it was mile 11.5 when we hit a water fountain for our 2nd water stop. This is a lot of water for us, but for Erika in particular, and I knew that this week, she was struggling a bit more than me. We headed out again and it was tough to start up with our tight legs. But we did and managed to pick up our pace again. Now all the crew teams were out in force, all over the river, and it was kind of cool to watch. I passed some time by telling a few of my ridiculous college stories, just to keep our minds off of the run for a few minutes, and it helped me anyway.

In mile 14, we crossed back over the Eliot Bridge, heading "home". I was wearing my Chicago Marathon shirt and passed by another runner with the exact same shirt and we exchanged greetings and talked very briefly about Chicago. Now we're both working very hard in this stretch. We decided to stop at the same water fountain as we did on the first loop, but it was a lot farther than either of us remembered. A lot farther! Really, really far. A long, long way. It took FOREVER. But we made it there and filled up our water bottles just before mile 17.

But at this point Erika was feeling some dizziness so we sat down for a few minutes to hopefully let it pass. It did eventually, but it took a bit and it was a really tough time for Erika, and for me by extension. While we were waiting, another guy with a Chicago Marathon shirt came by, saw mine and we talked about the race for a minute. I never knew that shirt would create so many connections!

We started back up slowly and cautiously. Not that we could do much more than that anyway given how tight our legs were. Fortunately Erika's dizziness faded and, while we never got back to our earlier paces, we were able to get back to a decent pace.

I asked Erika if she wanted to cut the run short given how she was feeling. I knew the answer before I asked, but I had to ask – just in case. As we neared the Museum of Science, we were forced to stop and rest, as the drawbridge was going up. And we thought, wow this is a shame, a forced break. Oh well, we'll just have to rest. After a couple of minutes, the bridge came down and we picked back up again. In mile 20, we stopped again because Erika was feeling nauseous. Man was this a trying run. After I struggled on our 16 miler last week, it was Erika's turn to have a tough run this week. And I felt for her. This was a trying run, a character test. Of course this is Erika we're talking about, and I know she can handle just about anything. But that still doesn't make it fun to have to deal with all this stuff.

We started up again without further incident. Given that our double loop was just over 10 miles each time and we were going 22, we had an extra loop winding through the MIT campus. We were just hanging on now and finished heading back along Memorial Drive. We finished in 2:58:26, at an 8:06 pace. That is a solid 22 mile run for us period, but given what we, and Erika in particular, went through from miles 17-22, this was an absolutely fantastic time!

I was so impressed with Erika today. Not a bit surprised, because I've come to know her well as a runner and a person this past year, and know very well how strong she is both physically and mentally. But this was a tough, tough run today – a true character test. And she absolutely

CRUSHED it. And, as I've thought many times before, I thought, man I have a tough running partner!

In the wake of the run, in the context of post run feelings, I am feeling great. I have my typical soreness and fatigue, but nothing bad. No Achilles, knee or ankle pain, which is absolutely awesome news. My biggest issue is chafing. Really, really bad chafing, I might add. But, in the hierarchy of running discomfort, I'll take that over a sore Achilles 10 times out of 10. It's superficial and it will feel better in a day or two. Until then, well, I'm a marathoner you know. It goes with the territory. If I can't absorb a bit of pain here and there, I wouldn't be doing this.

I focused on my hard work in this blog and that was 100 percent on target. I worked harder than ever training for Newmarket. I was working hard nearly every day. But through it all, as I pushed through every workout, I kept my eye on the big picture and kept everything in perspective. It's important to remember the incredible amount of hard work that goes into training for a marathon. And this is why success in a marathon is more gratifying than any other race.

Time For Pumpkin Coffee, September 22, 2015

I get my coffee at Bruegger's Bagels where I am a "Bottomless Mug" member. That means I get unlimited coffee for the year for a flat annual fee. And I make sure to get my money's worth. Wait a minute, you ask, "What does this have to do with running?" Silly, silly question. You should know better by now that everything has to do with running!

So Bruegger's has seasonal coffees and they just switched over to Pumpkin Spice. As a runner training for a fall marathon (two fall marathons) this means two very important things:

1. No more coconut coffee until the start of next summer.

2. It's almost time to race!

That 2nd thought sends a jolt of electricity through me, through my heart, my blood vessels, my muscles, my soul. But running a marathon takes a lot more than a shot of adrenaline. Running a marathon requires strength and stamina, both physically and psychologically. You can't get through a marathon with adrenaline. You need inner, core strength.

I've been working on building that strength for several years now, but especially since January of this year. And after a lot of ups and downs, I've become convinced that you have to fail to get that strong. You have to have runs when you fall short, when you struggle, when you feel awful, to really succeed. Because there will be a time in the marathon when your pace starts to flag, when you start to struggle a bit and when you feel awful. You have to get beat, to fail, to question your strength. And you've got to able to rebound, to not give up, and to run through that doubt and past it. And you need to KNOW that you can stare down adversity and beat it. And the only way that can work is if you've been there before and have run through that adversity before.

This means a lot of work. And in this training cycle, I am training harder than ever before. I am only running three days per week compared with four in the past. That may sound on the surface like I'm backing off my training, but nothing could be further from the truth. In the past, that fourth running day was just an easy 4-5 mile run. Now, that has been replaced by two hard days of cross training, one on the stationary bike and one on the elliptical. Combine that with the fact that all three of my runs are hard, that means five hard workouts per week. In addition to that, I've been doing core workouts regularly two times per week. While two core workouts per week is no big deal, it is significant when it's in addition to these five rigorous workouts. And now that I'm actually doing it regularly, I'm beginning to feel the results.

So, six days a week I'm working hard. Tonight, one day after running 22 miles, and after working a 10 hour day and enduring 3 hours of commuting, I was right back at it, doing a 45 minute tempo bike workout and a 45 minute core workout. I think this is the biggest difference with this training cycle compared with my prior training. In the past, Monday, the day after a long run, would be a rest day for me. Or I might have done an easy bike ride just to loosen up my legs. Now I'm going right back to work – HARD. I have never worked like this before.

Through this work my legs have gotten stronger and my core has gotten stronger. I have better endurance. And, most important of all, I know it. And that's really the key. As I look ahead to our two fall marathons, I'm continuing to cultivate that inner strength and confidence, that unshakable belief in myself that you just have to have to succeed in a marathon. Sometimes it's two steps forward and one step back but, in the long term, I'm continuing to progress and improve and getting very close to where I feel I need to be on race day.

In the meantime, I get to enjoy pumpkin spice coffee.

This was a great early morning mid-week long run. Any time I get a chance to run with Erika mid-week it is a bonus, so this was a good run right from the start. We ran this run very well together, including very solid tempo miles. We were just over a month from Race Day now, and everything was looking good.

It Stays Late Early Out There, September 23, 2015

This blog title is a tribute to Yogi Berra, the great, quotable, Yankee catcher who passed away yesterday. I modified the original quote, "It gets late early out there.", referring to playing outfield in Yankee Stadium, to fit my early morning context. Erika and I had a rare chance for a shared weekday run this morning and we headed out at 5:15. Earlier this summer, it would have been light then, but now it was pitch black out, and didn't start to get light until 6:00. Once I get up, I love running at this time of day. It's relatively quiet and peaceful and, with the exception of winter runs, the temperatures are awesome. It was in the low 50s and clear this AM with a star-filled sky – great running weather. The only downside of early AM weekday runs is that I have to go to work right afterwards. And I had a full busy day ahead of me at work today. So, it made for a long day in the end. But, the chance to run with Erika in these great conditions was too good to pass up.

Our planned run today was a 12 mile run, with 5 miles at a 7:30 tempo pace. That was actually longer than each of us had scheduled, but that's what we discussed, so we just ended up going with it. I think we were both a little concerned about how well we would hit our tempo pace and that translated into running pretty hard, to be sure we did. Turns out we didn't need to worry. We hit the first one in 7:20 and I thought OK, we can back off just a bit. We then went on to hit the 2nd one in 7:17. I said to Erika (jokingly), "7:17, we've got to pick it up now." Our watches never seem to quite match and she said she had 7:14 for this one, so I said, well at least that's a little better.

We kept going really solidly now and hit the 3rd tempo mile in 7:25. At that point, we were 5 miles into the run, my water was about 2/3 gone, and we had what would be our best water stop option at that point in Tedsechi's. This was a conservative water stop, but I've been burned twice recently running low on water and struggling to find water, so I decided to play it safe and grab water then. Anytime you stop a run like that, it's always a bit harder to get going again, but we hit the 4th tempo mile in 7:18 and the last one in 7:25. A great set of pretty consistent tempo miles, and a run to feel good about. From there, we pretty much cruised through the last 5 miles, not too fast, but not too slow either.

This will equal the longest mid-week run in my marathon training schedule and it went great. We are just 4 and 1/2 weeks away now from fall marathon #1. My legs felt weary today, but I didn't have any of the trouble signs that I watch for – foot, Achilles, and knee pain. So that's great news! Tomorrow is a core workout only and then I return to the track for an interval workout on Thursday.

Oh, and as far as Yogi, he was a key part of 10 Yankees World Series Championships and one of the most memorable baseball players ever. One of my favorites is when asked how many slices he wanted his pizza cut into, he said something along these lines, "You better cut it into 6. I don't think I can eat 8."

This is another blog that really requires no introduction. It captures the work ethic of marathon training really nicely.

Marathon Training is the Real Marathon, September 25, 2015

When you tell someone that you're running a marathon, they usually focus on how tough it is to run 26.2 miles. And, rightly so, that is a huge challenge. Even just to finish a marathon is a big challenge and requires a pretty good degree of training. But I've never run a marathon, or any race for that matter, just to finish it. I've always run marathons to race them, to run 26.2 miles as fast as I can. To do that successfully, or to even have a chance to come close, you have to train very hard for a very long time. And that really is the true marathon here.

I was thinking about this tonight when I was doing my core workout. I could easily skip a few reps, skip an exercise or two, or even miss a core workout and no one would know the difference. In fact, it probably would make very little difference to my strength or conditioning. But I would know. And that's the part that matters. While all of this training is designed to get us physically in shape to run a marathon at our target pace, the mental and psychological side of this is just as important. So, every time I do any work-out, I never cut a single corner. The only exception is if I'm injured. I don't mean sore, tired, or fatigued; I mean injured. So, every core workout I do, I finish every rep, of every set, of every exercise. Every stationary bike ride I finish every single second of my target time. And every run, I finish every 1/100th of every mile – even when my watch is clearly short. Because that's what this is all about – finishing, and finishing with purpose and strength. Following all the way through every single time. EVERY SINGLE TIME.

So when I struggle for motivation a bit, when my resolve falters, when my energy flags, I sometimes think, "You think this is hard, how do you think you're gonna feel in mile 25. GET IT DONE." This may not sound appealing, it may not sound like a lot of fun, and it may sound tedious. But this work, this struggle, this drive – this is what I love most about marathon training. The quest to be BETTER. Always. Not every day is the best, but every day is about trying to be. About the quest.

Erika and I have been in marathon training mode, for all intents and purposes, for nine months now, and it is a lot. And we've got two more full months to go. There are days when it feels awesome, and other days when it feels like an exhausting burden. To come home after a very long day and do a bike and core workout the day after running 22 miles. And then do a hard elliptical workout the next night, followed by a hard 12 mile tempo run early the next morning, followed by a core workout the next night, and then followed by repeat miles on the track the next night. Followed by a day off and then 20 more miles. Bringing my best every single time. And then doing it again the next week. For 11 months, with virtually no break at all. Now that's what I call a marathon.

This turned out to be quite a chaotic evening. But, as I always tell Eliza and Kevin to do, I focused like a laser. I didn't get upset or rattled, just went out and got the track workout done. And, yet again, I nailed the workout . I was crushing one workout after another these days, running so strong.

Oh, My Poor Addled Brain!, September 26, 2015

So I had an interesting day at work today. I put in a last minute request to attend the 5th International Symposium on Animal Mortality Management in Lancaster, PA next week. This was a really last minute request and, in our agency, out of state travel requests typically take weeks to get approved. This one got approved inside of 3 HOURS! This is a super high priority for us right now and I'm right in the thick of it. How did I get to be so lucky, you're probably asking yourself. Well, let's just say I have a really glamorous job – try not to get too jealous.

So, when I got home today, my head was spinning, trying to figure out how to morph my personal, professional, and running commitments around this new schedule commitment. And my mind was so mixed up and preoccupied when I get home that I just sat down to dinner and had a couple of tacos – completely forgetting my track interval tonight. By the time I finished, and realized what I had done, it was about 6:00. If it were earlier in the week, I might have been able to move some workouts around. But here it is Friday night, with a 20 mile run planned for Sunday AM. I was out of options, stuck between a rock and a hard place. (And not doing this run was not among the options.)

I chose the hard place. I waited about 30 minutes, but I couldn't wait much longer because it was already starting to get dark. Both Weymouth and Hingham had home football games tonight, but the Hingham track runs around a field adjacent to the football field, so that was the only viable choice tonight. I got there and started up about 6:45. My planned workout was a 1,000 meter (@ 4:00), a 2,000 meter (@ 8:30) and a 1,000 meter (@4:00), with a mile warm up before and a 1.5 mile cool down after.

I was apprehensive about this run because I knew this was way too much food way too close to the run. So I took a couple of preemptive Pepto Bismol before I left home. But I expected to suffer tonight. But amazingly, the stomach cramps and indigestion held off for the most part. I wouldn't say I felt good, but I felt decent. But in addition to feeling apprehensive, I felt determined.

To make a long story short, I ended up running these intervals in 3:56, 8:01, and 3:53. Even my warm up and cool down were fast. After those intervals, I ran my 1,5 mile cool down in 11:06, while dodging countless kids crossing the track. So on a night when I could have gotten frustrated and was facing adversity, I turned that right around and just crushed the workout.

I often like to look at the story or a run on different levels. At first, the story of this run was how my poor overwhelmed brain forgot about the run and how I ate dinner right before the run. Looking back in hindsight now, I'm over that and actually find it mildly amusing. If I had let it, that could have defined this run. it could have turned out to be a mediocre run that I felt frustrated about.

But the story didn't end there because I didn't let it. I went out, tossed aside those distractions and just absolutely nailed the run. And now the story of this run for me is how my determination and positive attitude turned what could have been a poor run into a strong, successful interval workout.

This run also made one more thing clear to me – I really need some more rest! This needs to be a restful weekend – because next week is going to be a tough one. So, my focus over the next 48 hours (other than a 20 mile run) is R&R – resting and preparing for a daunting week ahead. At least now I can relish a great run while I relax!

This was an early morning long run, and it was starting to get a little chilly on these early mornings. It was yet another strong run too and a significant PR for me. The highlight of this run was running the 18th and final mile in 7:28. Wow, just wow.

Running Strong, September 27, 2015

I've got to say, when that alarm went off at 4:30, my first thought was no, no, no. I do not want to get out of my warm bed! But I dragged myself out of bed and began the long pre-run process. Had a Cliff Bar and water, did a weather check and double check of the route, got dressed in all my running clothes, mixed my GU and water in my flasks, filled my water bottle, gave my watch a final booster charge, walked Napoleon, went to the bathroom, used the bathroom again, got my sunglasses on (even though it was totally dark out), and finally headed out to do my warm-up routine.

It was a chilly start to the day at 41 degrees, so I had a sweatshirt and sweatpants on warming up, and even had my winter running cap and light running gloves. I took the sweatpants off in favor of shorts, but decided to run with a light long sleeve shirt under my bright short sleeve shirt. All of that turned to be just about right today, as it stayed pretty cool throughout the whole run.

Erika and I started out at 5:30. It was cold and it was dark, but apparently we both felt pretty good as we ran the first mile in 7:38. Goodness gracious! We were going 18 miles today, so this was a little much. We headed through Jackson Square and turned past the Commuter Rail station, heading to Bare Cove Park. We were still cruising, with miles 2 and 3 at 7:47 and 7:51. We turned into Bare Cove Park and it was still pretty dark out. Because I wear prescription sunglasses, I have to choose whether I go with sunglasses or regular glasses at the start of the run. The sunglasses made the world look really dark right now, but I knew I would appreciate them later. We continued to run strong through Bare Cove, completing miles 4 and 5 in 7:57 and 7:43. This is fast for a long run, but it's feeling good today. And, not for the last time today, I thought I kind of wish it were race day today, because I am ON today.

We turned right onto 3A, slowing a bit in mile 6, at 8:07. We stopped for water at Tedeschi's just after mile 6 and started back up smoothly. We turned right onto Thaxter Street, a new route portion for us, and climbed a couple of hills. Mile 7 was a bit slower at 8:12, due to the hills, but we rebounded with a 7:59 mile in mile 8. We cut across North and South Street and continued on Hersey Street, all the way to Main Street/228. We passed a couple of small flocks of turkeys. The first ones made some kind of bird-like noise but it definitely wasn't a "gobble gobble" sound. Erika remarked on this and suggested that when we got to the next flock, I should try to teach them how to gobble. I tried and showed them, but it didn't help. I figured they just needed more time, but I was in a hurry today – no time to teach turkeys. Sorry Erika, I did my best.

228 brought us to miles 9 and 10, and we were running so steady and strong, finishing those miles in 7:52 and 8:09. We hung a left onto 3A,

going back down to Hingham Harbor, after another couple of "rolling hills". We finished mile 11 in 8:06 and stopped for a quick bathroom break just after that. I think we're going to learn all of the public bathrooms in the Weymouth/Hingham area soon! We turned back into "downtown" Hingham along South Street and hit mile 12 in 8:06. We're running a tad slower now, but so steady and strong and I'm loving how we're running today. It's not that it feels easy, but it feels solid and strong. We hung a right onto West Street/Beal Street and finished mile 13 in 8:05. I'm trying to take my GU out of the flask now, but it's so cold, that's it solidified and I have to shake it really hard to get anything out. As a result, I'm taking a little less GU than I normally would. Given how cool it was, we made a joint executive decision to skip our 2nd water stop.

We finished mile 14 in 8:07, just before turning left onto 3A, heading back to Weymouth and home. We crossed over the Back River and it feels just a bit warmer. But I'm still not hot in my running hat, gloves, and long sleeve shirt. Mile 15 featured yet another in a long parade of hills and we slowed a bit down to 8:20. The inside of my thighs/groin are killing me now, especially on down hills and I'm working very hard. But I still feel strong in spite of that. This is the part where running together with Erika was really important because we were both working hard over this series of hills.

We turned left onto North Street, crushed more hills, and finished mile 16 in 8:06. I feel like I'm really battling now, but I feel the strength in my legs and core. And, despite my soreness, I know I've got this. We turned onto East Street and, guess what? There was another hill. But what was really hurting me now were the down hills. We finished mile 17 in 8:21 and we're both working hard now.

Right before the end of mile 17, Erika told me to go ahead because her stomach was bothering her. So, after double checking to make sure it was nothing more serious than that, I took off. I mean, I really TOOK OFF. I think I was partially motivated by wanting to finish as fast as I could, so that I could double back and finish the last bit together with Erika. But I was feeling really strong. And fast. This is probably the strongest I've ever felt at the end of a long run, despite a fair amount of soreness and fatigue. I basically kicked the whole last mile and finished MILE 18 in 7:28! MILE 18 in 7:28! That is not just a good final mile for me. Even more than a great final mile. That was an exceptional final mile. 7:28 is half marathon race pace for me – that is nothing short of amazing for mile 18.

As soon as my watch stopped, I turned around, doubled back a bit and finished with Erika. I finished overall in 2:53:57, JUST under 8:00 average pace for 18 miles. And, although I don't run 18 miles often, that was a PR for me by more than 4:00, breaking a PR I set earlier this year. In the wake of the run, I'm icing a lot and eating and drinking to restore my energy. The rest of today is about rest and recovery. Funny how that 4:30 AM alarm seems like a distant memory now.

This blog and the track workout were representative of the effort I put into this marathon training. I worked so hard to train for Newmarket and ran so well. I was smart about my training, but when I had muscular soreness like this, I always pushed through it. And I consistently hit my goal times and target splits one run after another, even when I was much less than 100%.

Taking the Pain, October 7, 2015

When Erika and I were thinking about running two marathons this fall, we each sought advice from a few different people. One of the people I asked about this was my physical therapist, Jake, who is also a long time runner. The part of his advice that really stuck with me is that you can do it, but the marathon has to be almost like another long run. So, as my put my training plan together for these two marathons, I made it my toughest training plan yet with an emphasis on more really long, long runs. If my training plan had a tagline, it would be, "The Marathon: Just Another Long Run."

When you're a marathon runner, you learn to become accustomed to a certain level of pain. It's not that I'm the toughest guy in the world – I am not. But, with long runs in particular, I do experience some level of pain and discomfort before, during, and/or after every run. When that happens, some level of pain just becomes routine, ordinary, and almost like background noise. But, this past Sunday's long run was different.

Erika and I ran 22 miles at essentially race pace on Sunday. While those last four miles are the toughest ones, running 22 miles at race pace is pretty close to a marathon race experience. And, at the end of the run and afterwards, I felt almost like I had just finished a marathon. On Monday, my quads hurt, badly, when I went down stairs, upstairs, sat down, stood up, or walked. It even hurt when I lay down at night. The pain was so deep that, even though my hamstrings weren't sore, the pain extended so deep in my quads that it felt like my hamstrings were sore. I rolled and iced and felt a little bit better today. Today the only thing that really hurt intensely was going down stairs. But it still hurt to walk.

I had a track interval workout planned tonight, with 10 x 400 meter intervals. While I usually don't have a problem running through muscle soreness, I wasn't so sure about tonight's run. As I did my first two warm-up laps, my doubt continued to grow. I was sore with every stride and, through two laps, it wasn't going away at all. But I hung in and did my calisthenics and stretching. That all hurt too, but I wasn't giving up this quickly. So I headed out for my last two warm up laps and my legs finally started to loosen up and the pain began to fade. I did a couple of strides on the straightaways, gradually speeding up to a fast pace and then easing off, and I finally felt loose and fast. Hallelujah!

My target pace for these 400 meter intervals was 1:34 and I ended up beating that for all of them. As I went my legs loosened up and I felt very little pain. That is, until the 6th one, when I could feel the fatigue and pain starting to build again. I did another round of stretching for my calves and Achilles and felt that loosen up a bit more. But I was still feeling some quad pain in these final 400s.

Fortunately, I had gotten my flu shot earlier today and, as I got late in the workout, my shoulder began to feel sore from the flu shot. I say that only partially joking. When you have pain in your legs running, I really believe the best way to take your mind off of that pain is to have pain somewhere else to focus on. I really do think it helps – better to think about a sore shoulder than sore quad muscles. So I hung in through those last 400s and, as the darkness settled down upon the track, I had completed all 10 400s between 1:28 and 1:31.

As I did my cool down, the pain and tightness began to build again. But I feel like I got through this run without any real damage and can deal with this stuff by icing and rolling. And that's my post-run focus tonight. I was able to take the pain tonight and work through it for a successful run.

We were getting really close now and things were still going well. Although this run was a tough one, we pushed through it successfully and this ended up being a strong, successful run in the end. The key now was getting to the starting line healthy. It turns out that would be much tougher than we knew, not for me, but for Erika.

Winning Without Your Best Stuff, October 12, 2015

Erika and I have begun the dreaded taper. Fortunately I am so busy beyond running that I feel like I'm barely going to notice the taper this time. I am especially busy with work and, in spite of that, am actually taking a couple of extra days off to stay well rested leading up to race day.

On Sunday, we ran 16 miles after a very strong and fast 22 miles the week before. I was still feeling the effects of the 22 miler in my legs and neither one of us was at 100%. Sometimes these are the runs that I am most proud of. The days when I clearly don't have it but still stay strong and push through. I haven't written about a baseball analogy in a while, but 'tis the season. There are days when a starting pitcher goes out there and just doesn't have their best stuff. He probably knows that pretty early in the game, maybe even warming up in the bullpen. But if that pitcher goes out and, say gives up 3 runs in 6 innings, and keeps his team in the game, that could be a great start. In the box score, it looks just so-so, not really impressive at all. But the pitcher knows that, given the stuff he had that day, that may have been one of his best games ever. He was hanging his curveball, his slider was flat and he was missing his spots, and he still muddled his way through. And, sometimes, a battle of a game like that is even more impressive than a no-hitter.

That's how I feel about our run on Sunday. We were both struggling, early and often, but we just kept on pushing, never giving up, never settling. And in the end, we ended up running 16 miles at an 8:06 pace. Not super-fast for us, but not bad at all. And, now that you know the story behind the run, you know too that this was not just a good run, this was a great run. Runs like this are important because, unless you're extraordinarily lucky, you know you're going to feel this way at some point on RACE DAY. And you're going to need to run hard and push through fatigue when you're just not feeling it. And that's just what we did yesterday.

I took the rest of the day away from running, including writing about running. We went as a family to a huge cranberry festival in Wareham and now, as a result, have cranberry muffins. But, more importantly, we had a really nice day together as a family. Training for a marathon can be all-consuming and chew you up and spit you out. One of the lessons I've learned along the way is that it's really important to be able to step away from running, especially at this stage. An effective taper is as much about going into RACE DAY mentally fresh, as it is about being physically fresh and rested. I've often said that marathon training is an "all in" endeavor. But, sometimes being "all in" means being smart enough and aware enough to know when to back off a bit. Don't get me wrong, I did my elliptical workout today and Erika and I will do a track workout tomorrow. I'm still working hard. And doing all I possibly can to be 100% ready for RACE DAY. Looking for that magical day that I dream of, when I have my best stuff for 26.2 miles.

I was doing great with my running at this point and was feeling great physically. But this was a hard time emotionally for me. After all Erika and I had been through together, she was resting now due to a knee injury. So I was running on my own, and we really didn't know how Erika would do running Newmarket. So, lots of questions at this stage. So, while I focused on this run and ran it well, Erika was never far from my thoughts.

Staying to the Left, October 18, 2015

One week to go until the LOCO Marathon in Newmarket, NH! Today was our last long run before The Race. But since Erika has had some bad knee pain recently, she is resting and treating that injury now. No running until Race Day for her. So I was on my own today, kind of. I had a 10 mile run planned, with miles 3-6 at a 7:45 pace, and the rest at whatever pace felt right, just not too fast.

When Erika and I run together, I usually run on the left. That's just the way we typically run together and it's become our routine. So, while I was running on my own today, Erika was with me in spirit and in my thoughts. So, naturally I kept to the left whenever I could. May sound a little crazy, but I'm a marathoner, so a certain amount of craziness is part of my core character. Don't worry though, I wasn't too nuts. No imaginary conversations or high fives. I did not feel great today, and had some scattered soreness, but still felt solid and strong I ran my first two "easy" miles at 7:52 and 7:45. I really wasn't trying to push my pace, I am just strong now.

When I hit the tempo mile stretch, I also hit my target splits – 7:36, 7:44, 7:41, 7:38. I was slightly under, but not crazy fast, just where I wanted to be. After that, I eased up and ran 7:57, 8:04, 7:54, and 8:02 for the last 4 miles. Once again, I was pleased that the easy pace that I slipped into was about my marathon target race pace. And Erika was with me stride for stride.

So just 7 more days left to go. This will be a more conservative week for me. I've already planned to replace my planned speed interval track workout on Tuesday with an elliptical interval workout. I'll have another elliptical workout, a bike workout and then one short run before Newmarket. I'm also done with core workouts until after Newmarket. I'm taking a vacation day on Friday so that I can head into Sunday AM well rested and strong. The goal for this week is to rest and get to the start line strong and healthy. And to support Erika in her efforts to do the same. Fingers and toes crossed for a strong and healthy week ahead for both of us!

It took so many runs, so many workouts, so much work, pain, and sweat to get to this point. But I hadn't just trained hard, I had trained smart. And, despite the various little aches and pains, I was strong. I was fast. And I did believe.

The Final Tune Up, October 23, 2015

Tonight was my final run before the Loco Marathon in Newmarket, NH on Sunday. The plan for tonight was to run 5 miles easy. I don't mean easy like jogging, just running at a nice, steady, comfortable pace, whatever that turned out to be. I kept on checking myself as I went, was my breathing easy, did I feel relaxed, was I running at a conversational pace? And, while I got a little carried away at a few points, generally I was sticking to the script.

I've got to say I didn't feel 100% tonight. I had lots of little aches and pains. Nothing noteworthy but, at this point, you really want to feel 100%, and every little thing becomes a potential worry. They lessened as I went. But, nonetheless, I'm doing a full court press of icing, rolling and, later, heating, tonight. I'm also taking a short term high dosage of Advil to deal with any swelling that's going on.

But, with that said, man was I amped, and man was I strong tonight. My race goal is to run at under an 8:00 pace. And, my stretch goal for the marathon is to run at a 7:48 pace, which would give me a 3:25 time, and a Boston qualifying time – just barely. So tonight, running at what felt like an easy, comfortable pace, I ran 5 miles at a 7:50 pace. And I was running through a few hills too, hills that weren't really rigorous, but that will certainly be at least as tough as any we'll face in Newmarket.

Over the next couple of days, I'll be resting. Icing, rolling, heating and biking just a bit to loosen things up. While my tune up tonight wasn't all I expected with the minor aches and pains, I was thrilled with how strong and comfortable I felt at my target race pace tonight. In terms of that result, tonight couldn't be beat.

With any marathon, race day mantras are important. For now, I'll be keeping those to myself for Race Day. I want them to be fresh and powerful in my head on Race Day. But I will share my pre-race mantra which I will focus on over the next few days. It is short and sweet:

We are strong. We are fast. We believe.

So many of my blogs focused on the physical side of my running and that is absolutely important. But emotions are always at the core of my running, especially when training for a marathon. Going through this experience with Erika added to the emotions of marathon training, making the entire experience so much richer. While I worked hard to manage my emotions, I always welcomed them into my training, knowing that marathons are a matter of heart and will.

I'm No Robot, October 23, 2015

Running a marathon is, by its very nature, an emotional experience. The experience drags you through all sorts of emotional highs and lows. Running a marathon doesn't bring out just any emotion, it brings out all of them. It strips your soul bare. And that emotional experience is at least two orders of magnitude higher for marathon TRAINING. It is a long emotional journey and not for the faint of heart. If you do not get emotional training for and running a marathon, then you must be a robot. And I am no robot.

This training session has certainly been a roller coaster for Erika and me. We've both had down runs and we've both had nagging injuries. Erika has borne the worst of it recently. But, looking back at my training log, we've also had a lot of successes and high moments. Since Burlington, I've set training run PRs at 5 different distances – 14, 15, 18, 20, and 22 miles. That means that Erika and I both ran those runs faster than we did in our Burlington training. And, in general, even despite setbacks, we've both been running very strong.

Training for and running a marathon you learn a lot about managing emotions. You learn to take on, deal with and discard the negative emotions, frustration, disappointment, and lack of confidence. You cannot avoid them. You cannot ignore them. You have to face them, deal with them and move on. And, on the up side, and there is plenty of upside, you learn to channel the positive emotions, and manage them over time, kind of like a timed release medication. The emotions of running a marathon are unlike those of sports like basketball and football, where you have tremendous intensity in big moments. With a marathon, you have that same intensity, but you have to keep it level over the entire race, the entire training schedule. You have to be on for 3.5 hours straight – with no letup at all. It's intense, but not a rah-rah, smack 'em in the mouth kind of intense. It's a sustained level intensity. It can be draining and crushing, but also incredibly rewarding.

In the end, the emotions that always seem to take over for me are gratitude and joy. Running a marathon makes me grateful for so many things. Thankful for my family who lives with me through my marathon training. For my Mom and Uncle Jack who religiously read my blogs. For all of my friends and co-workers who have been supportive.

I am especially grateful just to be ABLE to run a marathon, regardless of the time I run in. To be physically healthy enough to endure a marathon. While I hope to run for many years, this is not something I take for granted. Each race is a gift to be treasured.

More recently, I am thankful for the running camaraderie, support and friendship of my running partner Erika. We have been through a lot together in a relatively short period of time. When you train for a marathon together, you spend A LOT of time together. Long runs take a long time. But, I always look forward to those shared long runs together. And I am always thankful to have Erika on my right.

I am building my emotions now looking towards Sunday. Gradually topping off the confidence, the mental energy, the motivation — getting ready to race. I know it will be an emotional day on Sunday, a day full of pride and gratitude. Probably a few tears. The difference is that this time, Erika and I will immediately begin recovering, not to rest, but to start getting ready for the Philadelphia Marathon – just four weeks later! Recovery week is just week 1 of a 4 week marathon training schedule.

No, we are not robots. But we are tough. We are strong. We are resilient. And we are ready for all the emotions that Race Day will bring.

I set a strong marathon PR in this race, by nearly 3 minutes. And even with that, I believe, looking back, I could have run even better. After all, this included probably about a 90 second bathroom break, among other things. But all in all, a great, great race for me and the race I had been looking for. I was proud and I was very happy with my race. Except that I so badly wanted to run the full race together with Erika. But I knew she wasn't 100% going into this, so that was kind of wishful thinking. But she had such a rough day. I just felt for her so much, knowing what she had gone through in this race. She is my running partner and my friend, and it's really true that her success means nearly as much to me as my own.

A Mixed Bag, October 25, 2015

Whenever someone says they have good news and bad news, I always pick the bad news first. So that's what you get. To frame this, when Erika and I run races together, while we're each trying to get the best time we can, the shared race matters a lot. And for me, Erika's race means virtually the same to me as my own. We had planned this race together, we were running it together, it was a joint effort. Almost every time I talked to someone about this marathon, I said WE were running it. And I meant it.

Today, after we had a GREAT first 11 miles together, I started to pull away in mile 12. I did this with some concern, but there were a couple of things going on here. First, I was on today. I knew early I was getting a PR today. I was so fast, so strong, and just relentless. I could have run a 1/2 PR if I wanted, I was flying and I was strong. And Erika was right with me. She started to flag a bit in miles 10 and 11, but we were still both running sub 8:00 paces. So, after asking 3 or 4 different ways if she was OK, I came away convinced she was. And, at that time, I think she really was OK. So she sent me on my way, told me to go get a PR, I told her to be safe, and off I went.

So I left her and let her continue on her way. And she hung in for a while, but eventually began struggling and ended up having a brutal second half of the race. Looking back, in hindsight, I would have pushed her to stop at the 1/2. But all the signs at that point were pretty positive and I figured if she eased off her pace in the second half, she would be fine. She had run a great half, was still running steady, and her knee that had been bothering her was feeling OK. Famous last words. Well, maybe not that famous, but you know. Those minutes waiting for Erika at the end were some of the longest minutes of my life. If you've ever been in that position, you know. If not, I'll sum it up by saying I was crushed, scared, worried, sad, anxious, and so on. And that doesn't do the feeling justice. It's just an awful feeling.

I will say that, for better or worse, and I think it was for worse in this case, Erika is about the toughest person I've ever known. She can run through just about anything. And, today she did. And, despite the negative outcome, I am proud of her and proud to have her as a running partner. Now, mostly I'm worried and concerned and just hoping that all the pain she went through is short term stuff that can be dealt with through icing, Advil, stretching, heating, rolling, PT, etc. Our second marathon in Philadelphia looms just 4 weeks away, but I'm not even thinking about that now. Now it's all about getting healthy and staying safe. So, send Erika healing wishes, say a prayer, whatever is your style.

But, like I said, there's good news too. First of all, the first 11 miles together and all of the pre-race prep were the most fun I've EVER had running a race. Great company, great fun, lots of smiles, lots of jokes, just a great time. And that will always be there. It was a blast.

But I ran too and, like I said earlier, I ran the race of my life today. I finished the 1/2 in under 1:40. While I struggled a bit coming out of the half, I was able to keep my pace up and stay strong. This was a two-loop course, so the second 13.1 miles were the same as the first. This was both good and bad, but overall I think I liked it, as I kind of knew what was coming. I had a sense of deja vu around mile 16 or so, as I needed to go to the bathroom badly. I had woken up at 3:00 this morning to try to take care of that, but it didn't work out. So, this time, I decided to stop at a porta pot on the course and was able to make it a quick stop. A very quick stop. I've got to say it's a weird feeling to go poop "on the clock". But I know it was the right decision because that would have wrecked the last 10 miles for me. And after that I felt much better.

My pace did start to flag not too long after that point, but I was keeping the pace decent, in the low 8:00s, so I wasn't fading too badly. And, I had built up so much banked time in the first 15 miles so I could afford to fade a bit. This is where I lost my Boston Qualifier time (I needed 3:25), and I knew it, but I had gone out so hard, it was all I could do to hang on like I did. This was a small race with a lot of wide open roads in the country. There were only 175 people running the full so, after we got past the 1/2, I was on my own quite a bit. But, I was still able to pass a few guys in those last 10 miles. We exchanged greetings and good wishes, one of the things that I love about running races.

The last three miles were on a rail trail, and it was excruciating. I was counting tenths of miles, and it was amazing how long each one seemed to take. I walked a couple of brief stretches, with the promise to myself that I would pick my pace back up faster after I walked, which I did. Finally, I got to the final turn and still had enough left in the tank for a decent kick.

I finished in 3:28:14, beating my previous marathon PR of 3:31:03, by nearly three minutes. This was the best race of my life to date, and I am incredibly proud of the result. I worked very, very hard for this one and know that every ounce of work paid off – and was needed to get this result. Even after getting some food and water at the race, and then having six slices of pizza, I had still lost two pounds compared to this morning! A very hard day's work, but an excellent day's work.

I expect I'll write a bit more about this one but, before I end for now, I need to thank Anne and Kevin, who drove both Erika and me up there, hung out in the rain for the first part of the race, and cheered us on. They also took my gloves, my hat, and extra GU flask when I got to the half. It was great to have them there and made the entire experience so much better. And I know they helped me to have this great race today.

So yeah, a mixed bag today. My heart is filled with joy and concern, pride and worry, thrills and heartbreak, exhilaration and fear. It's quite a combination and I'm even more fried emotionally than I am physically. But that's the life of a marathon runner. And I wouldn't trade it for anything.

I like this blog a lot. I think it captures this race experience really clearly. I still remember the free and easy feeling I had in the first half of the race. It was amazing. I really did define myself on this day. But, looking back, I realize, as I knew then, that I had truly defined myself over the course of months of training.

Defining Myself, October 26, 2015

Prior to the marathon, I mentioned in one of my blogs that I had a series of race day mantras. But since I wanted to keep them fresh for race day, I didn't want to write about them then. Well, since then, people have been literally breaking down my door asking about my race day mantras. Well not literally. And actually not even figuratively. But I figured everyone really wanted to know.

Actually, seriously, for a moment, I do want to write more about Newmarket, and my race day mantras were a big part of my day. Of course my training was the most important part, as I was physically strong and ready. But I also went into the race mentally strong and prepared and that matters a lot for a marathon. So now that the initial emotions have softened a bit, I'm going to take you through the race again, in a little more detail and tell you how it went down.

Pre-Race

When Erika and I arrived on the shuttle bus from the parking area, it felt like we were in the middle of nowhere. The glorified "Rockingham Ballroom" was really just like a small hall, a plain simple one, with the bathrooms closed. The only bathroom options were six porta-pots down the road a bit. So we waited in the rain, held each other's bags and took our turn. Then we got into the Ballroom (Newmarket style), picked up our bibs and shirts, stretched a bit, got our clothes together, etc. I took one more trip to the bathroom and waited for like 20 minutes, a ridiculous line. But I made it and got back to the ballroom with like 10 minutes to go. The temperatures were a bit borderline for what to wear. But I ended up with a short-sleeve shirt (my Chicago Marathon shirt) over a light long-sleeve running shirt, with a light winter running cap, light running gloves, and shorts. I had eaten less pre-race than usual because I was dealing with these bathroom concerns. It was still raining at the start, it was probably in the mid – upper 40s and we were chilly waiting to start.

Mile 1 – 7:38: We started off quickly. There was just a bit of congestion at the beginning, but it was nothing compared to Burlington. And it opened up quickly. There were a couple of rolling hills, but it was easy as advertised. And we both felt good, an auspicious start.

Mile 2- 7:36: More of the same. Still raining lightly but it wasn't bad at all and we were both running well and feeling good. At this point, it really felt like we were out on a long run together. Yeah, we were in a race, but there weren't that many people around us, and I felt so relaxed and comfortable. Just another long run with my running buddy. We were chatting and just enjoying the run together.

Mile 3- 7:31: The third negative split mile in a row to start the race and I was beginning to think we were getting a bit carried away. But the pace felt good for both of us, we both felt strong, and I didn't feel like we were pushing it. This was a lot like how I felt for Chicago. Except I am even stronger now.

Mile 4 – 7:25:OMG, are you kidding me, 7:25?! We actually thought we were slowing down, but uh-uh. And at this point, I thought, we're either gonna run ourselves into the ground or we're going to have the race of our lives. But I knew how strong we were, so I was betting on the latter. Again, we were so relaxed, just chatting like it was another long run. And that was the theme of my double marathon training, to get to the point where the marathon is just another long run. And, I thought, I've arrived!

Mile 5 – 7:44: Still a great pace, but a little more appropriate for mile 5 and I'm liking it. Somewhere along here, maybe it was a little later, I had given Erika my water bottle and stopped to pull up my compression socks. I had already pulled them up at the start, but they had fallen way down to my ankles again, so basically they were of no use. So I decided it was worth trying to stop quickly to pull them up one more time. Fortunately this time they seemed to stick!

Mile 6 – 7:38: Strong and fast again and running well. We're in a rural area, some small farms, and the fall foliage is pretty. I can't remember when the rain stopped, as that was kind of a blur, but I think it had stopped by now? Still having fun and chatting and just enjoying being out there with Erika. I could tell here she was starting to work a bit harder but that was not surprising as we were running a fast pace!

Mile 7 – 7:47: Fading just a tiny bit, but actually right where I want to be. Again, I'm an intense competitor, especially when racing, but I am still so relaxed. I just feel like Erika and I are out for a run and are having a great time. No pressure, no intensity, just enjoying the experience. The mantras and intensity are tucked away for when I need them. But right now, I'm just having fun, running free and easy – at an amazing target pace!

Mile 8 – 7:35: We are just crushing this. I know Erika's tiring a bit, but there are no real concerns at this point. We're still both running strong. Drinking water, taking GU, everything is going right at this stage.

Mile 9 – 7:50: We started to slow a bit here, and I could tell this pace was going to be too much eventually. That was kind of a given, but I could tell Erika was tiring a bit here. So we both slowed down a tad. Again, by slowing down, we were actually running at my target race pace, so this is still awesome. I'm still feeling virtually 100% at this point. I've logged 8 miles WAY ahead of my pace and I am feeling very strong. This has been an awesome start.

Mile 10 – 7:54: Again, a bit slower, though still a solid mile. We're both still running solidly at this point.

Mile 11- 7:54: We turned on to the rail trail right at the end of mile 10. This trail wasn't bad, it was pretty smooth and well-maintained. But it wasn't as smooth as the road, and it required a bit of focus to watch for the occasional rocks, which were spray painted. At this point, Erika told me to go ahead. We had been talking about how we were feeling and she said that, while the pace was getting to her a bit, and she was feeling it a bit in her legs, her knee that was bothering her was OK and generally she felt fine. I could tell this moment was coming and, after seeing this split, she told me to go get that PR, I told her to be safe and I took off.

Mile 12 – 7:29: Like I said I TOOK OFF. I was flying now. And still I felt strong and within myself. I knew this was too fast and for the first time I pulled out my mantras. "This is your day. This is your moment. Define Yourself." The last part of this was from a mantra that Deena Kastor used when she won the Chicago Marathon, and it really resonated with me. From this point forward, I recited this three part mantra often.

Mile 13- 7:14: I was defining myself alright. What in the world was that! So I reminded myself not to define myself as someone who burns out at the half. Yikes. 7:14?! Oh my goodness! Easy big fella. You're running the full today.

Mile 14 – 7:34: When I reached the halfway mark, Anne and Kevin were there cheering for me and I tossed them my hat, gloves, and the first GU flask that I had emptied. I was taking my GU right on schedule, so that was good. I wasn't hot, but I didn't think I needed the hat and gloves anymore, and I was right. I felt good and refreshed without them. I felt a bit of a letdown after I passed through the small crowd at the start/finish and ran immediately next to the 1/2 marathon finish chute. I mean I was a foot away from finishing. There were very few people running the full so when I passed the halfway mark, I was on my own a lot. I felt like I was fading a bit here, so I pushed myself and came up with another awesome mile. "This is your day. This is your moment. DEFINE YOURSELF."

Mile 15- 7:41: More definition – a strong mile again. I've got this, and am on BQ pace, and remind myself to keep pushing. Repeating my mantras. Focusing on drinking. Focusing on taking my GU. At this point, I had an issue come up. I had not been able to go to the bathroom (#2) that AM and despite taking a large pile of Pepto Bismol tablets, I had a feeling this moment was gonna come. Sure enough, I needed to go to the bathroom and I knew I was not going to make it through mile 26 like this.

Mile 16 – 9:04: The decision was an easy one. I stopped at an open porta-pot and went to the bathroom very quickly. But neatly. Honest. Then I got right back out there. The porta pot was right on the road and a car went by just as I was opening the door. Oh my, that's not what you expect! I picked my pace right back up and, even stopping to go to the bathroom, had a 9:04 mile. I smiled a bit about that and had to laugh. But, seriously, I was proud of my bathroom performance. And I felt a lot better!

Mile 17 – 7:42: This is your day. This is your moment. Define yourself. I am pounding away with my mantras and they are working. I am physically strong but I am also staying mentally strong and focused as my fatigue begins to build. I can feel myself getting tired now so the mantras matter now. My mental outlook and focus matters. Drink. Take your GU. Stay on pace. There have been a couple of runners ahead of me who have cheering squads in cars. They drive by, pull up ahead of us, cheer for these guys (and a bit for me sometimes) and then get back in their car to drive ahead again. Over and over. I had passed two of these guys before I went to the bathroom and have been working on catching up to them for a long time now. The road is long and straight, so I can see the guys far ahead of me and I'm working on reeling them in, over the course of miles. I soon learned the guy in front of me is Billy. I heard Billy's name endlessly. And I'm thinking, in a nice way of course, that I'm going to crush you Billy.

Mile 18 – 7:48: Still hanging in, and it's getting tougher to stick to the pace, but I'm motivated by Billy. Besides this is my day. I was thinking of Erika frequently in the second half, both wishing that she was safe and OK and knowing that she would be pushing me on to get this PR. Knowing how badly she wants this for me.

Mile 19 – 8:21: I didn't realize I was this slow in this mile, and right now, I know my BQ time of 3:25 is slipping away. But I'm staying in the moment here. No past, no future, just now. And I'm pushing myself relentlessly. Forget about the BQ – focus on NOW.

Mile 20- 8:02: The effort shows as my pace rebounds a bit. I'm trying to remember when I passed Billy, I think it was more like mile 21 or 22. If I recall right, I was right on his heels, like within 20 yards, for a while here. Drink. Take your GU. Stay quick. This is your day. This is your moment. Define yourself. And I add "RIGHT NOW." You are breaking 3:30 today.

Mile 22 – 8:32: The fatigue is eating away at me now My legs are still strong and I have something left, but I am hurting, I am worn and weary. But I am NOT GIVING IN. And I know that Erika is out there thinking of me while I think of her. No way am I letting down.

Mile 23 – 8:21: We enter the rail trail and my effort shows as my pace dropped down to 8:21. Just a 5k I tell myself now, but that image never seems to help me much. Never mind, this is your day!

Mile 24 – 8:17: I am working hard now, trying to push through this fatigue and it's working. Trying to just tick off the tenths of miles now, staying in the moment, my moment, defining myself. Thinking of Erika – no letting down now!

Mile 25- 8:50: Ugh, ouch, ouch, ouch. Defining yourself is hard work. I stopped to walk for a few seconds here, probably a bad idea. I picked back up again trying to boost my pace. But I am drained right now. I am hurting. My legs hurt. My shoulder and neck are stiff and tight. But I know how close I am and remind myself of that. This is your day. Define yourself. NOW.

Mile 26 – 8:24: I rebounded in this mile with sheer will. I know the mantra thing gets boring, but I'm giving you the real feel here. I repeated these mantras endlessly in my mind, just pounding away. And, it was working, and I knew it. This was going to be my day, my moment.

Mile 26.2 – 1:51: This was fast, because it showed as a 1/4 mile on my watch, so I ran this last stretch to the finish at sub 8:00 pace. Actually, more like 7:20! As I rounded the turn to the finish, the final 100 yards or so, I took off and had a pretty good kick to the finish line, reaching it in 3:28:14. A great, great race. And I had just defined myself as a sub 3:30 marathoner But, more importantly, I had run through the fatigue and beat it. And that's really how I defined myself today.

The transition from Newmarket to getting ready for Philadelphia was all about being ready to run Philly together with Erika. That was a bit in doubt, given how her legs felt after Newmarket. But all I could do was focus on getting myself ready while I supported Erika in her recovery from Newmarket.

A Short Bucket List, October 30, 2015

My mentality about post-marathon training has changed this year. After both Burlington and Newmarket I've been aggressive about cross training right after the race. And I feel that it's helped me a lot. So this week, after the marathon on Sunday, I've done workouts on four straight days, getting increasingly intense with each day. And, with each passing day, I feel better and stronger.

On Monday, I just did an easy 20 minutes on the exercise bike. Then, on Tuesday, I upped that to 30 minutes and did the middle 10 at a tempo pace. Then I switched to elliptical on Wednesday. I was planning these splits: 8:30/8:00/8:00/8:00/8:30. As it turned out, each of the middle three miles were at a sub 7:30 pace! And I felt strong! I added my hip lifting at the end for good measure. Tonight, I did 6 miles on the elliptical, with three of them at a 7:00 pace! It's been a great week.

For months I've been dreaming and daydreaming about how I would run in Newmarket. I had to work through some confidence dips along the way so my thoughts were not always positive. But I kept it up in my mind, especially focusing on how I would feel and how I would run and respond to fatigue late in the race. I went over this again and again in my head in the weeks leading up the race burning that determination into my mind. I was so ready for this race. The funny thing is I'm still doing it. The race is over and I'm still thinking about how I WILL run in Newmarket.

The thing is I'm still hungry. I am not mentally fatigued at all. Newmarket only increased my energy. It's not like I was disappointed in my time. I am happy and I am content. But I want to run. I want to run in my mind, in my heart and deep in my soul. I just want to run more. Fortunately Erika and I had the foresight to plan and register for a second marathon! Except this one is different. This one is about camaraderie, running partnership, and friendship. My one and only goal for this race is to run it together with Erika, entirely start to finish. I don't take that for granted after Newmarket. But I really don't care about the time at all this time. This one is for fun.

I've got a never ending list of running goals, races I'd like to do, PRs I'd like to get, and so on. I will have a busy year ahead next year. But right now, there's just one item on the list.

This run was hugely important, physically but especially emotionally and psychologically. The goal of this run was really just to get through it without any injuries, while feeling decent. And it was a great success! We were on our way to the start line in Philly and off to a good start. I'd say this was one of more important emotional runs of the year.

I Don't Know About You, But I'm Feeling 46, November 1, 2015

With apologies to Taylor Swift, I'm feeling all of my 46 years. This is not easy. I continue to work harder than I've ever worked before. It's not just the runs and workouts six days a week. It's also all of the pre-run/workout and post run/workout treatment. Icing, rolling, heating, and stretching – it goes on and on. It takes a lot of time and a lot of effort. Yeah, I'm feeling all of my 46 years. But I'm loving it! I've never been faster; I've never been stronger; and I've never been in better shape. It's not close. And I can feel it. I can feel that I'm continuing to get faster and stronger.

Today however, was not about speed. Erika and I cautiously set out to do a 10 mile run together today. We're just seven days away from the Loco Marathon in Newmarket, on one hand, and three weeks out from the Philly Marathon in the other direction. So we're working to balance a quick recovery with a careful and strong recovery. So, though we had a 10 mile run planned, we came back by home at the 5 mile mark, so we were never more than 2.5 miles away from home. We were not trying to run fast today, in fact we were specifically trying to go easy.

But we were both feeling OK today and no injuries reared their ugly heads, at least not much anyway. So we kept on plugging along, mile after methodical mile. This was our first run together since Newmarket and it was great to run together again and have us both feel decent. It was a lot of fun, but also a bit of a relief. In the end, we cut it short at 9 miles, as Erika's knee was beginning to bug her a bit more. It wasn't bad, but we didn't want it to get bad, so we stopped right then. In fact, I stopped and made us both stop. We walked that last bit home together (it was actually less than a mile as we were going to have to add on some distance to get to the full 10.) And then, since I was still feeling decent, I went out and finished my 10th mile.

I finished the 10 at an average 8:36 pace. But this was a highly successful run. Neither one of us seemed to aggravate any injuries and we basically got through the whole run together. It's one day at a time now, but today was a good one. And it sure is great to be 46!

Philly was different than any other marathon that I had ever run and trained for. This one was just for fun. I just wanted to get to the start line healthy. And, more than anything, I wanted to run the whole race together with Erika. I was still working hard, but my mindset was all about joy and gratitude.

My Mantra Shift, November 5, 2015

In Newmarket, although I ran hard, I ran a very confident, relaxed race. However, under the relaxed, smooth surface, my will and determination were rock solid. I ran that race with intensity and focus and I knew I would achieve my sub-3:30 goal. I was not going to be denied and I knew it was my day. Any my three-part mantra reflected that intensity — "This is Your Day. This is Your Moment. Define Yourself." And I did.

When Erika and I ran Burlington in May, she was strong like I was in Newmarket – it was her day and she ran great and met her goal on that day, while I struggled late. So in the two marathons we've run together, we've each had a great one, they just didn't happen on the same day for both of us. And, while we ran significant parts of both races together, we parted along the way and didn't finish together.

So, as we look towards the Philadelphia Marathon just four weeks after Newmarket, my mantra, goal, and mindset have changed dramatically. I have no time goal for Philly – none at all. My real hope and goal is for Erika and me to both be healthy and to be able to run the whole race together and finish together. If it's a decent time, that will be a plus, but I honestly don't care much about the time. So my mantra now is simply "Enjoy the Journey".

I have always felt a lot of gratitude about my running – thankful to be able to run in the first place, thankful to be able to run as well as I have and improve as much as I have, thankful for the support of my family and friends, thankful for the joy, satisfaction and pride that running brings me, and, now, thankful for Erika as a running partner. So, borrowing from a quote I read from John Bingham, I am running with a heart of gratitude. And I am thankful for all of it. This, combined with the fact that Philly is just four weeks after Newmarket, has led to a bit more relaxed training approach for me in this four-week transition. My pacing for my runs has been very conservative and cautious, no fast interval workouts, and, at least so far, no tempo runs either. I have also backed off of core workouts during this stretch, though I'm still doing a bit of lifting for my legs. It's a bit of a tricky time, as we're going from recovery to building back up to tapering, all in the course of 4 weeks and just three long runs.

Make no mistake though, I am still working hard. Very hard. In the 10 days since Newmarket, I have taken only one day off, and I'll be back at it again tomorrow, running early in the AM after an elliptical workout tonight. So, I'll have worked out in 10 of the first 11 days after my marathon. And, in the entire four-week stretch, I'll only have four days off. This is not over exuberance – this is planned. I've come to believe that these frequent bike and elliptical workouts post-marathon actually help to expedite the healing process. And, while I'm not being aggressive with my run pacing, I am still crushing it on the bike and elliptical, really going hard. It seems like it's working, as I've never recovered from a marathon this quickly before.

But, most important of all, I'm enjoying the journey, appreciating the moments, and savoring the experience. Every step of the way.

This was a nice, thoughtful, and insightful blog on the entire marathon experience. It meant so much to me as a runner, but also as a person overall. And now I was really enjoying the ride and how much it had meant.

A Sunday Without a Long Run, November 8, 2015

What kind of madness is this? A Sunday without a long run?! How can that be?

I know, it's a pretty strange feeling, but it's true. But it's not really a big deal, just a scheduling thing. Erika is out of town this weekend and, since we really wanted to do this one together, we decided to push it back to first thing Monday morning. This is an important run for us. We are at the halfway point between Newmarket and Philly and our plan is to run 16 miles tomorrow AM. This will be our only really true "long run" between Newmarket and Philly, a run we both felt we needed to build back up and transition from our recovery from Newmarket to tapering for Philly. But, in the meantime, it's a Sunday without a long run – strange. Fortunately, there are a lot of leaves outside waiting to be raked up, so I'll still stay busy and active today.

As I thought about this run, I thought back to all that Erika and I have been through together this year. And, being a numbers guy, I got curious – what exactly have we been through? So I checked my running journal and came up with 47 runs totaling 579.1 miles. As a note, Erika and I are both round numbers kinds of people when it comes to running – that decimal point there is a function of race mileage. So, beginning on January 3, we set out on a 30 degree day, running 8 miles to Wompatuck and back. That was the start of our long, arduous, and awesome journey to Burlington, VT. Little did we know what lay ahead! Along the way, we would conquer brutal cold, snow and ice, more snow and ice, a lot more snow and ice, badly bruised quads, strained Achilles, dizziness, strained ITs, heat and humidity, loads of PT appointments, and a host of other aches and pains. We are now getting ready to run our 6th race together this year, including our third marathon. In addition to all those miles, we also spent a bunch of time planning runs, discussing injuries, choosing races, preparing training plans, routing runs, and, in general, sharing this epic journey together. You might ask, knowing what I know now, if I had the choice, would I do it over again? The answer is an unequivocal 100% yes. In fact, the fact that it's been difficult and challenging is part of what has made it so meaningful.

When we run the Philadelphia Marathon, that will be our 50th run together this year and we will end up with 630.3 miles. Of course, we'll get out and do a 0.7 mile run to take care of that messy decimal point! But it seems fitting that, in our last meaningful run of the year, and perhaps the most meaningful run of all, will be our 50th together this year. 630 miles is a lot. It's really not possible to run 630 miles with someone and feel neutral about them. It's just too much time. You're either going to get sick of that person, or you're going to become friends. Fortunately, through pretty much blind luck, I've ended up with not just a great running partner, but also an important friend, on this journey.

Along the way, I have become a better runner. Faster and stronger. But also stronger mentally and emotionally. I'm better able to handle disappointment, failures, setbacks, and frustrations. I've had my experiences with falling short, with failing to meet my goals, with being disappointed in myself. I've taken a hard look at myself in the mirror along the way. And I believe I've become a better version of me along the way. I'm still the same person, but I'm more resilient, mentally stronger, more patient, more disciplined, more positive, better able to take on and handle adversity. Both Erika and I have had great successes this year, training runs and races that we've felt awesome about. But we've also had brutal runs that have humbled us and crushed us physically and emotionally. I believe that I, and I think we, have recovered from each setback and emerged stronger and better.

Like I said earlier, this running has taken a lot of time, and taken that away from other parts of my life at times. And that is hard at times. But, in spite of that, I think that this journey has not just made me a better runner. I believe I am a better version of me, prepared to be better in all facets of my life, as a parent, as a husband, as a friend, as a professional even as a dog owner. Yes, I am far from perfect and always will be. But that it is not the point of this journey. It is about always striving to be strong, striving to improve, and, all the while, appreciating the journey.

So, while I won't run today, no worries. The journey will continue at 6:00 AM tomorrow.

This was a pass/fail run for us and we passed. Again, the theme here was just to get to the starting line in Philly intact. We each had our share of aches and pains on this run, but we were able to work through without any real damage. And, on this day, that was a victory!

Our Third Dress Rehearsal, November 9, 2015

This is getting to be very familiar – another "dress rehearsal" marathon training run. But this one is much different since we're recovering from another marathon just 4 weeks prior. For one thing, normally our final long pre-marathon run has been 20 or 22 miles and it's been 3 weeks before Race Day. But, this time, it was only 16 miles, and just 2 weeks before Race Day.

Normally when you run 16 miles late in marathon training, you have this mindset that it's "only" a 16 miler. But today our mindset was that we just hoped to be able to get through 16 miles OK. As I wrote in my last blog this run was unusual for us because it was on a Monday AM. But it was a nice morning to run. A bit chilly to start (36 degrees) but about what we'll likely experience on Race Day. And it warmed up nicely to about 45 degrees by the time we were done.

Erika was battling through knee soreness today, but it actually went pretty well, all things considered. As for me, I've had ongoing groin soreness that cropped up in mile 12 today. And it got worse as we went, so it was pretty sore late in the run. And I ended up with a really sore toe nail as well. But Erika had nowhere near the soreness she had in Newmarket. And it didn't really get worse as we went. And, as for me, even though my pain got worse as I went, it was tolerable and I could run through it. And I have 2 weeks to aggressively treat my muscle soreness before Philly. So, in our twisted world, we felt great! Kind of.

So, stay with me here. It was a tough, painful run for both of us. But under the circumstances, it was a great run. We failed to set a new land speed record (average 8:26 pace) but we made it through this run reasonably intact. This was kind of a pass/fail run. We just needed to finish this feeling decent and it would be a success. For Philly, all we want to do is finish. That's it. I've never trained for a race like this before and, I have to say, it's a nice change of pace after all we've been through this year. It really reduces the pressure a lot.

So we both received a pass grade today. And I've never felt better about a passing grade! This run left me feeling very optimistic about Philly and with a sense of relief as well. The next two weeks will be very conservative from a training standpoint. Probably just two runs a week, lots of elliptical and biking, and lots of heating, rolling, stretching, and icing. The only goal for the next two weeks is to get to the start line healthy. Healthy enough to finish anyway. Once more, we're on our way!

Given how I was recovering from Newmarket while just trying to get to the start line in Philly, this run was a complete anomaly. But I know that running is meant to be enjoyed and, when you have days when you feel like this, you've got to just go with it and enjoy the moment. And I sure did!

Feeling Spunky, November 13, 2015

I'm not sure what it was today. Maybe it was that I had a PM work meeting cancelled, so I was able to get home early and run outside before dark – instead of on the dreaded treadmill. Or that I had a great work meeting this AM. Maybe it was the cool temperature combined with the misty rain in my face. Maybe I'm really starting to recover from Newmarket. Or maybe my heart grew two sizes today. But, whatever it was, I was feeling spunky today.

I was planning to run 8 miles today, and was hoping to sustain an 8:00 pace. But, I wasn't going to push it and, if I didn't feel up to that, I would take whatever pace my body was up for tonight. And, if I was sore, I had no problem cutting the run short either. Everything I'm doing now is just focused on getting ready to be able to run and finish the Philly Marathon – in less than 10 days now. So here's how it went.

Mile 1 – I felt a bit tight warming up and my sore toenail was bugging me a bit, so I wasn't sure what to think. It was about 47 degrees out and there was a light misty rain. I had a long sleeve shirt, with a bright yellow shirt over it for visibility purposes (my meaningless yellow shirt Erika), my winter running hat and gloves, and shorts. The temperature felt good to me and I think I was dressed just right for the weather. I headed down Chard Street into Jackson Square and felt OK. I was feeling things out in this mile and I felt good, but not great. I finished the mile in 7:55 and felt great about that for a first mile.

Mile 2 – I was headed out of Jackson Square up High Street. This is a stretch I've run a million times and it's very familiar. There's a slight uphill here and I'm not loving it. I'm feeling like I'm working pretty hard for mile 2, but feeling strong enough. I have a bit of soreness in my left knee and my right calf, but it's minor, background kind of pain. Doesn't affect my running, nor my stride, and it's neither sharp nor strong. I considered it, assessed it, and dismissed it as meaningless. I finished mile 2 in 8:03 and, while this was a slight dip, I'm feeling like maybe I can sustain this 8:00 pace after all.

Mile 3 – I hung a right onto Main Street/228 and after a quick downhill, had a slight climb. I really powered up that hill – hard – and I thought, huh. That was the first time I think I've really shifted into a high gear since Newmarket and it felt good. I'm running along Main Street on a nice smooth, flat stretch and, inspired by my strong climb, I feel like I'm running faster. Sure enough, turns out I finished mile 3 in 7:44! Pretty sure that was my fastest mile since Newmarket and I'm feeling a little stronger as I go.

Mile 4 – I turn right onto Cushing Street and it's starting to get dark given the overcast skies and rain. But I can still see fine, even despite the rain streaming down my glasses and face. And I feel like I'm getting stronger and running really well. Still feeling my knee, but it's just in the background and I figure I'll just ice it later. I finished mile 4 in 7:41 and now the complexion of this run has changed completely for me. Thinking of 8:00 pace is a distant memory and I'm now thinking faster.

Mile 5 – I stopped during this mile to stretch against a telephone pole, but I'm feeling it now. I turned from Cushing onto Ward Street. I haven't really opened it up since Newmarket, mostly because I haven't wanted to, didn't feel up to it, and didn't need it. I just wanted to get to the start line in Philly in one piece. But, running is a gift and, when there are days when you feel IT, I think sometimes you just have to run with it. So, even though my legs did not feel 100% still, my heart and soul are really stirring and I decided in this mile, to give myself a gift. To let myself have this run, to let go of the reins and just run with the joy and reckless abandon I'm feeling in my heart and soul. So I let go of the reins and effortlessly shifted gears. I'm running fast now and I know it, but it feels free and easy. This is pure running joy right now. Even so, I was surprised to finish mile 5 in 7:26 – I'm at my half-marathon race pace now. Yeah, HALF MARATHON RACE PACE.

Mile 6 – I am feeling absolutely zero fatigue. I'm running smooth, and really opening up my stride now. I feel like I'm gliding along. I turned left back down Main Street, back towards Jackson Square. Although I know my pace is good and I feel strong, I don't feel that I'm pushing it that hard. I just feel so smooth, and even with my lingering pains, this feels so good. When my watch beeped at the end of mile 6, it showed 7:06. This is FASTER than 10K race pace for me! In mile 6! Are you kidding me, this is crazy now. But I'm running with pure joy now, feeding my heart and soul and I'm hungry for this.

Mile 7 – I ran back through Jackson Square and, as I hit the hill coming out of Jackson Square, I shot up the hill. I mean I was flying. I have never run that hill this fast. As I turned right onto Commercial Street, I had a slight downhill before a continued climb. And, again, I was just flying up that hill. And, again I thought, I've never run this hill this fast in my life. I'm finally sensing some fatigue in my breathing, but now I am so locked into this run, I don't even care. I continue to fly up this hill and I know I'm having a special run tonight. As I finished mile 7, my watch showed 7:04! This is just unbelievable now.

Mile 8 – After such a hard run, I was going to ease up and let mile 8 be a cool down mile, but I can't do it. I am so pumped up and having so much fun, I want to keep on pushing it. To get to the even 8 miles, I added a little extra loop through the Abigail Adams School parking lot and I had to slow down a bit because there were a lot of cars and people walking. But I'm still feeling it and as I turn back out of the parking lot to home, I give one last push in the final 0.2 mile stretch. And, once again, I'm flying. I ended up finishing mile 8 in 7:30.

Wow. Under the circumstances, jammed between two marathons, when I'm just trying to recover and not even trying to run fast, this has got to be one of my best runs ever. I didn't even feel 100% and I ran faster than 10K race pace in miles 6 and 7. Honestly, that is just a stunning run for me. I ended up running the entire 8 miles at a 7:33 pace! I had no intention of running like this tonight, it just happened. And I've run enough runs by now to know that it's pretty special to feel this way. And, because this is all for fun, pretty much anytime I feel like THIS, I let myself have the moment. And man was it a good one.

This was our last long run before Philly. And I was feeling really sentimental about our year of running together. The run went OK, basically uneventful, which was perfect at this stage. And, as always, even when I didn't feel great, running with Erika was fun and the time passed quickly.

There's Just One Thing Left to Do, November 15, 2015

When the alarm went off at 4:30 this AM, the only thing I wanted was to stay curled up in my warm bed. But, Erika and I had a 6:00 AM run planned and my pre-long run routine has grown to be quite extensive these days, so I needed to get moving. Our heat hadn't come on yet this AM, so the house was chilly and I was cold as I got my running clothes on. I eventually added an extra long sleeve shirt for good measure. I really bundled up to take Napoleon out. Although 35 degrees is not really that cold, it felt colder given all of the mild weather we've had. So I'm still pretty wimpy about cold temperatures.

I've got to say, I did not have my normal pre-run energy this AM. We had a 10 mile run planned, again without any regard to pace. Just a run designed to ease us into Philly and serve as our final tune up. So the main goal today was to run and finish 10 miles without worsening any of our various aches and pains. On days like this, I am particularly thankful to have Erika as a running partner. First, just as incentive to get out the door. But then, when you're not feeling your best on a run and don't have a ton of energy, having good company is the best way to make the miles pass quickly. So, while I wasn't looking forward to the run itself that much, I was looking forward to running together.

In the end, the run was a success. We ran the 10 miles at an 8:16 pace, which is actually pretty good for us these days. And, while we each had aches and pains, none of them seemed particularly concerning. And as always, Erika's company was great and really made the miles pass by quickly and turn what could have been a long, tedious run into a fun outing. Once again, the theme of gratitude, especially poignant these days, returned to my running.

And now, here we are, on November 15, one week away from our final destination on this leg of our journey. Through our running journey, One Republic's "I Lived" has become our unofficial theme song. And man, have we lived. As the song goes, we really have done it all. We've had great runs, brutal runs, and everything in between. It has been full and it has been rich. Over the past week, I've begun to look in the rearview mirror a bit, reading back through emails between Erika and me about our runs, races, injuries, and just the whole experience. In the past few days, these have brought wide grins to my face, made me laugh out loud, and brought me to the brink of tears.

Of course, our running journey will continue beyond Philly. But for now, there's only one thing left to do. And, as I have throughout the journey, I plan to treasure these 26.2 miles full of moments, running with a heart full of gratitude and joy.

Each of my five marathons has meant a lot to me. Newport was the perfect first marathon. I met my time goal, ran strong, and had my family with me to celebrate before and after. Chicago was a fantastic experience, again highlighted by a great visit to Chicago with my Mom and Uncle Jack. And I ran an awesome, really fun race, beating my PR by more than 20 minutes! Burlington was so meaningful to run most of it together with Erika after so much hard training together. And again, my family was with me to share the experience. Newmarket was amazing because I ran my best marathon yet and ran so relaxed and strong. They are each different and hard to compare in that sense. But, even so, I would say that

Philly was the most meaningful of all because it was really a celebration of all Erika and I had been through this year.

The Perfect End to the Year, November 23, 2015

I often get asked "Why?", "Why do you do it?" And I give what feels like a logical, kind of a partial answer. But it never does the emotions of running and running marathons justice. And, this year, going through this three-marathon journey together with Erika. Well, THIS is why I do it. This marathon experience just made my running year complete. And I really don't think I can adequately describe it here. But I'm going to give it a shot.

To understand what yesterday meant, you have to start back in the summer of 2014, when Erika and I first began running together and found out we were really compatible running partners. That led to my decision to join Erika in running the Burlington Marathon in May of this year. And we went through incredibly difficult training for Burlington that really pounded both of us. But, along the way, through all that adversity, we were becoming a really good running team. And, though we didn't finish Burlington together, we ran a lot of it together, and it was a blast. It was kind of a celebration of all we had been through and conquered together. And while I faded at the end due to my digestive issues, Erika was really strong and came away meeting her goal of qualifying for Boston – by a lot! So I felt great about the time we had to run together and felt great about her achieving her goal, but felt bad that I had faded at the end, hadn't met my goal, and didn't finish together.

So we made the decision to run one and then eventually two fall marathons together. This was really, really tough and we almost didn't make it. Erika went into our first in Newmarket with an injury and, compounded by dehydration, it got a lot worse as she went. We had a great time running together for the first 11 miles, but then she faded badly after that. But that day, it was my turn to be strong, and I ran the best marathon of my life, beating my sub 3:30 goal by a good margin. But, again, the experience wasn't complete, because we weren't able to run the full race together, and because Erika had such an awful experience.

It's ironic because we run 99% of our training runs side by side but, up to this point, we had never run a full race together. For a while, it seemed like the third marathon together might be in doubt. But Erika went through PT, stretching and exercises and was healthy enough to at least get in our planned training runs. And she decided she could run the Gore Tex Philadelphia Marathon on November 22 – together. But there was still some doubt there about how it would go, especially since Newmarket was so awful. So we headed down to Philly with that doubt in the back of our minds, just hoping we could both get through this and run it 100% together.

While I've enjoyed the marathons I've run solo, running these ones with Erika has been such a rich shared experience. But I just wanted the chance to run one all the way though together. So for Philly, that was all I wanted. I didn't care a bit about time. This is the first race I've ever run like that and it's a liberating feeling. After a while we just stopped looking at our watches because we just didn't care. But, as it turns out we were running very steady and consistent. And, most important of all, while Erika had some knee pain, it was not strong, it was not sharp, it was not getting worse, and she was doing great. Neither one of us had any speed that day, but we were hanging in and running steady.

It was a cool day, pretty nice for running, though we were very cold at the start and late in the race too. In fact, Erika's hands were so numb at one point that I had to open one of her snacks for her. Then, later in the race, my hands were so cold and numb, I could barely open my water bottle. I won't sugarcoat this, this was the most pain and discomfort I've ever had running a marathon, especially late. But, it was also the most fun I've ever had. Even in the most painful moments, I was enjoying the experience, enjoying the journey, digging deep to get through the pain, but doing it in good spirits. We talked together throughout and it was so much fun and so gratifying to have Erika on my right hand side for every step through 26.2 miles. Running nearly four hours together, step for step, is a long time, especially when sandwiched with 6 hour drives before and after. But even at the toughest times, we never got down, always kept our spirits up, and worked through it together, heads held high, punctuated by smiles, jokes, and laughs. Just enjoying the journey.

This race together was so meaningful because it was really a celebration. A celebration of all we had been through together this year, all of the great runs, all of the brutal runs, and the running partnership, camaraderie and friendship that been forged through all of that shared experience. So, as we reached mile 25, and I could envision that shared finish together, my heart just soared. And, despite all the pain, I really enjoyed that final run to the finish line, finishing side by side, just as we had started.

It was another great year of running in 2015. I did not meet all of my goals, but I had so many great runs and so many fun runs. So many of them were memorable training runs with Erika, as we pursued this epic three marathon journey. It was a special year of running, which I will always treasure.

Top 10 Runs of 2015, December 9, 2015

Although 2015 isn't quite over, and I hope to have a few more good runs, I think it's safe to say that the most important runs are behind me. But, the term "top 10 runs" requires a bit of definition in this context. These are not my 10 best runs of 2015, though some of them were great runs. They weren't even always the most fun runs, though many were a blast. But some of them were really tough. In some cases, these were races. In other cases, they were training runs.

I think, in the end, what this boils down to is that these were the 10 most meaningful runs of the year for me. If you've read my writing along the way, you already know what #1 is. But some of the others may surprise you. There were many others that I considered and ultimately didn't include. If I went on to the top 20, many would be runs when Erika and/or

I struggled greatly. Some of these were downright brutal, but they meant a lot then and mean even more now If you enjoy these memories even just a fraction as much as I do, then this blog is a success!

#10. Kevin's First Half Marathon, 8/15/15

This wasn't actually a race, but it was the longest run that Kevin had ever done and, it turns out, the first time that he had run 13.1 miles. This was a 14 mile run overall, which we ran along the Paulinskill Valley Trail, while visiting my Dad in Blairstown, NJ. And, just by chance, this was run on my birthday. It was a nice summer day, but humid. This run for me was marked by its steadiness and consistency. Opportunities to run with Kevin have grown more rare since he started high school, so it was great to share 14 miles together side by side!

#9. My First Track Meet, 6/27/15

This was one of my most fun running days of the year. I headed up to Portland, ME with my co-worker Mike for the Maine Corporate Track Association Track Meet! And I took full advantage of the opportunity, competing in a 5K race, 1,600 meter, 800 meter, 400 meter and 200 meter! I ran all 5 races with reckless abandon, soaking up the experience, and I had a great, great time! As a result, I plan to run at least one more track meet next year, and look forward to many more!

#8. The Water Stop Run, 9/6/15

This may have been the funniest run of the year, sort of pathetic but funny. I had planned a very different route for this run than our usual routes. Therefore, I had, ironically, planned it out very carefully, driving a lot of it in advance, identifying specific water stops, and even arranging for Anne and Eliza to bring us water for our first water stop. It was a good thing I did, because the later planned water stops were a complete disaster! First, I had planned on going to the Wompatuck Visitor Center, but that was closed. Then we tried the general store on 228 and that was closed. And then a Hingham Fire station, but there was no sign of life there. Finally, we got ice water at the Atlantic Bagel Shop – I've never appreciated water more! Erika and I still joke about this run and I expect we will for years! And, by the way, after all that, we finished the 22 mile run at an 8:08 average pace!

#7. My Slowest Run Ever, 2/14/15

Erika and I ran A LOT of brutal runs this past winter, but I think this one may have been the toughest. And, in that sense, the best one of all! This was when there were many feet of snow piled up EVERYWHERE and we ran in Bare Cove Park, which was about the only place you could run at all. But, even then we were running single file in about 6 inches of packed snow. I had a cough and Erika was running for the fifth day in a row. It was 20 degrees and snowing, of course, and we had to dodge people and dogs along the single file path along the way. My water bottle froze and my GU was frozen solid, so I didn't even try to take that. We ended up going 10 miles at a 9:35 pace, my slowest run ever. But I have never been more proud of a run in my life!

#6. A Strong 18, No Wait 20, Mile Run, 8/29/15

This was the 5th run that Erika and I had done in 8 days and we were running so great together. We weren't sure about this run, so we planned it for 18 miles to start, with the possibility of extending it to 20 miles. Of course, knowing Erika and me , you know how this turned out. We ran so steady throughout this run, it was a beautiful day, and we had a great time. And, in the end, I wound up with a PR for 20 miles, in 2:42:15. It was runs like this that paved the way for my PR in Newmarket, NH on October 25. And, when I look back at 2015, it was runs like this that made this my most fun year of running ever!

#5. The Canal Run, 5/3/15

This run was so important and so meaningful for several reasons. We were just 3 weeks out from Burlington and we had had what I will describe as a bad 22 mile run two weeks before when we both struggled badly. Then, the week before this, I injured my Achilles on our long run. At that point, I wasn't even sure I could run Burlington, and had been working on recovery and treatment all week long. So we decided to head down to the Cape Cod Canal trail, which is perfectly flat, for this 22 miler. Erika's family joined us and her husband Mark carried their kids in a bike trailer, along with our water bottles. So this was kind of a make it or break it run, and it went great. We both had brand new compression socks and they helped a lot. We ran great, we both felt great, and this set the stage for a very successful race in Burlington! At the time, I think this was among my top 3 most meaningful runs ever. But, there were many more to come in 2015!

#4. Burlington Marathon, 5/24/15

Burlington was a mixed bag for me. But the story of the race, and the most meaningful part, was the first 19 miles that I ran with my running partner and friend. Erika and I had been through so much just to get to the start line. While I faded late due to digestive issues and the last few miles were, frankly, miserable, the first 19 were a celebration of all we had been through. And it was so much fun to run a marathon together with my running partner and friend and to celebrate our journey together. While it didn't end the way I wanted to for me, it did for Erika, and I was so happy for her. And, in addition to the race, I got to spend a great weekend with my family along with my Mom and Uncle Jack, which made the whole experience even more meaningful. In the end, it was a great race and a great weekend, for which I will always be thankful!

#3. The LOCO Marathon, Newmarket, NH, 10/25/15

This was a great, great race for me, and a brutal one for Erika. And that's what keeps it from being #1 on this list. We had a great time running together for the first 10 miles or so but then it became quite clear that Erika wasn't going to be able to keep up with me that day. And it continually went downhill for her from that point on. But, for me, I ran the race of my life finishing in 3:28:14, a PR by nearly 3 minutes. I ran so well and so strong and felt so great about my race. So it's right up there near the top. And it will always be among my most meaningful runs ever. But not quite the best.

#2. Bonus 800 Meter Intervals, Hingham Track, 8/25/15

This may seem like an odd choice for #2 for the year, unless you were there. Really, you might ask, this was more meaningful than your marathon PR? Seriously, you must be joking? I gave this one a lot of thought and, while this was a very different run than my marathon PR in Newmarket, thinking about the meaning of all these runs, I do feel like, in the end, this means even more.

This was the first track workout that Erika and I ran together, and it was a "bonus" run for us to do together. Running with Erika has been a core part of my running in 2015, and so much of my running experience this year was based on our shared running journey and partnership, and the friendship that sprouted from that shared experience. We were scheduled to do 6 x 800 meter intervals, and we ran them very well together, including kicking the last 100 meters of the final interval together. And it was a blast! But then, after we did our walking cool-down, Erika lined up for a 7th 800 with a big smile. And, of course, I joined her and we ran a great 7th interval together. She then asked what I wanted to do for a cool-down and I responded, "A mile, but it's not time for that yet." And it was my turn to have a big smile and line up for interval #8. And again, we ran it great.

While this probably seems like an odd choice to rank so high, I think this was the second most fun I had running all year. Those last two bonus intervals really captured the essence of our running partnership together this year. And I will always remember those moments fondly. And when I think about the runs that mattered the most, this one rises right to the top. Almost.

#1. Philadelphia Marathon, 11/22/15

I don't even know where to begin here, but this is an easy, clear-cut choice for me for my most meaningful run of the year. In all my runs this year, Philly stands alone on a pedestal, the most fun and most memorable race that I've ever done. In Philly, Erika and I accomplished what we had hoped to do in both Burlington and Newmarket – run the full 26.2 miles together. After running more than 600 miles together this year, it was so fitting that we ran the last 26.2 together. For Philly, we also drove down and back together, creating a whole additional set of memories, along with the race. This was a slow race for both of us, but we were both still reeling from Newmarket, Erika more than me, and we were thankful to be able to finish this race and run it together. This race was fun from start to finish, as well as before the start and after the finish. It was a celebration of a great year of running together, a celebration of all we had both been through along the way, and the celebration of a wonderful friendship forged through snow, ice, lots of pain, injuries, great individual and shared triumphs, brutal, crushing runs, and beautiful, glorious runs, all punctuated by great mutual support, seemingly endless smiles, laughs and long run stories. While I expect to have much faster races in the future and other very fun and meaningful races and training runs as well, I am not convinced that Philly will ever be topped.

I can't wait 'til next year to find out though!

The Beginning

I initially thought to write a conclusion to close out this book. I wanted to tie things up in a neat knot and bring my story to a close. But, as I thought more about what I would write in my conclusion, I realized I had it all wrong. This is not a conclusion at all. Rather I am just getting started.

I am now a Runner and the sky is the limit. The road is open and my next running adventures are up to me. Since I began my racing in 2009, my running has been a wonderful adventure and brought so much joy to my life. Not only have I become a much stronger and faster runner, but I believe I also have become a stronger person. I am more resilient and more confident. I have greater belief that, when I run into challenges, if I keep on working and keep on believing, I can beat them. Eventually.

I am proud. But I am also thankful. Thankful not just for the opportunity to run but thankful for all that I have in my life. I am already looking forward to my next running challenge to set new PRs in both 5ks and 10Ks this spring. And, to follow that, I will best my track times from my first track meet last year.

But there is so much more that I can do. Regardless of times, there are so many more adventures that await, so many opportunities to explore, to grow, to enjoy, to take on challenges and to beat them. It's hard to imagine now that, for 39 years of my life, I was not a Runner. But I am so thankful for this new aspect of my life now and have no regrets at all. Only satisfaction, pride, gratitude and joy. Better 39 years late than never!